by Elaine Biech

Other Titles by Elaine Biech:

Marketing Your Consulting Services, 2003
The Consultant's Quick Start Guide, 2001
Successful Team-Building Tools, 2001
The Consultant's Legal Guide, 2000
The Business of Consulting, 1999
Building High Performance, 1998
Interpersonal Skills: Understanding Your Impact on Others, 1996
The ASTD Sourcebook: Creativity and Innovation — Widen Your Spectrum, 1996
The HR Handbook, 1996
TQM for Training, 1994
Managing Teamwork, 1994
Business Communications, 1992
Delegating For Results, 1992
The Pfeiffer Annual, Training (1998, 1999, 2000, 2001, 2002, 2003, 2004, 2005, 2006)
The Pfeiffer Annual, Consulting (1998, 1999, 2000, 2001, 2002, 2003, 2004, 2005, 2006)

WILEY

Wiley Publishing, Inc.

Training For Dummies®

Published by
Wiley Publishing, Inc.
111 River St.
Hoboken, NJ 07030-5774
www.wiley.com

Copyright © 2005 by Wiley Publishing, Inc., Indianapolis, Indiana

Published by Wiley Publishing, Inc., Indianapolis, Indiana

Published simultaneously in Canada

For general information on our other products and services, please contact our Customer Care Department within the U.S. at 800-762-2974, outside the U.S. at 317-572-3993, or fax 317-572-4002.

For technical support, please visit www.wiley.com/techsupport.

Wiley also publishes its books in a variety of electronic formats. Some content that appears in print may not be available in electronic books.

Library of Congress Control Number: 2005921606

ISBN: 978-0-7645-5985-3

Manufactured in the United States of America

10   9   8   7   6   5

1O/RQ/QT/QV/IN

About the Author

Elaine Biech has been in the training and consulting field for more than a quarter of a century. She is president of ebb associates inc, an organization development and custom training design firm that helps organizations work through large-scale change. Known as the trainer's trainer, Elaine has been featured in *The Wall Street Journal, Harvard Management Update,* and *Fortune Magazine.* She is the author and editor of dozens of books, including *Marketing Your Consulting Services, The Business of Consulting*, and *The ASTD Sourcebook: Creativity and Innovation.*

An active American Society for Training and Development (ASTD) member, Elaine served on the National ASTD Board of Directors, initiated Consultant's Day at ASTD's International Conference and Expo, and writes ASTD's "Ask an Expert" Column. She is a past member of the ISA Board of Directors and currently serves on the Advisory Council for the Independent Consultants Association. Elaine is the recipient of the 1992 National ASTD Torch Award and was selected for the 1995 Wisconsin Women Entrepreneur's Mentor Award. In 2001, she received ISA's highest award, The Terry Broomfield Spirit Award. She is the editor for the prestigious *Training* and *Consulting Annuals* published by Pfeiffer.

You may reach her office at 757-588-3939 or by e-mail at elaine@ebbweb.com with inquiries about training or to request additional information.

About ASTD

ASTD is a leading association of workplace learning and performance professionals, forming a world-class community of practice. ASTD's 70,000 members and associates come from more than 100 countries and thousands of organizations — multinational corporations, medium-sized and small businesses, government, academia, consulting firms, and product and service suppliers.

ASTD marks its beginning in 1944, when the organization held its first annual conference. In recent years, ASTD has widened the industry's focus to connect learning and performance to measurable results, and is a sought-after voice on critical public-policy issues.

Dedication

For Shane and Thad, my best training projects.

Author's Acknowledgments

The words in this book were not created in a vacuum. To the many people who were an intricate part of authoring this book: "Thanks!"

Thanks to Dan Greene, my personal and professional support system. Thanks to Lorraine Kohart for your assistance and your sense of humor.

Thanks to the generous contributors to this book. You are the Names to Know in the profession: Jean Barbazette, Ann Herrmann-Nehdi, Don Kirkpatrick, Jack Phillips, Bob Pike, Dana Robinson, Mel Silberman, Thiagi, and Edie West.

Thanks to all the ebb associates clients who have challenged me to always design a better training and to conduct it under all kinds of conditions.

Thanks to Diane Steele and Kathleen Cox, the two professional women of Wiley who are as excited about this book as I am. Thanks to Susan Rachmeler for your editing expertise.

Thanks to everyone at ASTD who allow me to continue to grow and learn: Tony Bingham and Cat Russo for the special opportunity to publish under the respected ASTD brand; Jennifer Naughton for the expertise that you share with trainers everywhere and in Chapter 16; Elizabeth Hannah, Nancy Olson, and Linda David for allowing me to continue to expand my horizons.

Thanks to Kathleen Dolan Davies, Matt Davis, and Martin Delahoussaye of Pfeiffer who are always willing to help a struggling author.

Thanks to Celia Rocks, the best publicist anywhere, anytime; thanks for your brilliance-to-be on yet another book.

All of you deserve much more than the simple thank you that appears here. Thanks for helping me write *Training For Dummies*.

Publisher's Acknowledgments

We're proud of this book; please send us your comments through our Dummies online registration form located at www.dummies.com/register/.

Some of the people who helped bring this book to market include the following:

Acquisitions, Editorial, and Media Development

Project Editor: Tere Stouffer

Acquisitions Editor: Kathy Cox

General Reviewer: Priya Sharma, Ph.D.

Editorial Supervisor: Carmen Krikorian

Editorial Manager: Michelle Hacker

Editorial Assistant: Nadine Bell

Cover Photos: © Photodisc Collection/ Getty Images/Photodisc Blue

Cartoons: Rich Tennant, www.the5thwave.com

Composition

Project Coordinator: Adrienne Martinez, Emily Wichlinski

Layout and Graphics: Carl Byers, Andrea Dahl, Joyce Haughey, Jacque Roth, Heather Ryan, Janet Seib, Julie Trippetti

Proofreaders: Leeann Harney, Jessica Kramer, Carl Pierce, Dwight Ramsey, Aptara

Indexer: Aptara

Publishing and Editorial for Consumer Dummies

Diane Graves Steele, Vice President and Publisher, Consumer Dummies

Joyce Pepple, Acquisitions Director, Consumer Dummies

Kristin A. Cocks, Product Development Director, Consumer Dummies

Michael Spring, Vice President and Publisher, Travel

Kelly Regan, Editorial Director, Travel

Publishing for Technology Dummies

Andy Cummings, Vice President and Publisher, Dummies Technology/General User

Composition Services

Gerry Fahey, Vice President of Production Services

Debbie Stailey, Director of Composition Services

Contents at a Glance

Table of Contents

Foreword

*I*n the past ten years, the role of many trainers has slowly evolved from that of training "order taker" to a real participant in the strategic decisions made by senior management. Even with this exciting new role as a strategic partner, a vast group of talented trainers and other workplace learning and performance professionals spend their days designing, delivering, and evaluating training programs that will have a positive impact on job and organizational performance.

This group of dedicated and enthusiastic professionals often admit to falling into the profession from a wide variety of backgrounds. Teachers, human resource managers, subject matter experts (SMEs), managers, and supervisors have all become "accidental trainers." For some, this accident has turned into a lifelong passion for facilitating learning. For others, training is only a temporary, albeit critically important, assignment.

However, make no mistake. Both the accidental trainer and today's highly motivated workplace learning and performance professional share a common goal as a developer of human potential. They are powerful instruments to drive organizational performance that is ultimately hardwired directly to every company's bottom line.

When this book project started, author Elaine Biech—who has special ties to ASTD as a long-standing, active member and contributor—was busily involved as the author and developer of ASTD's highly demanded Training Certificate Program. We are proud to have our organization associated with this book and with Elaine. I encourage you to apply what you learn in this book, as well as to engage the resources our organization provides to the training and development profession. Seize the opportunity to make a positive impact on individual and organizational performance, and ultimately deliver ASTD's mission of "Creating a World that Works Better."

Tony Bingham
President and CEO
American Society for Training & Development (ASTD)

Introduction

. . . .

*T*raining is the best job I've ever had. That's because the training profession is one that touches almost everyone every day. Whether you're taking a golf lesson, finding out how to use new computer software, trying out a new recipe, or being coached by your boss, you're experiencing training. Your trainer doesn't need to be in the same room or on the same schedule.

What other job affords you the opportunity to increase an organization's bottom line, improve your country's productivity level, and enhance individuals' lives, all at the same time? It is truly a privilege to be a trainer, yet it's also a responsibility.

Training is a profession on the move, and those moves are ones to be proud of. As I finished this book, the American Society for Training and Development (ASTD), the trainers' professional association, was putting the finishing touches on the first internationally recognized Workplace Learning and Performance certification process. Based on the competency study completed in 2004, certification will be the final and most critical element, providing credentials for the profession and adding excitement to an already exciting profession. Chapter 16 describes the certification process in more detail.

About This Book

Training For Dummies is both practical and fun. It has been written in a logical sequence and is loaded with practical ideas. It is designed to take you through a training cycle from start to finish, and in sequential order. So, if you want to, you can start at the beginning of this book and move through to the end. If you're interested in finding only specific information, however, you can also use the index at the back of the book or the Table of Contents near the front.

This book is also fun to read, but don't let the conversational tone fool you. It is jam-packed with technical knowledge about the training profession as well as tips, tricks, and techniques for honing your training skills.

I feel fortunate that several gurus in the training profession have agreed to contribute snippets of content that focus on their areas of expertise. So as you read *Training For Dummies,* be sure to check out what experts like Thiagi say about facilitation and Ann Herrmann-Nehdi say about learning styles.

Foolish Assumptions

While writing this book, I imagine you, the reader, sitting next to me and telling me what you want to read about. And what did I hear you saying? "Practical. Make it practical." So I did.

I assume you fall into one of two categories: Either you're interested in becoming a trainer, or you're already a trainer and want to hone your skills. Perhaps you're even interested in obtaining professional certification from ASTD.

I also assume that you've been a participant in training and that some of those training sessions have been life-changing, while others have been a waste of your time. And I assume that you want to know how to conduct more of the former and none of the latter.

I assume that you know how important the training profession is to corporations' bottom lines as well as this country's productivity.

Finally, I make one other assumption: that is that you love (or will grow to love) training as much as I do!

How This Book Is Organized

Training For Dummies is divided into six parts, and the chapters within each part cover specific topics in detail. The parts and chapters follow a logical sequence — from thinking about becoming a trainer to designing, delivering, and evaluating a training session and, finally to ensuring that you continue to enhance your professionalism.

Part 1: So You're Going to Be a Trainer!

This part explores the field of training and uncovers what a trainer does. It introduces you to The Training Cycle and presents a quick list of training jargon. You can even explore whether you think you'd like a profession in training. And if you're already a trainer, a self-assessment provides data about your areas of strength and those that may need a bit of shoring up.

Part II: Designing the Best Darn Training in the World

Trainers must remember one very important rule: It's all about the learner. When you have this concept firmly planted in your mind, you're on the right path to designing a successful training session. This part helps you understand how to assess your learners' needs, how to write learning objectives, and how to design a training session that will knock their socks off! You also explore using off-the-shelf training programs and preparing for success.

Part III: Showtime: Delivering a Dynamic Training Session

Many trainers are born stage hounds. And while training is not always a circus, seeing people's eyes light up when you put knowledge in their hands, and seeing how their lives change with new skills, is often reward enough.

This part focuses on the implementation aspect of a trainer's job. It describes how to deliver success by ensuring that learning occurs. It also helps you become a master of audiovisuals and provides suggestions for how to address the many problems that occur in a classroom.

Part IV: It's Not Over Yet: The Follow-Up

Evaluation and other follow-up activities occur at the end of The Training Cycle, but they are of critical importance because only with evaluation can you be assured that the training is a success. The training session may be over, but your work is not. This part shows you how and why.

Part V: The Professional Trainer

The training profession is rapidly changing, and as a trainer, you must, too, if you want to stay in the game. This part addresses three key areas that encourage you to be a lifelong learner: ideas for continually upgrading your skills and knowledge; an explanation of the ASTD certification process; and a perspective on other aspects of the field of training.

Part VI: The Part of Tens

No *For Dummies* book is complete without The Part of Tens. This easy-to-read part includes six concise chapters that are filled with tips, techniques, and tidbits that are sure to enhance your training sessions instantly. In this part, you discover the best ways to start every training session, methods for increasing participation, tips for saving time in the classroom, ways to form small groups, ideas to add humor to your training, and icebreakers that you can implement immediately.

Look in this part first to find tips that are worth the price of the book. (Read the entire book to uncover a professional goldmine.)

Icons Used in This Book

Throughout this book, you find icons in the left margins that alert you to information you need to know. You find the following icons in this book.

Quick tips and tricks to make your job easier and ideas to help you apply the techniques and approaches discussed.

Important information that is critical to being a professional trainer.

A few words that impart wisdom you can rely on.

Many people have made the profession what it is today, and their names and notions are a part of the foundation that trainers rely on to deliver success.

Specific thoughts and ideas that guide what you need to know about ASTD certification.

Where to Go from Here

You can approach this book from several different angles. You can, of course, start with Chapter 1 and read straight through to the end. But you may not have time for that. Check out some other approaches:

- ✔ If you're brand-new to the training scene, you may wish to start with Part I. It grounds you in the topic.
- ✔ If you're looking for ways to enhance your skills in either the design or the delivery area, go directly to Part II or Part III.
- ✔ If you're looking for several fast ways to improve your training delivery or enhance your training session, check out the Part of Tens, where you find 60 ideas. You can also skim through the rest of the book and look for the Tip icon, reading each one.
- ✔ If you're thinking about beginning a professional certification process, you may wish to go directly to Chapter 16 and read all about it.

No matter where you start reading in this book, you find practical ideas. So my advice is to just start!

Part I
So You're Going to Be a Trainer!

In this part . . .

You explore some basic thoughts about training. Are you right for the job? What skills do you need to brush up? Why do adults learn? By what process does training occur? This part answers your most basic questions.

Chapter 1

What's a Trainer?

In This Chapter

▶ Introducing the training profession and a trainer's job

▶ Assessing your skills and abilities as a training professional

▶ Determining the importance of training

▶ Exploring a trainer's (a)typical day

So you want to be a trainer. Or perhaps you already are a trainer, and you've picked up this book to enhance your skills. In either case, this chapter helps you understand the training profession and what's expected of trainers.

Training is one of the most exciting jobs anyone can have. Although a trainer's role has changed substantially over the past decade and is currently going through another metamorphosis, many of the positive aspects always remain with the job. First, as a trainer you impact the work of many people — not only the learners with whom you work but also supervisors, senior management, clients, vendors, and perhaps even your company's board of directors. As a trainer, you have access to many people and can develop a broader picture of your organization's needs. Trainers are usually good communicators with good information. People listen to you.

In addition, training is exciting because it is a job that is an integral step in an organization's efforts toward change and improvement. You may be a part of defining the organization of today, envisioning the organization of the future, and helping to incorporate the changes necessary to create the new organization. As a trainer, you have the opportunity to influence the direction your organization takes and how it gets there.

Take a proactive stance in shaping your career. To be the most effective trainer, find out all you can about the organization in which you work. What are the primary issues it faces? Partner with those who lead your organization and find out how you help them. Where are the pressure points that affect the bottom line? Identify how your work can positively impact the bottom line, given that you're in a unique position to impact others. At the same time, remember to also take the opportunity to impact your career.

In this chapter, you answer three big questions.

- ✔ What is training and who uses it?
- ✔ What do trainers do?
- ✔ Do you have what it takes to be a trainer?

What Is Training?

You can say that a person has been in training since he was born. You have been learning and changing into the knowledgeable, skilled adults you currently are. Everyone has received training, and we have also all trained others. If you ever demonstrated the phone system to a new employee, advised your boss regarding changes in your department, or explained a shortcut for completing a task to a colleague, you were conducting training.

Training is about change. It is about transformation. It is all about learning. Training is a process designed to assist an individual to learn new skills, knowledge, or attitudes. As a result, these individuals make a change or transformation that improves or enhances their performance. These improvements ensure that people and organizations are able to do things better, faster, easier, and with higher quality and a better return on investment.

What forms does training take?

Learning is acquired in many training forums. You may have experienced some of these. You may have a one-on-one session with your supervisor to learn the benefits of a new product your company produces. You may attend a class to upgrade your negotiating skills. You may take an online course to learn how to use a new computer program. You may take a golf lesson to learn how to improve your use of long irons. You may be coached by someone in your company to learn to be more politically savvy. The key word in each of these examples is "learn." The reason training is provided is so that someone (or many people) learns something in order to make a change.

Trainers are necessary in every industry, from aardvark ranches to zipper manufacturers. Trainers have jobs in private industry, education, not-for-profit organizations, and government.

Trainers work with people in all positions and at all levels in an organization: executives, managers, supervisors, secretaries, production workers, scientists, artists, doctors, lawyers, instructors, security guards, salespeople, teachers, firefighters, authors, custodial workers, wait staff, and you. Even this book is a form of training — self-directed training as you learn your way through its pages.

NAMES TO KNOW

A brief history lesson

Training has been around since the Stone Age. It's not likely that train-the-trainer seminars existed in 2000 B.C. Yet without some natural way to transfer skills and knowledge, people would never have progressed from the first wheel on a muddy road to the computer chips that guide our exploration of outer space. Probably the first documented training occurred in the 18th century, when artisans and craftsmen formed apprenticeships that utilized a demonstration-practice-feedback-practice-again process.

It wasn't until 1944 that training was organized under one banner, The American Society for Training Directors (later changing its name to The American Society for Training and Development, and known simply as ASTD).

Two influential professionals helped to shape the early years of the profession. Malcolm Knowles advanced the idea of *andragogy,* a learning theory for adults, distinct from *pedagogy* for children. This tipped the scale toward a more learner-centered approach as opposed

to a content-centered approach. Len Nadler coined the term *Human Resource Development* and added structure and organization to the field.

The 1990s found many practitioners desiring to officially expand the field of training to incorporate identifying business goals at the top of the organization and ensuring that systems were in place to support the change required to achieve the business goals. Proponents felt that the field should include both non-learning as well as learning interventions (including traditional training activities). They also believed that the new model should measure its success based on performance.

But what to call this newly expanded field? Perhaps, *Workplace Learning and Performance.* Dana and Jim Robinson have led the practical implementation of these concepts to the field of training. They have been influential in helping others to understand the difference between learning and performance and how a trainer's role has expanded.

Why is training necessary?

Every year, most organizations budget money for training — over 50 billion dollars in the United States alone. The volume of money and effort suggests that corporations believe training is important. What do they know about training that justifies this much investment? For starters, training plays an important role in developing a productive workforce and finely tuning processes to increase profits. Training also helps people and organizations manage change. Because organizations are continuously changing techniques, goals, equipment, people, and locations, all members of the workforce require training to support these changes.

There are four critical aspects of a coordinated comprehensive training approach. In the most efficient organizations, the four are aligned toward the same corporate goals.

✔ **There is a business need or requirement.** This is the starting point. Effective training starts with the clarification (or creation) of organizational goals. This enables the training department to provide a strategic approach to the services it offers the organization. Examples of business needs include increasing customer satisfaction, increasing market share, and improving quality.

✔ **There is a need to improve or change performance.** Performance is usually tied to a specific job and a task or set of tasks within that job. It is what the employee must do to achieve the organizational goal. For example, if improving quality is a business goal, each employee must know what process to use to ensure delivery of a quality product or service.

✔ **There is a need to gain knowledge or to learn new skills.** In order to change performance, employees may need to learn something new. This learning may take many forms such as coaching, classroom training, computer-based training (CBT), on-the-job training (OJT), or self-study.

✔ **There is a need for change in the environment.** At times, employees may possess the skills and knowledge required to change their performance, but some aspect of the environment either prevents or discourages individuals from making the change. For example, if an organization's goal is to improve quality, there will be little change if the reward system focuses on quantity, not quality.

Trainers are involved in providing services that address all these aspects. If you're a beginning trainer, you'll most likely start with interventions that deliver knowledge and new skills (the third bullet in the preceding list). This is the traditional "training" role. However, as you grow professionally, you may be required to provide training for all of the other needs that affect an organization.

What do organizations expect to accomplish by investing in training efforts? They desire change in performance of employees in order to:

✔ Reduce employee turnover

✔ Maintain current customers

✔ Create new customers

✔ Increase customer satisfaction

✔ Reduce errors

✔ Reduce expenses

✔ Save time

✔ Add dollars to the bottom line

Training is experiencing growing pains

As training enters the 21st century, the training field is experiencing growing pains in three ways.

✔ **The field of training is expanding its role.** In the "Why is training necessary?" section earlier in this chapter, I mention the importance of aligning the four requirements of the organization when budgeting for training: business, performance, learning, and environmental needs. This alignment is one of the important aspects that the Workplace Learning and Performance movement has brought to the field of training.

✔ **The field is indecisive about what to call itself.** At this time, the training profession is having an identity crisis — partially brought on by the expanded role. Whether it will be called Training and Development, Human Resource Development, or Workplace Learning and Performance is yet to be seen. But that doesn't bring the practitioners to a halt. Training must go on!

✔ **Certification is finally available for those practicing in the field.** This is beneficial because it provides the credentials to support the training field and adds credibility to the professional trainer. ASTD administers the process and approved the effort as this book went to press in early 2005. Details for how you can be certified as a Workplace Learning and Performance professional are available from ASTD. You may wish to begin to find out more about the ASTD Certification design by checking the ASTD Web site at www.astd.org. Also check out Chapter 16.

What's causing the growing pains? The evolution has to do with the difference between activity and results. In the past, the best measure of training was how many people were trained. Today, the measures go beyond the training room and directly to those things that affect the bottom line: increased productivity, improved sales, better quality, fewer errors, decreased employee turnover, and others. Businesses are finding ways to measure the effects of training on the business and are interested in their return on investment (ROI).

There are many reasons people require training in the workplace. Some of these reasons include:

✔ Orient new employees

✔ Provide long-term professional development

✔ Upgrade knowledge required for the job

✔ Introduce new skills to experienced employees

✔ Change career paths due to job elimination

But won't trainers run out of people to train? Not likely. Organizations are required to continually make changes. Technology advances continue to influence how trainers do their jobs. The skilled labor pool continues to shrink worldwide. Thousands of new employees enter the workforce every week. That keeps at least a few trainers busy.

Is training just for business?

You experience training in other parts of your life in addition to the workplace. For example, you may decide you want to play the piano or practice yoga. You may want to find out more about your ancestors or Italian artists. If so, you'll likely locate someone who teaches these subjects at your local college, community center, or in the Yellow Pages. In this way, individuals seek training for a variety of reasons outside the workplace:

- ✔ Learn new skills (try a new hobby such as painting or growing bonsai)
- ✔ Enhance skills you already have (take a tennis lesson to improve your game or a gourmet-cooking lesson to learn new techniques)
- ✔ Acquire knowledge about a subject that interests you (attend a class about African history or investing in the stock market)
- ✔ Gain information you require due to a life change (attend a class to learn to care for your elderly parent or learn how to prepare for retirement)

Training is available for all areas of your life.

What Do Trainers Do?

The trainers' roles, they are a changing, and many new roles are currently being defined in the training arena. The following list provides just a sample of the trainer roles and titles that are emerging.

- ✔ Career coach
- ✔ Chief learning officer
- ✔ Competency expert
- ✔ Computer-based training designer
- ✔ Continuous learning coach
- ✔ Corporate trainer
- ✔ Courseware designer
- ✔ Curriculum development specialist
- ✔ Employee development specialist
- ✔ Executive coach
- ✔ Facilitator
- ✔ Instructional designer
- ✔ Instructional technologist
- ✔ Instructor
- ✔ Knowledge manager
- ✔ Leadership trainer
- ✔ Manager of strategic initiatives
- ✔ Media designer
- ✔ Multimedia engineer
- ✔ Organization development specialist
- ✔ Performance analyst

✔ Performance consultant

✔ Performance technologist

✔ Performance improvement
technologist

✔ Technical trainer

✔ Training leader

✔ Workforce diversity director

Even though the preceding list uses wildly different words and appears to be quite diverse, all of these roles play a part in ensuring that people gain knowledge or skills, or change attitudes. In the "Why is training necessary?" section earlier in this chapter, I mention that beginning trainers usually start with interventions that design and deliver knowledge and new skills. This traditional "training" role remains the mainstay of the training field. In addition, classroom training continues to be the most used delivery method, hovering around 70 percent. Technology in the form of computer-based training (no instructor) and instructor-led training from a remote site (via Web conferencing or videoconferencing) have each grown slightly — around one percent — each year since 2000.

The two roles (design and delivery) can be further subdivided into two main categories. All training professionals are involved with designing and/or presenting a learning experience. Whether you design, deliver, or do a bit of both, you have two aspects to master: content and process.

✔ **Content:** Whether you're designing or presenting, you need to truly understand what others need to know about the topic. Get inside the topic and find out more than what's offered in your instructor's manual. Ask more questions of more people if you're designing. Talk to *subject matter experts,* often called *SMEs* in the training world. The content is based on your organization's needs.

✔ **Process:** Both design and delivery have methods that you incorporate into your training task. Design methods incorporate skills such as designing participant materials, incorporating adult learning principles, and selecting methods for the perfect blended learning program. Delivery methods incorporate skills such as facilitating group process, presentation skills, and managing disruptive participants.

This book provides tips and techniques for both content and process.

Assessing your training potential

Every career has its own set of characteristics that increase the chances that someone will enjoy the job and have a natural aptitude for the work that is done. The following list identifies a number of those characteristics for a trainer.

✔ Able to relate to specific situations

✔ Assertive and influencing

✔ Both logical and creative

✔ Builds trust

✔ Confident and poised

✔ Customer-focused

✔ Enjoys presenting information; articulate

✔ Enthusiastic

✔ Excellent communicator (verbal and written)

✔ Flexible and spontaneous

✔ Good listener

✔ Impartial and objective

✔ Lifelong learner

✔ Patient

✔ People-oriented, warm, and approachable

✔ Process-oriented

✔ Self-sufficient

✔ Sense of humor

✔ Solution- and results-oriented

✔ Strong business sense

✔ Team player and partners well

✔ Tolerant of ambiguity

✔ Well-organized

Examine the list of characteristics. Which of these are natural for you? Which do you need to work harder at to be a successful and satisfied trainer?

Take stock of your skills

In addition to natural aptitude, every job also requires a specific skill set. The skills required of a trainer are many and varied. ASTD completed a Competency Study for the Workplace Learning and Performance profession in 2004. This study identified the roles, competencies, and areas of expertise for the profession. The Competency Study further defines the skills that are required. The Training Knowledge and Skills Inventory that follows incorporates these skills.

Complete the Training Knowledge and Skills Inventory in Table 1-1 to identify your current strengths and the skills you need to improve to perform your job effectively. This activity assists you in setting specific objectives for your professional development.

Complete this inventory by evaluating your ability to perform each skill using two rating scales. You evaluate each skill from two perspectives. In Column 1 you rate your ability, and in Column 2 you rate the importance of the skill to your particular job.

Evaluate your ability by completing column 1 using this rating scale:

5   Outstanding ability (one of my talents)

4   Above-average ability

3   Average or moderate ability

2   Minimal ability

1   No experience or training in this area

Describe the importance of each skill to the job you currently have:

5   One of the most important aspects of the job

4   Above-average importance

3   Average importance

2   Occasional importance

1   Minimal importance

0   No importance

Table 1-1	Training Knowledge and Skills Inventory		
Professional Foundation			
Skills	*Column 1* *Your Ability*	*Column 2* *Importance on the Job*	*Column 3* *Difference (Col 1 – 2 = 3)*
Communicates effectively, verbally and in writing			
Continuous learner, improving and updating skills and knowledge			
Establishes professional credibility			
Promotes collaboration, partnerships and teamwork throughout the organization			
Is knowledgeable about the organization's vision, strategy, goals, business issues, and culture			

(continued)

Table 1-1 *(continued)*

Assessing Needs

Skills	*Column 1* *Your Ability*	*Column 2* *Importance* *on the Job*	*Column 3* *Difference* *(Col 1 – 2 = 3)*
Designs a plan for assessing needs using appropriate methodologies			
Conducts a needs assessment			
Analyzes needs to determine priorities			
Able to determine whether training or some other intervention is required			
Assesses learning and performance before and after to measure training effectiveness			

Designing Learning

Skills	*Column 1* *Your Ability*	*Column 2* *Importance* *on the Job*	*Column 3* *Difference* *(Col 1 – 2 = 3)*
Establishes effective learning objectives			
Selects, adapts, or creates a design appropriate for the project			
Selects and sequences content and instructional methods appropriate for the project and learners' diversity			
Designs blended learning solutions that incorporate online, classroom, on-the-job, self-paced, and other options			
Incorporates media and technology appropriately			
Determines whether to buy off-the-shelf or develop training materials			
Applies adult learning theory and principles in developing a curriculum			

Skills	Column 1 Your Ability	Column 2 Importance on the Job	Column 3 Difference (Col 1 – 2 = 3)
Develops and evaluates instructional materials and media support			
Designs participant-oriented learning activities			
Understands legal and ethical issues relevant to designing training			
Uses various techniques to prepare for training delivery			

Presenting and Facilitating

Skills	Column 1 Your Ability	Column 2 Importance on the Job	Column 3 Difference (Col 1 – 2 = 3)
Establishes credibility appropriately			
Arranges room/environment for optimal learning			
Creates positive learning environment			
Aligns learning methodologies with learners' styles and preferences			
Aligns objectives and learning with business and participant needs			
Demonstrates effective presentation and facilitation skills			
Demonstrates effective questioning skills			
Uses a variety of learning methodologies			
Stimulates and sustains learner motivation and encourages participation			
Uses audiovisuals effectively			
Demonstrates understanding of group dynamics			

(continued)

Table 1-1 *(continued)*

Presenting and Facilitating

Skills	Column 1 Your Ability	Column 2 Importance on the Job	Column 3 Difference (Col 1 – 2 = 3)
Manages difficult participants			
Manages unexpected events in the classroom and learning environment			
Promotes transfer of knowledge and skills to the workplace			

Evaluating Performance

Skills	Column 1 Your Ability	Column 2 Importance on the Job	Column 3 Difference (Col 1 – 2 = 3)
Evaluates learning, performance and instructional effectiveness			
Develops evaluations instruments, such as questionnaires, tests			
Incorporates feedback and data for future improvement			
Analyzes evaluation results			
Explains the four levels of evaluation			
Total			

Your self-assessment

So how did you do? Perhaps you did not know what some of the skills meant. That's okay for now. Each is more clearly defined throughout the book.

Take a few minutes to review the inventory you completed. First put a plus (+) next to the items for which you rated yourself at 5. These are the talents that form a foundation for your role as a trainer. Circle your three strongest in Table 1-1.

Next total Column 1. The maximum score is 200. In general a score of 150 or more indicates a well-rounded, proficient trainer. Not there? Not to worry. That's what this book is all about.

Next subtract Column 2 from Column 1 for each of the 40 skills. Write the difference in Column 3. Note that you have a negative number if Column 2 has a larger number than Column 1. If the difference is negative, it means that the task is important in your job and your skill level may not measure up. These areas clearly need improvement. Put squares around them in Table 1-1. If you have no negative numbers, identify those items that have the lowest numbers.

Your results provide you with a general direction for skills and knowledge you may wish to acquire.

The 2004 ASTD Competency Study provides a more extensive discussion of the skills and an explanation of the different skills required for other roles in the Workplace Learning and Performance profession. ASTD offers classes and other learning opportunities for new trainers or trainers desiring to brush up on their skills.

How do you become a trainer?

There are as many paths to a career in training as there are types of training. Many trainers, like me, can tell you they "came in the back door." I was a trainer for over a year before I realized that training was a profession in its own right. Because training became a collateral duty to the "real" job I had, I didn't consider that someone may have studied the training process to ensure effectiveness! It was only after I started messing around with the curriculum and experimenting with various training methodologies that my research led me to an entire body of knowledge. Until then, I thought I was inventing Adult Learning Theory! I must admit I was a bit disappointed when I first discovered Malcolm Knowles!

Most trainers work for organizations in other departments. They may drift over to the performance improvement department or the human resources department and apply for a job. Sometime they have taken a class and decide they want to be at the training end of the classroom rather than the learner end. In other cases they may have been tapped to conduct training on a new product, service, or procedure. Enjoying the experience, they followed up on how to do it full time. Some individuals enroll in adult learning degree programs.

No matter how you have gotten to this point in your career, and whether you're a part-time trainer, full-time trainer, or wannabe trainer, remember that a professional certification is available to you through ASTD, providing you with the foundation for becoming a trainer.

A Day in the Life of a Trainer

What's a typical day in the life of a trainer like? For most trainers, every day is different, so *atypical* is probably a better description. Here's what happens if you follow Jose for a day:

Jose has been with Honesty Parts and Services (HPS) for several years. He started out in the marketing department but enjoyed one of his interpersonal communications classes so much that he decided to apply for a job as a trainer in the human performance improvement department.

Jose's director reports to the Chief Learning Officer, who works with other leaders in the organization to determine a strategic direction and goals. Everything that the department does is aligned with the organization's strategic direction. When one of the department heads contacted Jose's director requesting the department to dcsign a training program, she first checked to ensure alignment. Next she conducted a performance assessment. After she determined that training was the solution, she turned the project over to Jose and a team that included an instructional designer, a subject matter expert, and a computer-based training designer.

Jose and his team spent the last few weeks designing a blended training program that would meet the needs of the department. The team started with the assessment results, conducted additional research on the topic, and interviewed additional people in the department. They considered the content, time available, the audience, and the locations. As a result, they designed a classroom module that included participant materials and a PowerPoint presentation, follow-up self-paced e-learning content, and a job aid. Jose put in long hours during the design and development stage.

The program pilot, a trial run, for the classroom module has been scheduled for today. Yesterday Jose and his team finalized the session materials, set up the room, checked out the audiovisual equipment, and arranged for lunch to be brought in from the cafeteria.

This morning, Jose arrived at the training site an hour before the session so that he could be certain everything was ready to go. Participants started arriving 45 minutes before the sessions started. As he introduced himself to individuals, he learned that many of them were uncertain of the location and that this was a first training opportunity for a few. The early arrivals did not give him any time to himself, so Jose was glad that he spent the past week preparing for the session. He had practiced the materials out loud, conducted a dry run with his team, tried out the activities with his peers, and even delivered some of the content to his family. He felt ready.

Jose had told his wife that he would be late getting home tonight. Following the session, which ends at 4:30 p.m., his team will meet to critique the day and to determine whether any adjustments need to be made in the agenda or the content for the next day.

Following the two-day session, he and his team will make any minor modifications to the session based on feedback from the participants, ensure that participants use the follow-up materials, follow up with the department head, and begin to schedule the other classes locally and at remote sites. He will travel overnight for several of the sessions but is looking forward to seeing some of the organization's branch offices.

Now, at 7:59 a.m., Jose looked out to the participants before starting. He felt satisfied that he was in a position to contribute to HPS's bottom line and that he had a job that gave him so much pleasure and satisfaction. With those thoughts on his mind, he smiled at the group and said, "Good morning!"

Do You Have What It Takes?

Although training may seem like a glamorous profession to an observer, like any other profession, it has its hidden challenges. Having the skills to be a trainer is only one prerequisite. A much more difficult requirement for a successful trainer is to have strong mental and emotional composure. Training is a demanding profession. It requires constant energy output. If you tire quickly, become discouraged easily, or become frustrated if things do not go according to plan, training may not be for you. Here are some aspects to consider about training.

✔ **Are you willing to work longer than an 8-hour day?** Even though a training program may be scheduled from 9 to 5, you may find yourself going to the training room much earlier than 9:00 a.m. and staying much later than 5:00 p.m. A well-prepared training session takes thoughtful room and material setup. If you arrive at the training room at the same time as the trainees, you will feel disorganized and unprepared. You may even start late because of last-minute preparations.

✔ **Are you also willing to stay later than your official "ending" time?** The same principle applies after the training program has ended. It is usually the trainer's responsibility to ensure that all items you used for the training are removed from the training room. You may need to replace tables and chairs the way you found them. You may need to straighten the room. Also, many trainees stay after the program is over so that they can ask questions they did not wish to ask in front of the rest of the participants. They expect the trainer to be there cheerfully ready to answer their questions. In addition, you may have many details to wrap up at the end of the day: add notes to your training manual, review your PowerPoint presentation for the next day, clean your transparencies, revise your schedule for the next day, complete administrative tasks, file your materials in order, send additional resources to a participant, or prepare a flip chart for the next day.

✔ **Can you stand on your feet all day?** Trainers do not often have the opportunity to sit down. Because they are facilitating the program in one way or another, they stand during all presentations and during most discussions. Even when the participants are in small groups, trainers move from group to group ready to answer questions, address problems, or know when to move on to the next subject.

✔ **Even if you can literally stand on your feet all day, can you figuratively stand on your feet all day?** No amount of preparation can equip a trainer for everything that can happen in a training session. The trainer must be prepared to respond to unexpected questions and events. A trainer must be flexible. Sometimes, the planned agenda doesn't fit the needs of the audience. A good trainer adjusts the agenda and changes the material so that it meets the needs of the audience. An effective trainer also reads the audience and adjusts the level of the training to fit the level of the audience.

✔ **Can you perform even when you feel lousy?** Trainers don't often have the discretion to call in sick. When a session is scheduled, it often has been done long in advance, and often learners travel from long distances to attend training. Therefore, trainers must be able to present enthusiastically even when they are a little under the weather. The show must go on!

✔ **Are you prepared to constantly give of yourself without expecting to receive anything in return?** Trainers are often viewed by others as "healers" — those people who always have the answers and who can perform "magic." Conversely, trainers are not often perceived as people who have their own needs. As a result, participants may use your training program to get some bad feelings off their chests. Giving may extend to time as well, such as having time for breaks and lunch that may be used by participants wanting to discuss their personal situations.

✔ **Can you be the perfect role model all the time?** It is a trainer's job to teach the "right" way to do things. You must also be prepared to practice what you preach. Trainers run the risk of losing their credibility if they are not perceived to be a perfect example of what they teach. And, because no one is perfect, trainers must also admit it when they make a mistake. Trainers cannot allow participants to leave a training session with incorrect information.

✔ **Can you cope with constant logistic problems?** Even though it may be someone else's responsibility to make room and equipment arrangements, it becomes the trainer's problem if something is not right. Are you prepared to deal with malfunctioning equipment, rooms that are not set up, reservations clerks who say you never reserved a room, materials that do not arrive, materials that have been typed or collated incorrectly, or any mess-up in general? A good trainer takes full accountability for ensuring that all logistics of a training program are in order.

✔ **Can you be a big lug?** Although it would be nice to have all the training materials, supplies, and equipment just magically show up at the training site, it is more likely that you will be the person responsible for getting it all there. Packing, loading, unloading, and unpacking (and then doing it all over again) is simply a part of a trainer's job.

✔ **Are you prepared to encourage your participants even when there is a lack of management commitment?** Sometimes, people are sent to training because their managers think that it is "a good thing to do." There may be little serious commitment to support and encourage these employees when the training is completed. Can you provide support and understanding in the absence of managers' commitment?

✔ **Can you deliver hard feedback?** Trainees do not learn effectively if during their training process they are not given honest feedback. Are you able to give this feedback, even when it is not good and even if it may impact an employee's job?

✔ **Are you able to process failure, identify solutions, and make improvements?** Not every training program is a smashing success. In fact, some are downright bad. Successful trainers are those who analyze what went wrong in the bad sessions and then design changes in the program so that it improves the next time around.

Many of the preceding questions are certainly not meant to discourage you, but rather to introduce the reality of a sometimes glamorous-appearing job. It may be challenging. It usually requires a great deal of work. And it can be riddled with problems. However, you forget all the difficulties when former participants tell you that "you changed their lives." Or that "you inspired them." Of course this doesn't happen on a weekly basis, but it does happen often enough to make it all worthwhile.

Yes, training is a demanding, sometimes hectic, often ambiguous job. There is never a dull moment. It is exciting. It is the catalyst for improvement. It is the process to the future. Training exists to facilitate change and to encourage transformation for a better future. The late Christa McAuliffe, teacher and NASA astronaut, summed it up this way: "I touch the future; I teach."

Chapter 2

Why Adults Learn

In This Chapter

▶ Examining the basic principles of adult learning

▶ Identifying a trainer's responsibility to ensure adults learn

▶ Identifying types of learning

▶ Defining training roles

*T*hink back to the past 60 days. What is one thing you learned?

Before reading ahead, try to recall what you learned and why you learned it. Perhaps you learned to play racquetball because you always wanted to learn to play the game. Perhaps you had a flat tire on the way home, and you had to learn to change the tire because you had to do it. You didn't want to, but you had no choice.

If you're like most adults, you learn to do most things as an adult because you want to learn it or you need to learn it.

This chapter explores adult learning theory, how people learn, and how trainers can assist participants to learn in the classroom.

Adult Learning Theory

Trainers are most successful when they understand conditions under which adults learn best. Therefore, it is important to understand the difference between why adults learn and how adults are traditionally taught.

The traditional style of teaching is based on a didactic model, a synonym for lecturing. Generally this model is teacher-led and content-centered. Another word used is *pedagogy,* which literally means the art of teaching children.

In the introduction to this chapter, you discovered that most adults learn things because they want to or need to. Children do, too. However, children's formal learning is usually led by someone else and is based on their learning specific tasks to prepare them to learn additional, more complicated tasks.

For example, you learned to count to 100 in kindergarten so that you could learn to add and subtract in first grade, so that you could learn to multiply and divide in third grade, so that you could learn algebra in eighth grade, so that you could learn trigonometry in high school, so that you could learn calculus in college.

Most people have experienced the pedagogical model of learning. It has dominated education for centuries and assumes the following:

- ✔ The instructor is the expert. Because the learner has little experience, it is up to the instructor to impart wisdom.

- ✔ The instructor is responsible for all aspects of the learning process, including what, how, and when the learners learn.

- ✔ Learning is content-centered. Objectives establish goals, and a logical sequence of material is presented to the learners.

- ✔ Motivation is external, and learners learn because they must reach the next level of understanding, pass a test, or acquire certification.

Does this sound familiar? It should. Unless you had an atypical learning situation, it is most likely how you were taught starting in kindergarten and through college. Some schools are changing however. Although the lecture method is still used, it is frequently enhanced with other learning methods. This suggests that someone has identified a better method for teaching.

Who is Malcolm Knowles?

Malcolm Knowles is considered the father of adult learning theory. Because pedagogy is defined as the art and science of teaching children, European adult educators coined the word *andragogy* to identify the growing body of knowledge about adult learning. It was Dr. Knowles' highly readable book, *The Adult Learner: A Neglected Species,* published in 1973, that took the topic from theoretical to practical. Table 2-1 compares the differences between andragogy and pedagogy. Trainers and adult educators began to implement practical applications based on Dr. Knowles' six assumptions.

The following list summarizes Malcolm Knowles' six assumptions and adds a practical application from a trainer's perspective. Although there is some duplication of ideas, I have presented all six assumptions to you as Knowles identified them. Many authors distill the six to five, four, and even three.

- ✔ Adults have a need to know why they should learn something before investing time in a learning event. Trainers must ensure that the learners know the purpose for training as early as possible.

- ✔ Adults enter any learning situation with an image of themselves as self-directing, responsible grown-ups. Trainers must help adults identify their needs and direct their own learning experience.

✔ Adults come to a learning opportunity with a wealth of experience and a great deal to contribute. Trainers are successful when they identify ways to build on and make use of adults' hard-earned experience.

✔ Adults have a strong readiness to learn those things that help them cope with daily life effectively. Training that relates directly to situations adults face is viewed as relevant.

✔ Adults are willing to devote energy to learning those things that they believe help them perform a task or solve a problem. Trainers who determine needs and interests and develop content in response to these needs are most helpful to adult learners.

✔ Adults are more responsive to internal motivators such as increased self-esteem than external motivators such as higher salaries. Trainers can ensure that this internal motivation is not blocked by barriers such as a poor self-concept or time constraints by creating a safe learning climate.

Table 2-1   Andragogical and Pedagogical Training: A Comparison

Andragogy	*Pedagogy*
Learners are called "participants" or "learners."	Learners are called "students."
Independent learning style.	Dependent learning style.
Objectives are flexible.	Objectives are predetermined and inflexible.
It is assumed that the learners have experience to contribute.	It is assumed that the learners are inexperienced and/or uninformed.
Active training methods are used.	Passive training methods, such as lecture, are used.
Learners influence timing and pace in a learner-centered approach.	Trainer controls timing and pace.
Participant involvement is vital to success.	Participants contribute little to the experience.
Learning is real-life problem-centered.	Learning is content-centered.
Participants are seen as primary resources for ideas and examples.	Trainer is seen as the primary resource who provides ideas and examples.

Applying adult learning theory to training

I don't know whether Malcolm Knowles had this in mind when he presented his adult learning theory to the world, but it seems that he is talking about responsibility. Furthermore, whether you're the trainer or the learner you have responsibility to ensure that the training is successful, that learning occurs, and that change takes place.

If you're the trainer

✔ Create a learning environment that is safe.

✔ Be organized, have well-defined objectives, and establish a clear direction for your session based on the participants' needs. Be so well organized that it is easy to be flexible when the participants' needs are different from what you anticipated.

✔ Ensure that your content is meaningful and transferable to the learners' world.

✔ Treat your learners with respect, understanding, and genuine concern.

✔ Invite learners to share their knowledge and experiences.

If you're the learner

✔ Be an active learner, participating in the interactive exercises.

✔ Be critical of poorly defined sessions, an unprepared trainer, or processes that prevent your learning; provide constructive feedback to the trainer.

✔ Ensure your personal success by encouraging feedback from the trainer.

Delivering constructive feedback is a key action expected of all professional trainers. Learners have a right to receive feedback from their trainers.

✔ Recognize that you're responsible for your own learning, so ensure that all your questions are answered.

✔ Contribute to your own success by clearly identifying a learning plan for yourself; then do your part to achieve your objectives.

Trainers beware! Note that I encourage learners to be critical of you if you're not prepared or the session doesn't meet their needs. Why? Professional trainers profess to build on the foundation of adult learning theory. If something is not working, step back, determine why, and fix it. If you're not doing that, you're not practicing good adult learning principles. You may need another trainer to guide you.

How Do People Learn?

The adult learning theory presented in the previous section provides a foundation of principles of adult learning. However, there are additional considerations to enhance results when training adults. In the following sections, I examine them.

Bloom's Taxonomy

In the early '60s, Benjamin Bloom and a university committee identified three learning domains: cognitive, psychomotor, and affective. Because the project was completed by university folks, the terms may seem a bit abstract.

Trainers typically use knowledge (cognitive), skills (psychomotor), and attitude (affective) to describe the three categories of learning. In addition, trainers frequently refer to these three learning categories as the KSAs. You may think of these as the ultimate goals of the training process — what your learner acquires as a result of training.

Bloom's group further expanded on the domains. They created a hierarchical ordering of the cognitive and affective learning outcomes. Their work subdivided each domain, starting from the simplest behavior to the most complex: Knowledge, Comprehension, Application, Analysis, Synthesis, and Evaluation. Each of these levels builds on the earlier one. For example, knowledge must occur prior to comprehension; comprehension must occur before application. Each level of learning identified the desired specific, observable, and measurable result.

This work is known as *Bloom's Taxonomy*. The divisions are not absolutes, and other systems and hierarchies have been developed since then. Bloom's Taxonomy, however, is easily understood and may be the most widely applied. The following table explains what it means.

Behavioral Levels	Skills	Examples
Knowledge	Define, list, name, recall, repeat knowledge or information	Can name six levels of Bloom's Taxonomy
Comprehension	Translate, describe, explain information in one's own words	Can compare and explain Bloom's six levels
Application	Apply, demonstrate, use knowledge in new situations	Can apply Bloom's theory to write learning objectives
Analysis	Analyze, compare, question, break knowledge into parts	Can compare and contrast aspects of Bloom's model
Synthesis	Arrange, create, plan, prepare a new whole from parts	Can design a new learning model
Evaluation	Appraise, assess, judge, score information based on knowledge	Can evaluate and defend the benefits of Bloom's Taxonomy

It is interesting to note that although the committee actually identified three domains of learning, they applied the six levels to only the cognitive and affective learning domains. They did not elaborate on psychomotor (skills). Their explanation for this was that they had little experience teaching manual skills at the college level.

Three types of learning: KSAs

Trainers address three types of learning: knowledge (K), skills (S), and influencing attitude (A). Trainers frequently shorten this to the KSA acronym. (If you want the research to support this, it is called *Bloom's Taxonomy.*)

Knowledge (Bloom called this *cognitive*) involves the development of intellectual skills. Examples of knowledge include understanding the principles of accounting, knowing the stages of childhood, understanding how interest rates affect the economy, or knowing how to get a book published.

Skills (Bloom called this *psychomotor*) refers to physical movement, coordination, and the use of the motor-skills area. Examples of skills you may learn include the ability to use a digital camera, operate a backhoe, supervise staff, listen effectively, or kick a soccer ball.

Attitude (Bloom called this *affective*) refers to how you deal with things emotionally, such as feelings, motivation, and enthusiasm. Although attitude is not "taught," training may affect it. Trainers cannot change attitudes, but they frequently have the opportunity to influence attitudes.

Trainers sometimes discuss whether it is the learner's skill or will that prevents topnotch performance following a training session. This refers to the fact that an employee may have learned the skill but is unwilling to use it. Therefore, the real reason an employee may not be using what was learned may not be skill-based at all. It may be that the employee won't use the skill that was learned.

Knowing that there are three types of learning means that you need to use different methods to address each. I discuss this in more depth in Chapter 5 when I address design.

Other considerations for learning

How do you gain information? Hear? See? Do you also touch? Smell and taste, too? You bet you do! We all gain information through our five senses. The highest percent of information usually comes through seeing and hearing.

Many people have theories about how humans learn best. David Kolb, for example, presents four learning styles: the converger, the diverger, the assimilator, and the accommodator. Another theory was developed by W. E. (Ned) Herrmann. His research shows brain specialization in four quadrants and that each quadrant has its own preferred way of learning. Ned's daughter Ann Herrmann-Nehdi continues to enhance her father's work.

Still a third theory, *Neurolinguistic Programming (NLP),* proposes that everyone takes information in through three modalities: visual, auditory, and kinesthetic. Most people use a combination of all three modalities. Preferred learning styles determine how your participants assimilate, sort, retain, retrieve, and reproduce new information.

Visual learners, for example, prefer pictures, diagrams, and other visuals. They probably need to "see it" to "know it." They may have artistic ability and a strong sense of color. They may have difficulty following directions or learning from lectures. They may overreact to noise or misinterpret words.

How can you create a learning environment that is conducive for the visual learner? Consider these suggestions.

- ✔ Provide written directions when possible.
- ✔ Enhance presentations with visuals, graphics, illustrations, diagrams, props, or flowcharts.
- ✔ Create a colorful classroom with neon sticky-back notes, posters, colorful and coordinated markers, crayons, and participant materials.
- ✔ Provide paper (colorful) and markers for doodling and taking notes.
- ✔ Help participants visualize a process using films, demonstrations, or role plays to "show" how.
- ✔ Color code participant materials or use icons to help them find their way.

Auditory learners, on the other hand, prefer to get information by listening. They need to "hear it" to "know it." They may have difficulty following written directions or any activity that includes reading.

How can you create a learning environment that is conducive for the auditory learner? Consider these suggestions.

- ✔ Provide spoken directions, when possible.
- ✔ Use discussions, tapes, debates, panels, interviews, and other verbal methods for transferring knowledge.
- ✔ Plan for buzz groups, small group discussion, teach-backs, and presentations that allow participants to talk through the information.
- ✔ Avoid using subtle body language or facial expression to make a point.
- ✔ Create learning activities in which learners repeat the information.

Finally, kinesthetic learners prefer hands-on learning. They need to "do it" to "know it." They assemble things without reading directions and usually have good spatial perception. They learn best when they are actively involved.

How can you create a learning environment that is conducive for the kinesthetic learner? Consider these suggestions.

- ✔ Provide physically active learning opportunities.
- ✔ Engage them in experiential, hands-on learning activities.
- ✔ Provide things for them to touch and "play with" such as Play Doh, tactile toys, koosh balls, and crayons.
- ✔ Take frequent breaks or allow informal movement during the session that doesn't disturb other participants.
- ✔ Build in activities such as making models, role playing, scavenger hunts, relay races, and other active review and practice methods.
- ✔ Use computers to reinforce learning.
- ✔ Find ways other than testing to express knowledge and skills, such as demonstrations.

You usually encounter all of these learning styles in a training session at one time.

So what does a trainer do? It is not usually possible to address all the learning preferences all the time in a group. Do what all good trainers do.

- ✔ Accept that people learn in different ways.
- ✔ Use different methods that facilitate learning for different preferences.
- ✔ And, finally, when designing or delivering training, strive to create a variety of approaches that utilize techniques and activities from all learning preferences.

Helping Adults Learn in the Classroom

You may have a difficult time finding practical advice to ensure that the training room — your workplace — maximizes adult learning. However, in 25 years of experience in classrooms, I've discovered practical tips for applying Malcolm Knowles' principles to ensure that participants learn. I've grouped them in four categories for you.

- ✔ Create a safe haven for learning.
- ✔ Create a comfortable environment.
- ✔ Encourage participation.
- ✔ Facilitate more than you lecture.

In the following sections, I examine each of these and help you decide how you can address them.

Create a safe haven for learning

It would be great if everything you did as a trainer went just the way it was supposed to, but it won't. Trust me. Some learners may arrive thinking that training is punishment. Others may arrive with memories of past learning experiences in mind, such as failing tests. Yet others may arrive bringing their daily burdens with them. You can create a safe haven for everyone by using some of these ideas.

- ✔ Be prepared early enough so that you can greet participants at the door, welcome them, learn their names, and allow time for them to tell you something that's important to them.

- ✔ Share the objectives of the training early, prior to the session, if possible.

- ✔ Let participants know how they stand to benefit from the information.

- ✔ Demonstrate your respect for each individual.

- ✔ Ensure confidentiality — "what's said in the room stays in the room."

- ✔ Add something whimsical to pique curiosity and add a smile. This may be crayons, clay, koosh balls, or manipulative toys.

- ✔ Use names and sincere reinforcement to build rapport.

I like to use table tents (card stock folded in half length-wise) on which participants write their names. Some trainers prefer to use name badges. Whatever your choice, be sure that you can read them. For example, ask participants to write their first names large enough so that everyone can read them from across the room. If you use preprinted table tents, ensure that the type size is bold and can be read from 40 feet. Also, if water glasses are placed on the tables, bunch them up in one spot so that participants take them as they need them. Otherwise, there will be one sitting in front of each table tent, and you will be unable to read the names.

Create a comfortable environment

I prefer to arrive in a training room early enough to make it mine so that I can welcome the learners in as my guests. As a trainer, be sensitive to the mood of the room — created by both the physical aspects as well as each participant's demeanor. To create a comfortable environment, consider these suggestions before your next training session.

- ✔ Turn the lights on bright. There is nothing more depressing to me than walking into a ballroom where the lights have been left on romantic dim from the party the night before.

Ask for a room with natural light. Even on a sunless day, natural light is more pleasant than any artificial lighting.

✔ Learn how to adjust the thermostat for the most comfortable level for most of the participants. Remember, you can never please all of them all the time. Do your best.

✔ Ensure that the environment "looks" comfortable. Hide empty boxes. Chairs should be straight. Place materials neatly and uniformly at each seat. This order tells the learners that you care and went to the trouble of getting ready for them.

✔ Ensure that you and your visuals can be seen and heard by all learners. Go ahead try it out. Sit in their seats. Will all participants be able to see your visuals and hear you?

✔ Arrange to have the most comfortable chairs available.

✔ Arrange the tables to be conducive to learning. Chapter 7 provides a number of suggestions.

✔ Ensure that everyone has adequate personal space.

✔ Have extra supplies, pens, and paper available.

✔ Have coffee, tea, and water waiting in the morning.

✔ Plan for ample breaks.

Learning with style: Seven things trainers do

by Ann Herrmann-Nehdi

It has been widely established that people have preferred learning styles and teaching styles, so what is a trainer to do in response?

✔ **Expect difference!** Research has shown that men and women, different age groups, different brain dominance styles, and different personalities all learn differently! If you design and train knowing that your learners all process information differently, you won't be caught off guard and will be better equipped from the start to respond to those differing styles.

Do some research about your learners to better know in advance how diverse they may be. Look for data on occupations, age, gender, culture, and anything you can learn about their background. Look for ways to make links in your content to the different interests and backgrounds you're working

with. Brain research has shown that the more the context fits with your learning, the better your learners will remember what you have taught .

✔ **Do not follow the Golden Rule.** Most kids grew up being told to "do to others as you want them to do to you." Why ignore the Golden Rule? The way *you like* to learn may be opposite from the way your learners like to learn. It is easy to assume that everyone will find your approach as interesting as you do. Think of the times you were frustrated with the style of an instructor or trainer! Don't let that happen to your learners!

Look for new ideas by observing other trainers doing similar content, how do they approach it? Ask your group about they way they prefer to learn; get them involved. Try cofacilitating and designing with a partner who does things differently.

✔ **Remember to be a learner yourself!** How easy it is to forget what it is like to be a participant. Putting yourself into learning situations will provide you with a very good reminder. Be willing to experiment, attend programs, and stay current with new approaches and techniques you can learn by observing others in action. It is very easy to get stuck in a "rut" and teach a program you know well the same way every time.

Sign up for conferences (check out www. vnulearning.com/about-trg.htm or www.astd.org) and go to a wide variety of sessions, network with others in the training profession, and attend as many learning experiences as you can.

✔ **Give learners enough time to learn.** It is very important to provide time for application and practice in different formats. Brain studies have shown that in order for learning to "stick" in memory, many learners need "mental rehearsal," time to apply and practice. If you have a learner who is learning outside of his/her preferred style, this time is even more critical. Too often, in today's hurried world, people eliminate or shorten the time needed to apply, practice, and "rehearse" mentally what has been learned.

Provide context-specific practice to allow learners to take in the learning in their own formats and contexts. Be sure to allow for questions and clarification after the practice.

✔ **Watch your reactions — both verbal and nonverbal.** Gestures, tone, facial expressions, and eye contact are all taken in by your audience, often at a subconscious level. You may be inadvertently reacting in a negative way to a learner with a style you find uncomfortable.

Videotape yourself and observe your verbal and nonverbal reactions — especially to learners whom you may find irritating or different — and/or get feedback from others. It may be necessary to practice changing your expression, tone, or gestures.

✔ **Don't load your questions.** Many questions are preloaded with the answer and may be only suited to a specific type of learner. Ask questions in varied ways and give enough time for answers. Questions provide a great opportunity for learners to participate.

Think of as many ways as you can to ask questions. Observe other trainers. Have a partner capture the type of questions you typically ask and look for variety the next time you train. Be aware that leaving a five-second pause after the question provides a much greater opportunity for your learners to process and respond more effectively. You may also find ways to draw in other learners who are not as quick to offer an answer.

✔ **Multiple ways of training equals multiple learning options.** Too often, trainers train with only one approach — it may be comfortable, what you're used to, or just what you have had available. Examples may include PowerPoint slides with text bullets, lectures, games, discussion, and so on. To honor different learning styles, it is essential to use different delivery approaches. Experiment with different ways to get across your learning messages.

Use a whole-brain approach. For the Left Brain, use lecture, theories, data, case studies, problem-solving activities, and debate for logical learners; use outlines, structured quizzes, reference material, step-by-step practice, and detailed study for structured learners. For the Right Brain, use collaborative activities, role play, presentations, writing, and music for interpersonal learners. For holistic learners, try visualization, games, creative activities, props, metaphors and visuals, conceptual models, and brainstorming.

Encourage participation

I believe that creating active and ample participation is the most important thing you can do to enhance learning. You find this thread running through the entire book. Here are a couple of thoughts to get you started.

- Use small break-out groups to overcome any reluctance to share ideas or concerns.
- Use participants' names as often as possible.
- Use body language to encourage participation; positive nods, smiles, and eye contact all show that you're interested in others' ideas.
- Share something of yourself to begin a trusted exchange of ideas.
- Learn and apply techniques to get learners to open up. You'll discover numerous ideas later in this book.

Facilitate more than you lecture

There are few times when straight lecture is required. Perhaps when rules or laws must be imparted word for word, when safety is an issue, or when your learners have no knowledge of the subject. But for the most part, facilitating experiential activities and discussions lead to the same end, enhancing learning for everyone.

- Create discussion. Not just between you and the learners, but among the learners.
- Get opinions and ideas out in the open before you deliver your message. You may be surprised at how much "training" the learners can do for you.
- Share personal experiences to build rapport and trust.
- Provide opportunities for participants to evaluate their own learning throughout the session.
- Create experiential learning activities in which the learners discover the learning on their own.

One Last Note: Who's Who and What's What

What is the difference between trainers, teachers, instructors, facilitators, and others? What distinguishes learners, participants, trainees, and students? How about the difference between training, educating, and instructing? And last, what's the difference between learning, knowledge, skills, and performance?

Who's who?

First, examine those who are delivering the training:

- **Trainers:** Title given to adults who are the learning catalysts so other adults may learn new skills and knowledge. Often, but not always, the skills and knowledge taught by trainers are required to enhance the learner's performance on the job.

- **Facilitators:** Title given adults who ensure learners' participation; sometimes interchangeable with trainers but more often used when little knowledge or skill is dispensed. Often used for describing a person who conducts team-building or strategic-planning sessions.

- **Presenters:** Title given adults who deliver speeches at conferences or to larger groups; minimal emphasis on two-way communication.

- **Instructors:** Title used for teachers in academia. May also be used for specific skill sets, such as tennis instructors or flight instructors.

- **Teachers:** Title most often given those who are instructing children; pedagogical.

How about those who are receiving the training?

- **Learners:** A neutral term that can be used for anyone gaining information.

- **Participants:** A general term used by trainers to refer to anyone in a learning or intervention session; a learner.

- **Trainees:** Synonymous with participants; most recently has been replaced by "learners" or "participants."

- **Students:** Used for young children; pedagogical.

Avoid using the word "student" when discussing your participants. Learners or participants best define the adults whom you're training.

What's what?

The activity that occurs between the two *whos* in the preceding section may be called any of these.

- **Training:** The activity conducted by adults who are learning new skills. (Of course this can refer to animals as well!) Knowledge is generally put to immediate use. Hands-on practice is included.

- **Facilitating:** May be interchanged with the term "training." Usually refers to taking less of a leading role and being more of a catalyst.

> I was once given a great bit of advice that I pass on to you. To be the most successful trainer/facilitator, don't be a sage on stage, but be a guide on the side.

✔ **Instructing:** Allows participants to generalize beyond what has been taught. Minimal hands-on practice.

✔ **Educating:** Imparting knowledge generally in a broader context with delayed implementation. Very little hands-on practice.

The results of the activity just discussed may be called some of these:

✔ **Learning:** Gaining knowledge and skills to make change.

✔ **Knowledge:** Gaining cognitive competence and information assimilation.

✔ **Skill development:** Gaining psychomotor competence.

✔ **Performance:** Implementing the knowledge and skills that have been gained.

You may find other labels for these roles and what occurs, and as the profession grows and changes you're likely to find even more. What you call yourself is not nearly as important as the significant work you accomplish: Helping adults learn so they can improve their performance.

Again, why do adults learn? Because everyone wants or needs to learn. We are all trainers, all learners. Carl Rogers said, "The degree to which I can create relationships which facilitate the growth of others as separate persons is a measure of the growth I have achieved in myself."

Chapter 3

The Training Cycle

● ●

In This Chapter

▶ Introducing The Training Cycle

▶ Defining training jargon

▶ Ensuring learning occurs in The Training Cycle

● ●

*T*he most widely used method for developing new training programs is called *Instructional Systems Design (ISD)*. ISD was originally developed by and for the military to effectively create training programs. There are about 100 different ISD models and as many names, but most are based on four to seven steps represented by the acronym ADDIE:

✔ Analysis

✔ Design

✔ Development

✔ Implementation

✔ Evaluation

These steps are logically sequenced and ensure a practical approach to designing a training program. Some ISD models are linear; some are circular. They all accomplish the same thing: design a training program that gets results. The Training Cycle presented in the next section represents the ISD model that guides you through the rest of the book.

This chapter is dedicated to understanding The Training Cycle, its background, its moving parts, and how learning fits into it.

The Training Cycle: An Overview

Anytime you attended a training program, whether it was off-the-shelf or developed from scratch, whether it was taught by someone inside your organization or an external vendor, whether it was a program teaching management development skills or word processing skills, chances are that the program was designed by following a specific process, or a representative ISD model. I refer to this process as *The Training Cycle.* The Training Cycle begins long before the training program is conducted and continues after the program has been completed. Figure 3-1 is an illustration of the five stages of The Training Cycle. In this chapter, you get a brief overview of each stage of the Cycle. Subsequent chapters provide the depth you need to begin to implement each stage yourself.

It is critical for all trainers to be well rounded and understand the training process from start to finish. The Training Cycle provides you with a big picture of the process. You can fill in the details as you move through this book.

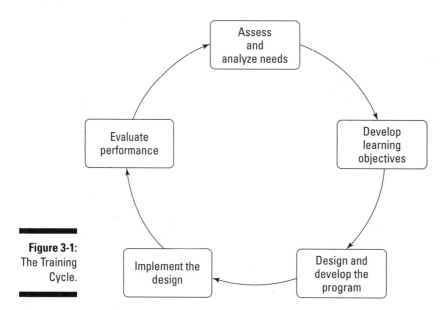

Figure 3-1:
The Training
Cycle.

Assess and analyze needs

This stage of The Training Cycle is called *analysis* in the ADDIE acronym. Generally, you need to conduct an assessment and analyze the data to identify specific needs. There are two main reasons for completing an assessment and analysis.

✔ First, you want to make sure there is a reason to conduct training. You may discover, after conducting the analysis, that the relevant issue can be addressed by something other than training. For example, you may be able to do on-the-job coaching, or you may feel that an article in the company newsletter alerts employees to the information needed.

✔ Second, if you do determine that training is necessary, the analysis should tell you exactly what should be taught in the training session. It should also help you determine your training objectives.

There are many ways to conduct assessments. You can use a formal instrument that measures a person's skill or knowledge or one that simply measures a person's preference. You can use written questionnaires or you can use personal interviews. If you use interviews, you can meet with individuals one-on-one, or you can conduct small focus groups. Another way to assess a need is to observe an employee working or to take a work sample. You can also use records or reports that already exist.

Your goal in collecting this data is to determine the gap between a job requirement and an individual's actual skill or knowledge. Bottom line is to determine what is preventing the desired performance. You use this information in the next stage of The Training Cycle.

Develop learning objectives

After you have determined that there is a legitimate training need, your next step is to state exactly what you want the training to accomplish. You do this by writing objectives. There are two kinds of objectives from two perspectives used in training:

✔ **The learning objective:** This is a statement of the performance (knowledge or skill) that is desired after the training has been conducted. Learning objectives should be based on the information you discovered during the analysis step. For example, "At the end of this training session, participants will be able to design participant-focused learning activities."

✔ **The training objective:** This is a statement of what the instructor hopes to accomplish during the training session. This may be an outcome, or it may be a description of what the instructor plans to do in order to accomplish the learning objectives. For example, "This session will create a positive learning climate that encourages participants to get involved and to ask questions."

Some trainers include both learning and training objectives in their design. Learning objectives are a required step in every good training design. Training objectives help the trainer to focus on designing and delivering a first-class training program by setting targets for the trainer to achieve.

Learners are told what the learning objectives are at the beginning of a training session. And preferably at the same time they are told about the training. But wait, I am getting ahead of myself. I have not yet begun the design process! That's what the next stage of The Training Cycle is all about.

Design and develop the program

After you determine the objectives, you can begin the program design. This is the stage of The Training Cycle that I like best. You decide exactly what you're going to do to accomplish the objectives you set. There are many things to consider in designing a training program.

Your first decision is whether to design it at all. You may decide instead to buy it off the shelf and customize it. Whether you design or customize, you want to consider who your audience is, what the best training techniques are, how to add creativity to the program, and how to ensure that learning objectives are met. You also build in methods to ensure that the learning is applied back on the job and a process to evaluate the program's effectiveness.

If you design it, a big task ahead of you is developing the materials. What paper handouts do the learners need? What audiovisual materials and equipment will you use? If it is an online course, what technical support will you require? Will your learners require job aids — either paper or online? While this stage can be exciting, it can also be exhausting.

Implement the design

This is The Training Cycle stage where you actually conduct the program. A trainer completes a huge amount of preparation before the program. Even after an excellent job of preparing, there is no guarantee that the program will go off without a hitch. That's why some trainers pilot a program with a group of pseudo-learners who provide feedback before the session is ready for prime time.

You use both presentation and facilitation skills. As a trainer, you're a presenter and a facilitator:

- **Presenters provide more information.** If much of the information is new or technical, you may need to present. The preferred role, however, is as a facilitator.
- **Facilitators play more of a catalyst role and ensure learners' participation.** A good trainer is often synonymous with the term "facilitator."

While you're conducting the training, you want to constantly read your audience to see whether you're meeting their needs. If you see that an approach isn't working, stop and try another. Don't be afraid to stray from the agenda if that seems to be the audience's need. This is the stage where platform experience and good facilitation skills are required.

Evaluate performance

When it's over, it's not over. The evaluation stage is an important part of The Training Cycle for three reasons:

✔ First, the evaluation tells you whether or not the objectives were accomplished.

✔ Second, information from the evaluation stage should be fed into the assess and analyze stage. It is used to improve the training program should it be conducted again. This is why this model is circular.

✔ Finally, evaluation information serves as the basis for determining needs for future programs or other changes an organization may need to make.

Thus the cycle is complete and the process starts all over again. I examine each of the five stages in depth starting in Chapter 4.

Training Jargon

Is it soup yet? Alphabet, that is. If you associate with training types, I am sure you may at times think they are speaking in a foreign tongue.

Perhaps it is time to introduce a few of the acronyms and technical terms you hear in the training field.

✔ **ADDIE:** This is a classic model of a training design process. The acronym is formed by the steps in the process: Analysis, Design, Development, Implementation, and Evaluation.

✔ **Andragogy:** A term developed in Europe to describe the art and science of adult learning. Malcolm Knowles is sometimes incorrectly credited with coining the word. He actually introduced and promoted it through his work and writing. Typically refers to adults' capacity to direct and motivate their learning, utilize past experience and knowledge, and evaluate the relevance of training content to their personal needs.

✔ **Assessment:** Usually refers to a questionnaire, exam, test, or other evaluation process.

✔ **Asynchronous Training/Learning:** Typically a self-paced, online tutorial that doesn't require the trainer and instructor to participate at the same time.

✔ **Audiovisuals:** Any medium used to deliver information that enhances the presentation through auditory and/or visual means, for example, PowerPoint presentations, video clips, overhead transparencies, flipcharts. Frequently abbreviated as AV.

✔ **Blended learning:** The practice of using several mediums in one curriculum. Typically refers to a combination of classroom and self-paced computer training.

✔ **Bloom's Taxonomy:** A hierarchical ordering of cognitive and affective learning outcomes developed by Benjamin Bloom and a university committee. An interesting fact is that the committee actually identified a third domain of learning, psychomotor, but did not elaborate on it. The explanation for this oversight was that committee members had little experience teaching manual skills at the college level. The three learning outcomes — cognitive (knowledge), psychomotor (skills), and affective (attitude) — are frequently referred to as the KSAs.

✔ **CBT:** Computer-based training, a generic term for any learning delivered via a computer.

✔ **Chunking:** Separating learning information into small sections to improve learner comprehension and retention.

✔ **Criterion-referenced instruction:** A system of training developed by Bob Mager where the results are measured by the learner's ability to meet specified performance objectives (criterion) upon completion.

✔ **Delivery method:** The way a training is provided to learners, for example, classroom, videoconference, CD-ROM, audio tape.

✔ **Design:** The formulation of a plan or outline for training.

✔ **Development:** The stage of creating a training program in which the materials are created and training methods are finalized.

✔ **Evaluation:** The final step in The Training Cycle used to measure results.

✔ **Hard skills:** Refers to technical or information technology (IT) related skills.

✔ **Icebreaker:** An activity conducted at the beginning of a training program that introduces participants to each other, may introduce content, and in general helps participants ease into the program.

✔ **ISD:** Instructional Systems Design, a process used to analyze, design, develop, implement, and evaluate training. Hey, isn't that the ADDIE model? It is also The Training Cycle, discussed in this chapter.

✔ **Job aid:** A tool to provide on-the-job direction for a specific task; may be in paper or computer format.

✔ **KSA:** Knowledge, skills, attitude — the three learning categories based on Bloom's Taxonomy.

✔ **Learning objective:** A clear, measurable statement of behavior that a learner demonstrates when the training is considered a success. May also be called *performance objective*.

✔ **Learning style:** Numerous models abound suggesting individuals' approaches to learning based on strengths and preferences.

- ✔ **SME:** Subject matter expert, the most knowledgeable person regarding specific content for a training program.

- ✔ **Soft skills:** Term used to describe a type of training that is not technical or IT related, for example, communication, leadership, listening, stress management.

- ✔ **Task analysis:** The process of identifying the specific steps to correctly perform a task.

Perhaps this short trip through my trainer's dictionary answers questions you may have had up to this point and prepares you for the rest of the book.

Learning and The Training Cycle

The Training Cycle is so orderly and straightforward, it seems like it would be impossible to miss anything important. That's true, but keep in mind that training is really about the learner.

Adults learn differently. In Chapter 2, I briefly mentioned several bright minds that have all arrived at various models for learning preferences. Although they do not agree on any one measure or model, they do agree that learners have different preferences for learning. In addition, everyone favors different senses for recognizing and processing information. If the experts can't arrive at a solution for how people learn, how can you be expected to train people with vastly different learning preferences in the same group? You can!

Variety and flexibility

You can successfully get in touch with all learning styles in your group if you remember two things:

- ✔ **Add variety.** Lots! Research suggests that varying your delivery methods and using different training methods enhances learning for everyone. In fact, most recent research goes even further to say that training that affects more than one preference actually has a greater impact than focusing on the one preference for each specific learner (as if you could do that, anyway!). Lots of variety has a greater payoff. Therefore, you should also vary the delivery itself, changing pace, control, complexity, or timing.

- ✔ **Be flexible.** Just as your learners have a preference for learning, you also have a preference for training. You may prefer small group activities or informal discussion or even lectures. You may tend to be more people focused or content focused. You may prefer to be entertaining or professorial, coaching or directing. Whatever your preference, be flexible. Move outside your comfort zone at times to improve learner comprehension and retention.

Conditions of learning

Before leaving this discussion about incorporating learning into The Training Cycle, I must mention Robert Gagne and his Conditions of Learning. He identified nine instructional events. Applying these events to your training helps to ensure learning occurs. Here are Gagne's Instructional Events:

- ✔ Gain the learners' attention.
- ✔ Share the objectives of the session.
- ✔ Ask learners to recall prior learning.
- ✔ Deliver the content.
- ✔ Use methods to enhance understanding, for example, case studies, examples, graphs.
- ✔ Provide an opportunity to practice.
- ✔ Provide feedback.
- ✔ Assess performance.
- ✔ Provide job aids or references to ensure transfer to the job.

If you've been around the training field for a while, you know that these events are commonplace and are assumed to be a part of any effective training program.

As a trainer, you're responsible for doing everything you can to ensure that learning takes place: Use a theory-based design model like The Training Cycle presented in this chapter, adapt to learners' preferences, and incorporate conditions of learning. Yet remember these words from Galileo Galilei (1564–1642), an Italian astronomer and physicist: "You cannot teach a man anything. You can only help him discover it within himself."

Part II
Designing the Best Darn Training in the World

The 5th Wave   By Rich Tennant

"Nothing serious. I'm still trying to use a pair of nun-chucks in my PowerPoint presentations."

In this part . . .

Y ou find out that training is all about the learner. Keeping that in mind, you find answers to questions about designing training. How do you write an effective learning objective? How do you design a training session that is both effective and fun? How do you tap into the wealth of off-the-shelf materials available to you? And how can you find time to complete all the preparation that's required?

Chapter 4

Assessing Needs and Developing Learning Objectives

In This Chapter

▶ Identifying how to conduct needs assessments

▶ Determining whether it is a training need

▶ Gathering data about your audience

▶ Identifying how to write learning objectives

*I*f you remember nothing else about training from this book, remember this: It's all about the learner.

In this chapter, I begin the design of a training program *for the learner*. The design follows the five stages in The Training Cycle presented in the last chapter. This chapter addresses the first two stages of the cycle:

✔ Assess and analyze needs

✔ Develop learning objectives

Conducting Needs Assessments

Designing training may be like planning a sightseeing tour in a strange country. You have lots of things you would like to do, many things you would like to learn, but you have no idea how far apart any of these things are, what the people will be like, how long it will take, what attire is appropriate, or which activities should be higher priority.

When you plan a sightseeing tour, you most likely read a travel guide or two, contact a travel agency and other experts, talk to people who live there, discuss the possibilities with others who have taken a similar tour, and check out the Internet to get the greatest bang for your buck.

You want answers about why to go, how to go, what to see, when to go, and with whom you should confer. You collect data about a potential tour. Next, you analyze that data and make a decision. You may consider the cost, required time, and your safety. Your analysis may suggest that the tour you had hoped for is not a good idea, and you may stop planning. On the other hand, the data may suggest that you modify your original ideas. In any case, you have to make a decision about what to do next.

You have just followed the steps of conducting a needs assessment.

1. **Identify a need or data to investigate a problem (you need information about a tour).**

2. **Determine a plan for gathering data (decide whom you will contact and what to read).**

3. **Gather the data (talk to people, read books).**

4. **Analyze the data you collected (can you afford it? is the timing right?).**

5. **Make a decision (decide to go or not; if yes, use the data to create a travel plan).**

The why, how, what, who, and when of needs assessment

Like your sightseeing tour, a trainer wants to get the most bang for the buck. That means conducting a needs assessment and analyzing the data. What's the root cause of the problem? Is training even the issue? Figure 4-1 highlights the first stage of The Training Cycle.

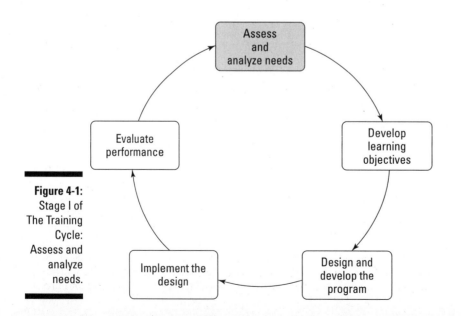

Figure 4-1:
Stage I of
The Training
Cycle:
Assess and
analyze
needs.

Why conduct a needs assessment?

Why a needs assessment? The ultimate goal of a needs assessment is to determine the current and the desired performance. The difference or the gap between the two is the learning that must occur and the basis for a good training design.

Supervisors and managers may approach trainers and request that they conduct training because of some incident that has happened. For example, the cafeteria is getting an unusually high number of customer complaints. Because of this, the trainer may be asked to develop a customer service skills program. Although it may be tempting to quickly put together a customer service training program, it would be much wiser to first determine whether there is really a need for it. An assessment can help you make such a determination.

Several more specific reasons for conducting a needs assessment include these:

- ✔ Determine whether there is a training requirement.
- ✔ Determine root causes of a poor performance level.
- ✔ Determine desired performance (training results).
- ✔ Provide baseline data.
- ✔ Identify content and scope of training.
- ✔ Gain participant and organizational support. (Often, folks get on board when they have involvement from the start.)

How to collect data?

There are many tools you may use to conduct a needs assessment. Following are a few of the most commonly used approaches.

- ✔ **Interviews:** The trainer uses this technique/tool to identify people who can provide information about the need and then interviews them. The advantage to this type of interview is that you can obtain in-depth information about the situation and you can get others' ideas about how to handle the situation. If you do end up providing a training program, you also have some early commitment because people have had input in shaping the program. The disadvantage to this type of needs assessment is that it is labor intensive. By the way, although it isn't ideal, interviews may be conducted by telephone as well.

- ✔ **Focus groups:** Another approach is a focus group. Somewhat like the interview, the trainer identifies key people who can provide information about the need. However, instead of interviewing them individually, the trainer interviews them in groups. There are two advantages to this method. First, the trainer can interview more people in a shorter period of time. Second, the members of the focus group can piggyback off each others' ideas. The disadvantage to this approach is that a quiet person may not give his/her point of view. The result may be that the trainer has information provided only by the outspoken members of the group.

✔ **Questionnaires:** This tool is used when a trainer wants to collect specific information from a large group or a widely dispersed group. The advantages are that you can include many people and the results are clear cut. The disadvantage is that questionnaires may not allow for free expression or unanticipated information; therefore, the trainer may miss some critical data points.

Your data is only as good as the questions you create. You probably want to test a new questionnaire on a small group of people to determine what works and what doesn't. Sometimes, questions can be misinterpreted. Sometimes, questions ask for things they never intended. Sometimes, typos prevent collection of good data also.

✔ **Observation:** This is a good needs assessment technique in two circumstances. First, it is useful when a trainer is assessing the need for skill-based training. Second, it is a good technique to use when a trainer is asked to conduct a program that changes behavior (for example, customer service, giving constructive feedback, flipping flapjacks, welding an I-beam). The most important advantage to this technique is that it provides the trainer with a realistic view of the situation. The disadvantages are that it takes a long time and it is labor intensive. In addition, observation can only indicate behavior, not the reasons behind the behavior or action.

✔ **Performance data reviews:** This technique is used when performance criteria are clear and there is sufficient data available to measure the performance criteria. The advantage to this approach is that the training topics and goals are easier to determine. The trainer need only look at the gap between the criteria and the actual performance. The disadvantage to this approach is that the data may be confounded by other variables, such as equipment downtime or external expectations.

✔ **Informal discussions:** In this approach, the trainer gathers data about training needs through informal conversations with other employees, supervisors, and managers in the organization. The advantage of this approach is that the trainer can get candid information that may help in choosing a more formal needs assessment approach. The disadvantage is that it may be biased due to its unsystematic approach.

✔ **Knowledge tests:** Tests are beneficial in helping trainers identify what to include in a knowledge-based program. The advantage to a skill test is that it measures knowledge versus attitude. A potential disadvantage is that the items on the skill test may not actually reflect the knowledge used on the job.

Note that you may use a combination of the tools listed. Every assessment is different. You don't use the same assessment you used to plan your foreign tour to determine how to remodel your bathroom. You may not use the same needs assessment and analysis tool for two training programs, either.

What criteria will be used to select a data gathering method?

Many factors determine which method you use. The following list provides an idea of what you, your department, or the organization want to consider.

- ✔ **Time:** What is your turnaround time?

- ✔ **Cost:** How much money is available for the assessment? Hiring someone from the outside to conduct focus groups can be costly.

- ✔ **Comfort level and trust:** What is the climate within your organization? Can you rely on the data?

- ✔ **Size of the population to be surveyed:** How many people need to be involved in the assessment?

- ✔ **Confidentiality required:** Is confidentiality an issue for individuals in the organization?

- ✔ **Reliability and validity needed:** To what extent is this critical? How will the assessment methodology affect reliability and validity?

- ✔ **Culture of the organization:** What have employees been used to in the past, and how may different methods be perceived? What about the culture? For example, an open organizational structure may encourage focus groups while an hierarchical organization is more likely to administer anonymous surveys.

- ✔ **Location of those to be surveyed:** Are a large number of people located remotely?

Who will be trained?

As important as it is to determine whether there is a training need, it is equally important to learn as much about your audience as you can. You discover much about your audience in the data-gathering part of your needs assessment.

However, in some instances, someone else will have completed the assessment and the analysis. Your job may be to just deliver the program. At those times, you may find it useful to gain additional information about your participants before the training occurs.

Use these questions as a starting point to find out more about your participants. It is doubtful that you would ever need to know all the information. Consider it a data smorgasbord. Select those that you want to know more about.

- ✔ **Background**

  - Why were you asked to provide training for them?

  - Have they had other training on the same topic?

  - What do they know (and need to know) about you?

- How many of the participants are personally acquainted with you?

- Are they aware of the level of expertise or experience you bring to the situation?

- Who are the key players in their department and organization?

✔ **Demographics**

- How many will attend your session?

- Is their attendance voluntary? Required? Requested? Invited?

- What is the demographic makeup of the participants? Age? Gender? Other descriptive factors?

- What information sources do they depend on? Magazines? TV? Books? Newspapers?

✔ **Level of expertise**

- How familiar are they with the subject matter?

- What do they want to know?

- Are all individuals at the same skill and knowledge level with respect to the topic?

- Who are the experts in the group?

- What is their level of responsibility or authority?

- How does their level compare to yours? Does it determine the subject level or delivery style?

✔ **Attitudes**

- Are they interested in the subject? Should they be interested?

- What successes and issues have they encountered?

- What are their attitudes and beliefs relevant to the topic?

- Do they know why they are coming to training?

- May their minds already be made up?

- What are their opinions about you?

- Will they be friendly? Hostile?

✔ **Design considerations**

- Will they ask many questions?

- Do you expect them to raise objections?

- Did the participants and their managers help to identify the objectives of the training?

- Are you aware of anything that may antagonize them? Hot buttons? Taboo words or subjects? Gestures? Past experiences?

- What is special about these participants?

- Is there anything special about the location where you will be presenting?

- Is there anything unusual about the date or timing of your training, for example, vacation, recent performance appraisals, downsizing effort?

✔ **Expected results**

- How can you meet their needs?

- How does this training benefit the participants?

- May there be disadvantages to the participants?

- What changes do their supervisors expect as a result of the training?

- Does the organization's culture encourage participants to use what they learn in training? What may get in the way of learners' applying their new knowledge or skill?

When do you begin the needs assessment?

As quickly as you can!

You want as much time as possible to design and develop the training. It's a big job.

No matter how extensive and complete your assessment and analysis are, it is always a good idea to conduct a mini needs assessment at the beginning of each session. I like to chart responses to the question, "What are your hopes and fears for this session?" Other trainers simply ask for each participant's expectation. This does two things:

> ✔ It helps you determine whether your design is on the mark.
> ✔ It gives participants an opportunity to state their expectations.

Besides, it's a great way for people to start participating early using the subject as the topic.

Note that you may uncover a few misperceptions. You may also need to make a few slight modifications to meet all the needs. This is all in a day's work for a trainer. Even if participants have expectations that you cannot meet during this session, you can discuss this with them at the first break to determine how you may help them.

Potential questions to ask

Each needs assessment is different. Questions you may consider asking include these:

- What performance gap needs to be addressed?
- Is training the best solution?
- What type of training is required?
- What other solutions have been considered?
- How is the performance impacting the organization?
- What knowledge or skills need to be addressed?
- What are the specific job requirements?
- What instruments, materials, and equipment arc used by the employees?
- Who needs this knowledge or skill?
- What is the skill level for these individuals? (may include a list of specific skills)
- What materials should be included in the training instruction?
- How do these individuals (employees, participants) feel about their performance?
- How do these individuals perceive an impending training? What value is it to them?
- How supportive are the participants' direct supervisors? Other management?
- What resources are available for the training?

Potentially thousands of questions may be asked. As a trainer, you need to determine what is most important and what you need to know so that you can recommend a learning event that is most beneficial to the participants as well as the organization. Note that I did not say so that you can design and conduct a training session. One of the most important reasons for conducting a needs assessment and analyzing the data is to determine whether training is the answer.

Is it training?

It isn't over until you know whether it is a training need. These three quick questions help you pinpoint the answer:

- ✔ Does the individual have the skill to do the job?
- ✔ Does the individual have the will to do the job?
- ✔ Is the individual allowed to do the job?

If the answer to the first question is "no," training may be a solution but not necessarily. If the answer to all of the questions is "yes," it is definitely not a training solution.

Well, what else could it be?

- ✔ A "no" to the second question means you may have a motivation problem; training doesn't solve that.
- ✔ A "no" to the third question means there is probably a procedure or policy problem; training doesn't solve that.
- ✔ A "yes" to all three questions could mean that it is an equipment problem that prevents individuals from producing quality on time.
- ✔ Even a "no" to the first question doesn't necessarily mean training is required; perhaps coaching is a solution. In other instances, individuals may not have received feedback and may not even know they are doing something incorrectly.

Before anyone jumps to the assumption that a performance problem requires training, consider that it may be due to dozens of other things: inadequate materials, tools, or workspace; unreliable equipment; unclear expectations; inappropriate consequences or incentives; lack of feedback or coaching; inappropriate job assignment; work environment; or others.

Before you finalize your needs assessment, be certain to know whether training is the solution. Don't make the mistake of presupposing that training is the solution to a performance issue prior to completing your needs assessment.

If your time is limited

You may wish to believe that The Training Cycle is always followed and that a thorough needs assessment is always completed. That just isn't the real world. If you've been in the training field during the past few years you know that timelines are shorter, demand is more frequent, and expectations are higher. Although training should start with the business goal, it doesn't always.

So what can you do? You could skip the needs assessment stage completely, but later, you may wish that you hadn't. I've done all of the following at one time or another. While they are not the same as a complete needs assessment, one or two can provide you with some basic information so that you can better understand the situation.

- ✔ Get as much information from the contact person as possible. This at least gives you a foundation.

- ✔ Talk to several participants. If I need information fast, I ask the contact person to line up a couple of phone interviews for me. I ask each person several of the questions discussed in the "The why, how, what, who, and when of needs assessment" section in this chapter.

- ✔ E-mail a simple questionnaire to all the participants. You get a better response if you attach it to a friendly note from you that welcomes the participants to the training, informs them of the objectives, and lets them know what they may expect, for example, practical, hands-on; ten ways to express your creativity; action-packed day filled with tips you can implement immediately.

- ✔ Ask your contact to provide any materials that may be relevant for the session, for example, meeting agendas and notes, survey results.

- ✔ If you know others in the organization, you may wish to contact them for any "inside scoop."

- ✔ Contact other trainers or colleagues who may have worked with this group in the past. Do this especially if you're filling in for someone.

- ✔ If you really have no time, you probably want to add opening activities that help you gain information about the group. You may ask about their expectations, their hopes and fears for the session, their greatest problem and greatest success as it relates to the content, or any other activity that helps to fill the needs assessment gap.

- ✔ I may also pack a few backup materials and activities in case the session takes a turn for something different from what I had planned.

Do what you can. An hour or two on the telephone with knowledgeable people makes a huge difference. At least you have some data. Walking in with even a small amount of data in your hip pocket is always better than walking into a big void.

Check with your local college or university. Frequently marketing classes are looking for assessment or survey design projects. You need to allow time for both the design as well as educating the group or individual about you and your organization. If you have time but a minimum amount of money, this can be an elegant solution.

Writing Objectives

After you complete the needs assessment, analyze the data, and ascertain the need for training, you develop the objectives for the training. Figure 4-2 shows that developing objectives is the second stage of The Training Cycle.

Learning objectives are written for the learner. You may also choose to write training objectives which are for the design and development of the training. Learning objectives are a requirement. Many trainers do not write training objectives.

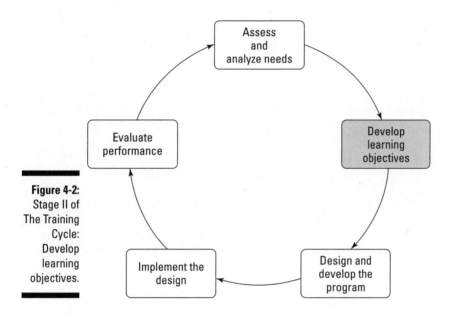

Figure 4-2:
Stage II of
The Training
Cycle:
Develop
learning
objectives.

What objectives should do

Learning objectives are written to specify the performance (knowledge or skill) that is desired after the training has been completed. The following sections spell out the four elements you want to include in your learning objectives.

Specifying exactly what the learner will be able to do

In Chapter 2, you can read about Bloom's Taxonomy, the hierarchy of learning outcomes. This is the point in The Training Cycle where Bloom's Taxonomy comes in handy: specifying exactly what the learner will know or be able to do at the end of the training experience.

Do you want the learners to have knowledge about the subject? Comprehension? Be able to apply the information? Analyze or synthesize it? Or do you want them to be able to make judgments about the information?

Because the goal of most training that you conduct is to improve skills, you most often select verbs from the application column. However, there are other objectives to training programs that may not require application, but merely comprehension. And, of course, there are also times when you want the learner to go beyond application.

The list of verbs associated with the six levels in Table 4-1 helps you to select a verb that fits the level of learning.

Table 4-1	**Bloom's Cognitive Domain**				
Knowledge	*Comprehension*	*Application*	*Analysis*	*Synthesis*	*Evaluation*
Recalling information	Interpreting information in one's own words	Applying or generalizing knowledge to new situations	Breaking knowledge into parts and showing relationships	Bringing together parts of knowledge to form a new whole	Making judgments based on given criteria
Arrange	Describe	Apply	Analyze	Arrange	Appraise
Cite	Differentiate	Calculate	Appraise	Assemble	Assess
Define	Discuss	Choose	Categorize	Collect	Compare
Duplicate	Explain	Classify	Compare	Combine	Conclude
Label	Express	Complete	Contrast	Compile	Critique
List	Generalize	Compute	Criticize	Compose	Defend
Match	Identify	Demonstrate	Detect	Construct	Estimate
Memorize	Indicate	Dramatize	Diagram	Create	Evaluate
Name	Locate	Employ	Differentiate	Design	Grade
Order	Paraphrase	Illustrate	Discriminate	Formulate	Judge
Outline	Recognize	Interpret	Examine	Generate	Justify
Recall	Report	Modify	Experiment	Manage	Measure
Record	Restate	Operate	Group	Organize	Predict
Relate	Review	Practice	Inventory	Plan	Prescribe
Repeat	Select	Prepare	Question	Prepare	Rank
Reproduce	Sort	Schedule	Subdivide	Propose	Rate
Select	Tell	Sketch	Summarize	Rearrange	Recommend
State	Translate	Solve	Test	Set up	Score
Tabulate		Use		Synthesize	Select
Write				Write	Support
					Validate
					Value

Deciding whether you've written a good objective

An objective should meet several criteria. It should be specific so that there is no question about what you mean. It should be measurable, meaning you should be able to count it or determine with a distinct yes or no whether it was accomplished. An objective should be attainable — no pie in the sky statement, yet it should not be so easy to attain that it isn't worth the paper on which it is written. An objective should be relevant to the mission of the organization, to the change that is desired, to achieve the greater goal. And finally, it should be time bound, meaning: When is the individual expected to achieve the objective: by the end of the training session, within a month? Objectives should be SMART, as follows:

- ✔ **S**pecific
- ✔ **M**easurable
- ✔ **A**ttainable, yet a stretch
- ✔ **R**elevant
- ✔ **T**ime-bound

Getting additional guidance

Use these additional ideas for writing objectives:

- ✔ Be brief and to the point; include only one major item in each objective.
- ✔ Use an observable action verb to describe the expected result. You can see (or hear) "list," "demonstrate," and "calculate." You cannot see someone "remember," "believe," or "learn."
- ✔ Specify a time frame or target date of completion; generally, this occurs at the end of the training session.
- ✔ Specify resource limitations (money, personnel, equipment) as appropriate.
- ✔ Describe the participants' expected performance.
- ✔ Specify results to be achieved in measurable or observable terms.
- ✔ Choose areas over which you have direct influence or control; don't write objectives for which your training program has no accountability.
- ✔ Make objectives realistic in terms of what can actually be accomplished in the training as well as in terms of resources you have available to you.
- ✔ Include enough challenge in the objective to make it worth formulating.
- ✔ Indicate the minimum level of acceptable performance.
- ✔ Specify the conditions (if any) under which the action must be performed.

✔ Specify degree of success if less than 100 percent is acceptable.

✔ Select objectives that are supportive and consistent with overall organization missions and goals.

Using this formula to easily write objectives

A correctly written objective includes four components, sometimes called the *ABCD*s of a good objective:

✔ Audience (who)

✔ Behavior (will do what)

✔ Condition (by when or some other condition, such as with assistance)

✔ Degree (how well, if not 100 percent of the time)

To easily write an objective, fill in the blanks. Use this formula to help you out.

Who will do what, by when, and how well?

_____ will _____, by _____, _____.

"You will be able to write good learning objectives, by the time you finish this chapter, 100 percent of the time."

Is it a SMART objective?

✔ **S**pecific? Yes, I can see you "write objectives."

✔ **M**easurable? Yes, 100 percent.

✔ **A**ttainable, yet a stretch? Yes, not that much of a stretch for you.

✔ **R**elevant? Yes, that's what this chapter is about.

✔ **T**ime-bound? Yes, depending on how fast you read.

Trainers design the training based on the learning objectives. Typically, trainers also post the objectives at the beginning of their sessions. They may word the objective less clinically and begin it with, "By the end of this training. . . ." If the learners are expected to be able to do the task 100 percent of the time, the trainers may not include it in the objective. Therefore, the objective may be rewritten.

"By the end of this training, you will be able to write learning objectives."

Task analysis

At some point in your career you're likely to find folks who are involved in task analysis. In its simplest form, task analysis breaks a job (task) down into observable steps. It also reveals the knowledge and skills the employee needs to complete each step. At times task analysis is used to determine training needs. It may be a part of the analysis completed during the needs assessment. Learning objectives may be written based on the task analysis.

I understand, for example, that the task of tying a shoe can be broken down into 214 steps! Task analysis steps are completed to determine which aspects of the job to include in a training program.

1. **Identify tasks that are required for performing the job.**

2. **For each task, list the exact steps that a person must do to complete the task. List every step from start to finish in order, no matter how small the step.**

3. **When listing the steps, make them as clear as possible. Even the smallest assumption can create confusion in the actual performance of the task.**

4. **After you have completed all steps for every task, go back and identify each step in one of three ways:**

   - **Common knowledge:** Trainee will know how to do this step because of common knowledge. No training is necessary for this step.

   - **On-the-job training:** The step is simple enough that the trainee can learn it on the job. No training is necessary for this step, but you may want to consider developing a job aid such as a check sheet or a list of procedures.

   - **Training topic:** The trainee will not know how to do this step without training. Your technical training program should be based around these topics.

5. **Ask a subject matter expert (SME) to review your task analysis to see whether you have analyzed the job(s) correctly.**

6. **Design your training program around those topics you identified as requiring training.**

7. **If you also develop job aids, make sure they are integrated into the training program so that trainees know they are available and so that they can ask questions, if they have them.**

Task analysis and training objectives are used prior to designing the training program. Both are critical steps between conducting the needs assessment and designing the training program. Both play a part in setting the goals of the training session and ultimately achieving them. As David Campbell says, "Aim at nothing and you'll hit it every time."

Chapter 5

Developing the Training Design

. . . .

In This Chapter

▶ Creating a supportive learning environment

▶ Designing materials to ensure that learning occurs

▶ Examining the pros and cons of lecturing

▶ Identifying a variety of activities

▶ Considering the purpose for using visuals

▶ Wrapping up an effective training session

. . . .

*T*raining is serious business. Or is it?

Educators know that children learn from play. Adults do, too. This chapter addresses the design and development of training. While the design and development of a training program is a lot of work, you should remember throughout to ensure that the design creates training that is learner-focused. That is, the participant learns all the KSAs (knowledge, skills, attitudes — remember?) while enjoying the process along the way.

This chapter discusses the third stage of The Training Cycle, design and development (see Figure 5-1). The training you design and develop is built on a foundation formed by two important aspects: adult learning principles and the learning objectives.

✔ The adult learning principles, developed by Malcolm Knowles and discussed in Chapter 2, are the basic characteristics that distinguish adult learning from how children learn.

✔ The learning objectives, created as a result of the needs assessment and analysis discussed in Chapter 4, describe what the participant knows or does as a result of the training.

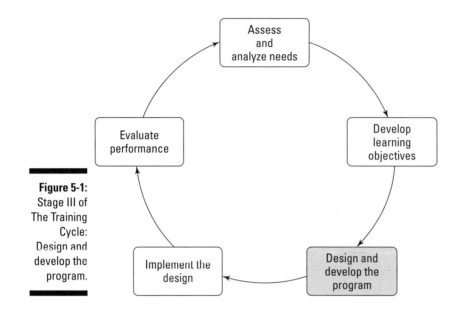

Figure 5-1:
Stage III of
The Training
Cycle:
Design and
develop the
program.

You may discover that some training designers create a distinct split between the "design" and the "development" of a training program. The distinctions for these folks focus on a couple of things.

- ✔ Design focuses on preparing the designer for selecting and writing the materials. Actions include writing objectives, deciding on the sequence of content, identifying documentation, and planning the evaluation.

- ✔ Development focuses on selecting and creating the materials. Actions include selecting and writing materials for the participants' and the trainer's use, documentation, and the evaluation of materials.

Do you see the similarities and the small difference? Other than writing the objectives, the design stage provides direction for what to do in the development stage. At any rate, this model combines the two.

In this chapter, I divide the design of training into three segments: what you need to accomplish at the beginning of the training, what you need to accomplish in the middle of the training, and what you need to accomplish at the end of the training. Beginning, middle, end. That's logical.

- ✔ **Beginning:** An opening that establishes a climate conducive to learning.

- ✔ **Middle:** A body that ensures learning occurs.

- ✔ **End:** A conclusion that provides a sense of closure to the training and an anticipation for applying what was learned after the training experience.

Are you ready to begin the design and development process? Remember to have some fun along the way.

Designing Learning is one of the Areas of Expertise as identified by the Competency Study from the American Society for Training and Development (ASTD) 2004. It is one of the areas that trainers may have as an emphasis in certification.

How Do I Begin?

Your training design starts with the end first: the expected improved performance of each participant. The learning objectives act as your guide to the design. List the learning objectives in the order in which you will teach them. You want to break some of the objectives down to the more specific skills and knowledge participants will acquire to improve their performance. Can you see an outline taking shape? That's exactly what you need to begin the design process! Consider the following abbreviated outline of the topics used for a train-the-trainer session.

 I. Opening and Introduction

 II. Overview of The Training Cycle

    A. Define training and trainers' roles

    B. Five stages

 III. Stage I: Needs assessment and analysis

    A. Conducting needs assessments

    B. Data-collection methods

    C. Analyzing the data

 IV. Stage II: Learning objectives

    A. Types of objectives

    B. Writing effective objectives

 V. Stage III: Design and Development

    A. Adult learning theory

    B. Sequence and structure

    C. Learning methods and activities

    D. Customizing off-the-shelf

VI. Stage IV: Facilitate the Design

    A. Trainer preparation

    B. Difference between presenting and facilitating

    C. Group dynamics

    D. Media delivery skills

    E. Conducting activities

VII. Stage V: Evaluation

    A. Kirkpatrick's four levels of evaluation

    B. Return on investment

    C. Designing evaluation instruments

    D. Using the data

VIII. Training session follow-up

IX. Closing and wrap-up activities

How do you turn an outline into a training session? Entire books are written on the subject of designing a training program. Some designers want you to use a specific model, identify confirming and corrective feedback, identify the rationale, create task listings, list the resources (a.k.a. *markers*), determine a task criticality rating, develop a process map, identify evaluation criteria, identify units, create an information map, compare to an organizational scheme, and on and on. I don't know about you, but I can't keep that many concepts in my head all at once.

What I can do is organize the content in a logical flow and figure out the best way to assist the participants to acquire the skill or knowledge required to achieve the desired performance. And that's what you need to focus on for now. If you want to go into more depth, I suggest you contact your local chapter of ASTD for a design course recommendation.

Oh, and one more thing. Before you continue too far with the design process, you need to find out how the training will be delivered. Someone else will most likely make that decision. The choices include trainer-led classroom, trainer-led from a remote location, on-the-job training (OJT), self-paced, or technology-based training. Instructor-led classroom continues to be the most implemented at about 70 percent. Both instructor-led from a remote location (for example, Webconferencing, videoconferencing) and technology-based (with no instructor) are growing slightly each year. Blended learning, a contemporary term, is a combination of two or more delivery systems.

The rest of this book focuses on the trainer-led classroom delivery. However, most of the information and techniques are also directly transferable to the trainer-led from a remote location.

You have been asked to develop a training program that will occur in a classroom setting. What's next? These are the steps I use to design and develop a learning experience. I think you will find them easy to follow.

Before you dive in to design and develop the training program, obtain a clear definition of the limitations. Many a trainer has been headed in a direction only to learn that resources are not available in the form of time, money, or people. Clarify the limitations first.

1. **List all the learning objectives for the session. This is the basis for the content.**

2. **If you need to break the objectives down to smaller, more manageable units, do so now.**

3. **Arrange the learning objectives into a logical learning sequence. The sequences that are most often used include these:**

   - Chronological

   - Procedural order

   - Problem/solution

   - Categories

   - General to specific

   - Simple to complex

   - Less risky to more risky

   - Known to unknown

4. **Determine content, ensuring that you have enough, but not too much. What do your learners need to know? Need to do? What specific knowledge and skills will help them achieve the learning objectives?**

5. **Identify the best methodology, for example, role play, discussion, or practice, to use to transmit the content to the learner.**

6. **Develop or purchase the support material you need to go along with what will happen during the learning experience. This includes some or all of these.**

   - Participant materials, for example, manual, handouts, job aids, texts

   - Visual and media support, for example, overhead transparencies, PowerPoint presentation, videos, software

   - Activity support, for example, role-play cards, scripts, exercises, props, case studies

   - Trainer materials, for example, trainer's guide, markers

• Administrative support, for example, agenda, roster, supply check-list, evaluations

7. Conduct a pilot to determine what needs to be changed or improved to achieve success.

If you need to play with the sequence of the learning objectives, you can do it on your computer. Another possibility is to write each objective on a separate index card. Lay the cards on a table and move them around until you achieve what you're looking for.

The rest of this chapter is devoted to how you fill in the gaps of the design outline you have created. It is divided into the three different parts of the session: the beginning, middle, and the end. (How's that for a logical sequence?)

This chapter also discusses some of the methodologies you may use: lecturettes and over 50 types of activities. It provides you with tips for designing media and visual materials.

Designing a Dynamic Opening

The first ten minutes of your training design may be the most important ten minutes of the entire session.

A successful opening should accomplish several things.

✔ Establish a participative climate

✔ Introduce participants

✔ Introduce the agenda

✔ Clarify the participants' expectations

✔ List objectives of the training

✔ Build interest and excitement

✔ Learn something about the participants

✔ Determine some minimum rules of engagement and ground rules

✔ Establish your credibility

All about icebreakers

Have you ever attended a training session when someone droned on for the first 15 minutes about the procedure for completing the sign-in sheet, where the bathrooms are located, how to get to the cafeteria, how to get your parking pass stamped, and on and on? Really got you excited about the training session, I'll bet!

My hero of icebreakers is Edie West, author, training consultant, and long-time expert on the creation of icebreakers and energizers.

I like to start my sessions with something that surprises or shocks the participants. For example, after being introduced, I have started by walking in with a large shopping bag full of T-shirts and saying, "They say you can't tell a book by its cover. But I believe you can tell a person by her T-shirt!" I proceed to pull T-shirts out of the bag and read the funny sayings to the group. I hand them a bright sheet of paper (several different colors are used) with the outline of a T-shirt and ask them to use the crayons on the table to draw a picture or write a slogan on the T-shirt that represents their motto or what they stand for.

When participants have all finished designing their T-shirts — and it may take some prodding — I ask them to get up and find all the other participants whose paper is the same color as theirs, to introduce themselves to each other, and to explain their T-shirts (about 5 minutes). I ask them to sit down and have each person introduce themselves and their T-shirts to the rest of the group. At the end I have them all hang their T-shirts on the wall.

Icebreakers, a delicacy

by Edie West

Successful icebreakers are the proverbial frosting on the cake. They enhance the delicate flavor of a training program and help preserve its freshness. Don't worry if everyone's taste is different — a well-designed, well-executed icebreaker achieves its purpose anyway. What would a birthday party be without a cake?

Just as a German chocolate cake needs a coconut frosting, the success in using icebreakers is in choosing ones with the right ingredients to help set the venue and tone:

✔ Choose or create an icebreaker that has a real purpose tied to the program outcomes.

✔ Select icebreaker types that are relevant to participants, the program, and the facilitator.

✔ Conduct with lighthearted instructions that raise levels of comfort and acceptance.

✔ Use appropriate humor to enhance the experience.

✔ Assist participants to draw conclusions that underscore the intent.

Happy baking!

You discover in the "Selecting activities" section in this chapter how I use the T-shirt theme throughout the session. But for now, what have I done?

✔ Grabbed their attention

✔ Established a participative climate, instant involvement

✔ Set the pace — fast

✔ Put people at ease (including the trainer)

✔ Initiated personal interaction and individual introductions

✔ Heard everyone's names

✔ Had everyone speak once in the large group

✔ Started to define the group's personality (trainer observation)

✔ Started to identify thc individual personalities

✔ Everyone learned something about each other (shortens the path to find other participants with similar interests)

✔ Established a transition to the content

Design content-related icebreakers

Icebreakers should have something to do with the content. These four ideas show you just how easy it can be.

✔ When participants introduce themselves, ask them to state their names, which department (or company) they are from, and to add one piece of information that relates to the session content. For example, if you're training problem-solving skills, ask them to identify one example of how they hope to use the skills they are about to learn.

✔ Ask participants to get into small groups (three to four people) around the table, to introduce themselves to each other, and as a group to decide on the biggest challenge they have that relates to the session content. For example, if you're teaching listening skills to front desk hotel personnel, you may ask them to decide the biggest chal-

lenge they face where listening skills may be useful.

✔ In any training session, you can ask participants to identify their expectations for the class.

✔ You can always bring in a box of "things" (dollar stores are great places to find "things") and have them select one "thing" and relate it to the content. For example, if you're training team-building skills, you can provide a box of tools (tape measure, hammer, ice scraper, measuring cup, pancake turner, wire whip, level, scissors, stapler, calculator). Pass the box around and ask each person to select a tool. When participants introduce themselves, they are to complete the statement, "As a team player I am like a _____ because...," filling in the blank with the tool they selected.

What!?! The content? Yes. I use this icebreaker for the train-the-trainer course that I teach, and after the final introduction, the class begins to process the icebreaker itself. And this is where I slip in a few references about my credibility: "As a trainer for the last 20 years, I. . ." or "As the training director for. . ." or "As I discuss in my last book. . . ."

As I write this I am staring at a quote written by someone who published an article in a training journal: "Icebreakers have nothing to do with course content, but they're essential if you want people to work together." Right on the last part, but absolutely wrong on the first part. With a little planning, you should be able to design an icebreaker that introduces the content. See the "Design content-related icebreakers" sidebar for further information.

If a group is composed of people who know each other well, an icebreaker may not be necessary for getting acquainted; there are other opening activities you may need to conduct. The first ten minutes is a very important time for your session. A well-designed opening and icebreaker establish a climate that is conducive to learning.

What else will your participants expect in your design?

Your participants will expect you to design several orientation tasks to get the session started. If I am facilitating a session that lasts at least one full day, I generally allow a little more than an hour for the opening activities. I find that investing time up front prevents other problems from happening later on. Okay, so how do I plan for that time?

- ✔ **Icebreaker:** 15 minutes
- ✔ **Introductions:** 20 minutes (1 minute per person)
- ✔ **Review agenda:** 2 minutes
- ✔ **Mini needs assessment:** 3 minutes
- ✔ **Introduce learning objectives:** 10 minutes
- ✔ **Clarify their expectations:** 10 minutes
- ✔ **Establish ground rules:** 7 minutes
- ✔ **Housekeeping information:** 1 minute

Remember these are estimates. Sometimes, the icebreaker takes longer or participants get wordy with their introductions. Build some slippage in the rest of the morning. Believe me, this opening time is worth it.

If you examine this list of opening activities, what must be developed?

✔ You need to design the icebreaker, and if you need a handout (see information about Bingo in Chapter 23), you need to develop it.

✔ You most likely want table tents (cardstock folded in half lengthwise) on which participants write their names; the markers should have a broad-enough tip so that participants' names can be seen from all places around the room.

✔ You want an agenda printed on paper so that each participant can have one.

 I do not put specific times on the agenda. Participants get nervous if they see that you're behind by 30 minutes. They don't understand that you may be currently covering something that was planned for later or that you know that what they are addressing now is much more important than something later and that you can decrease time on another activity.

 I print my personal agenda on brightly colored paper with time required for each activity. I use bright paper so that I can see it if it gets lost under handouts or whatever. And I need to have those times so that I keep the class on track. I like to allow flexibility to meet participants' needs, but I also need to take full responsibility for achieving the learning objectives.

✔ You need to know what information you need for the mini needs assessment. In the case of the train-the-trainer, I wanted to know how long they had been trainers, whether they had ever attended a train-the-trainer, whether they had designed training, and finally whether they thought that training was their destined profession.

✔ You may want to post the learning objectives on a flipchart pad so that you can hang them on the wall after you discuss them, keeping them visible.

✔ You need blank flipchart pages to note participants' expectations and the ground rules. I do not dictate ground rules. The groups establish their own. I find that they follow them better that way.

That wraps up the design for the opening.

Designing the Body to Ensure Learning Occurs

Perhaps you have designed an opening for the training session that meets the requirements to establish a climate that is conducive to learning. Now get started on the middle, which is the bulk of the training. It requires that you design factors into the training that ensure that learning occurs. The purpose of the body is to ensure that your participants

- ✔ Accomplish the stated objectives.
- ✔ Learn all the concepts presented.
- ✔ Practice the skills.
- ✔ Acquire feedback.
- ✔ Understand the application to the job (or beyond the training experience).

Lectures

You know how important it is for learners to be actively involved in the training. Yet there may be times when you need to deliver a larger amount of information. A lecture may be unavoidable. In that case, you need to present the information. Even so, I never use the word "lecture." I use a made-up word, *lecturette,* for these special times. It gives the illusion of being less tedious and a bit more playful! And that's exactly what I am recommending you do with your lecturettes. Make them playful and learner-centered.

Problems with a lecture

"So what's so bad about lectures?" you may ask. You've probably heard hundreds of lectures in school, and you survived that. It's not that they are bad, but there are better ways. First, consider some of the problems.

- ✔ It doesn't involve the participants.
- ✔ It ignores participants' experience.
- ✔ It rarely stimulates excitement and involvement.
- ✔ The trainer, due to minimal feedback, has no way of knowing whether participants are understanding the concepts.
- ✔ It is one-way communication, often resulting in passive learners who do not have an opportunity to clarify material.
- ✔ People may leave with incorrect information.
- ✔ It may be physically uncomfortable.
- ✔ It can be dull and boring.
- ✔ It is impossible to hold individuals' attention for long periods of time.
- ✔ Success is dependent on speaking ability.
- ✔ It doesn't account for various learning styles.

- ✔ It creates a poor transfer of learning.
- ✔ It is difficult to reinforce an audience.

Can you think of other problems with lecturing?

Some appropriate times for a lecture

On the other hand, there may be times when it is best for you to lecture. Perhaps you have been in situations like these:

- ✔ A short lecture followed by another activity can be appropriate for introducing key conceptual ideas.
- ✔ When used in conjunction with a variety of activities, a lecture can be a refreshing way for participants to relax while they learn.
- ✔ If you need to disseminate a large amount of information in a short period of time, a lecture may be appropriate. However, it should be accompanied by a job aid or some other materials for future reference.
- ✔ A lecture may be appropriate if you need to maintain control of the group and reduce verbal resistance.
- ✔ A lecture is appropriate when specific information must be disseminated that affects ethics, legal aspects, safety, and so on.
- ✔ A well-prepared, humorous lecture may stimulate a group.
- ✔ A lecture may be an easier technique for some trainers.
- ✔ Guest speakers, who are known for their expertise in a given content area, may be admired for their lecture. This can backfire, however, if the speaker loses the group.
- ✔ You may use a lecture when a group is so large that participative methods would be chaotic.

Are there other times when lecture may be appropriate?

If you must use a lecturette, make it participative

How in the world can you design a participative lecturette? Try these suggestions. Most are practical and easy to build in to any lecturette.

- ✔ Design pop quizzes in the middle.
- ✔ Plan to ask questions regarding predictions or recall of information.
- ✔ Create a conversation between trainer and participants.
- ✔ Intersperse tasks or demonstrations.
- ✔ Develop a guided note-taking page in the form of questions or fill in the blanks.

✔ Develop handouts with a key-word outline of the presentation with room to write.

✔ Design visuals to go with the lecturette so that participants can follow your words visually.

✔ Plan to stop at various points to ask whether everyone is with you.

✔ Present a partial story at the beginning and complete the story after the end of the lecturette.

✔ Find ways to interject humor, such as creating a cartoon to match the content you present.

Lecture if you must, but build participation into your lecturettes.

Countless alternatives to lecture

There are hundreds of alternative methods you can use to replace a lecture. Recognize that many of these methods usually take longer than a lecturette, but a well-constructed activity enhances learning because the participant experiences the learning by being personally involved. For example, in the classic NASA "Lost on the Moon" exercise, participants experience the power and value of group decision-making.

Why would you use an activity anyway?

✔ **Activities are energizing.** Use games in your design to give people a break, time to stretch (their brains, as well as their bodies), to relieve stress, and to just get energized.

✔ **Activities get people working together.** Build rapport among participants to increase the amount of knowledge floating around the room. More learning occurs when everyone is sharing and learning from each other. As the trainer/facilitator, you have a body of knowledge, but the compiled knowledge of your group far outweighs what you know.

✔ **Activities promote learning by doing.** Your participants retain the knowledge better if you can engage as many of their senses as possible.

✔ **Activities provide you with a way to reinforce information.** It would be pretty boring if you stated the same things over and over in the same way, even though you know that repetition is good. Activities allow participants to experience the same information in another way.

✔ **Activities are motivational.** Learners respond because they are actively involved. It is a pleasant way to learn.

Thousands of activities, games, and exercises exist. Or you can create your own. One of the best resources for games is *The Games Trainers Play* series by

Ed Scannell and John Newstrom. The best resource for experiential learning activities is *The Pfeiffer Annual.* Two volumes are published each year, one for trainers and one for consultants. These resources and many others publish activities that you can easily adapt to the training program you're designing.

Presentation variations

Presentations refer to any method that gives information to the participants with less interaction than many of the other methods.

- ✔ **Panel:** Made up of participants, managers, customers, or top executives, providing a unique opportunity for an intimate discussion or a question-and-answer period.

- ✔ **Tour:** Visit someplace in the organization where a host guides you through the information you need to know, for example, the organization's library, to demonstrate how to retrieve information.

- ✔ **Lecturette:** A mini lecture because I believe all lectures should be interactive and so brief that it's over before anyone notices.

- ✔ **Guided note-taking:** Create handouts that have spaces available to add information. Information is gleaned during a lecturette, while watching a role play, or while viewing a video.

- ✔ **Storytelling:** Telling an event (true or fictitious) that has a moral or lesson or demonstrates consequences. The punch line leaves the listener inspired, influenced, or improved, without necessarily explaining the learning point.

- ✔ **Debate:** Two teams address two different sides of an issue to explore perspectives from both sides.

Experiential learning activities

Experiential learning activities (ELAs), sometimes called *structured experiences,* are in a category of their own. ELAs are activities that are specifically designed for inductive learning through the five-stage cycle associated with them: experiencing, publishing, processing, generalizing, and applying. More information can be found in Chapter 8. ELAs are especially useful in a change-management situation or when attitudes are an issue.

Demonstrations

Demonstrations typically involve someone showing the participants a process or modeling a procedure.

- ✔ **Instructor role play:** Role play by two instructors to demonstrate a technique or make a point, followed with discussion.

- ✔ **Field trips:** Visit the location where the action takes place. If you're teaching customer service, visit your call center and listen in on a few live calls to discuss technique.

✔ **Video, DVD:** Use clips from training or commercial videos for participants to identify issues, solve problems, and rewrite the scripts. Be sure to follow copyright laws.

✔ **Magic tricks:** Use magic tricks to help you make an analogous point within the training.

✔ **Coaching:** Sometimes conducted outside a training event, it could be used as participants practice a particularly difficult skill. Participants are in pairs during role plays or other skill practice.

✔ **Interviews:** Participants ask questions of a resource person who attends the training session at a designated time. Purpose is to obtain another perspective, hear from the expert, or add knowledge.

✔ **Props:** Oh my gosh! So many possibilities! Bring tools: "As a team player I am most like a _____." Bring chunks of two by fours for participants to write the skills they have acquired and "build" the final structure. Bring packets of seeds and use as a metaphor for the "seeds of communication." Well, you get the idea.

Reading

Reading refers to any method that pertains to interacting with the printed word.

✔ **Read ahead:** Materials provided to participants to read prior to the session.

✔ **Letters to each other:** Participants write letters to each other to provide feedback, as a summary of what each has learned in the session, or as follow-up after the training.

✔ **Story starters:** Participants are given a partial situation and then complete it practicing the skills and knowledge they are learning in the training.

Drama

Drama refers to methods that require the participants or the facilitator to act out a role.

✔ **Skits:** A short presentation presented by small groups to demonstrate skill or knowledge learned.

✔ **Survival problem solving:** Usually used as a team-building activity in which a team is placed in a situation that represents danger. Team members need to work together using specified criteria to make decisions.

✔ **Costumes:** Can be used by the trainer to make a point or play a role. Partial costumes, hats for example, could be analogies for the different roles people play on the job.

✔ **Writing a script:** Participants can script a role play for other participants based on the content.

Discussions

Discussion methods refer to two-way discussions that occur between participants and/or the facilitator.

- ✔ **Buzz groups:** Two people "buzz" for one to two minutes about a topic before sharing their ideas with the larger group.

- ✔ **Round robin:** Trainer gets opinions from everyone in the training session. Discussion or rebuttal is held until everyone's ideas have been stated.

- ✔ **Brainstorming:** A process for identifying a large number of ideas without judgment.

- ✔ **Nominal group technique:** A problem-solving tool where ideas are initially generated in silence, then weighted, and prioritized.

- ✔ **Fishbowl:** Group is divided with half the participants sitting in a circle (the fishbowl) discussing a topic. The other half of the group is sitting around the outside and can coach during the discussion, can silently motion to replace someone, or can offer feedback at the end. Several variations.

- ✔ **Develop a theory:** Participants make up a theory related to the knowledge or skills they are learning.

Cases

Cases generally refer to learning methods in which the participants are presented with scenarios that require analysis and suggestions for improvement.

- ✔ **Case studies:** A real or fictional situation is presented to the participants to analyze and recommend solutions. If an actual situation was presented, the facilitator usually shares the actual outcome.

- ✔ **In-baskets:** Items are given to participants that replicate problems, messages, and tasks that could actually show up in someone's in-basket. Participants must make decisions, manage their time, and establish priorities as they address the items.

- ✔ **Critical incidents:** A short version of a case study, which focuses on the most vital aspects of a problem situation, and so on.

- ✔ **Sequential case studies:** Participants are given a portion of a case study. Depending on the decision they make on the first portion, a second, third and perhaps even a fourth set of data is distributed. All groups may end up in different places.

- ✔ **Problem-solving clinic:** Participants bring real-world problems for the rest of the group to solve.

Art

Art entails more creative methods involving drawing, design, sculpting, or other nonword events.

> ✔ **Portraits:** Participants create portraits of themselves being successful at learning the content of the session or as an opening activity to introduce themselves to the group.

> ✔ **Cartoons:** Can be used as energizers or to reinforce knowledge or skills that are being taught.

> ✔ **Posters:** Participants create posters to make a point, summarize information, and so on.

> ✔ **Draw how you feel about _____:** Exactly what it says, draw how you feel about whatever the topic is. Can be reworded such as draw a logo that represents teamwork.

Playlikes

Playlikes are learning methods that are similar to dramatizations but less serious and more open ended.

> ✔ **Role plays:** Participants act out roles, attitudes, or behaviors that are not their own to practice skills or apply what they have learned. Frequently an observer provides feedback to those in character.

> ✔ **Role reversals:** Participants assume the role of the person with whom they interact daily, for example, their bosses.

> ✔ **Video feedback:** Participants are videotaped during a role play or presentation situation. They view their own tapes and complete a self-critique.

> ✔ **Outdoor adventure learning:** Sometimes called *ropes courses;* used for problem solving and team building.

> ✔ **Improv:** Actors create a skit without a script. Input and ideas are gleaned from the audience.

> ✔ **Simulations:** A training environment that closely represents the real environment to allow participants to practice skills.

Games

Games refer to any board, card, television, computer, or physical event that leads to learning or review of material.

> ✔ **Crossword puzzles:** Computer software can take a list of terms from the session and arrange clues and words into a crossword puzzle.

> ✔ **Relays:** Teams set up in a relay to compete to be the first to complete a set of instructions. Good for review of concepts to test skill acquisition.

- ✔ **Card games:** As many variations as there are cards! Various pieces of data can be placed on cards to solve a problem.

- ✔ **Computer games:** Good for reinforcing skills back at the workplace after the session.

- ✔ **Any board-game adaptation:** Many board games such as Trivial Pursuit can be adapted to the content of the training.

- ✔ **Any game-show adaptation:** Game shows such as *Jeopardy!* can be adapted to the content of the training.

Participant directed

The method refers to situations where participants take the leadership role in the delivery of training to others or the analysis of their own learning.

- ✔ **Skill centers:** Several areas are set up around the training room to practice skills or test knowledge. Trainees move from one area to another, selecting the ones most appropriate for them.

- ✔ **Teaching teams:** Usually pairs select a topic from the agenda and teach the rest of the group.

- ✔ **Self-analysis:** Usually a series of questions with correct answers to review knowledge. May also be a set of thought-provoking concepts or questions that allow participants to examine their personal attitudes.

- ✔ **Teach backs:** Participants are given a small portion of content that they study and "teach back" to the rest of the participants. This can be conducted in small groups or the larger group.

- ✔ **Journaling:** Participants keep a written record of thoughts, feelings, reactions, successes, plans, and action items.

- ✔ **Research:** Challenge given in the classroom for participants to track down the correct answer between sessions. Can be used to locate information on the internet as well.

Participant events

Participant events refers to learning methods that have a specific placement in a training session.

- ✔ **Icebreakers:** A structured activity usually used at the beginning of a training session to initiate participation and introductions.

- ✔ **Energizers:** A brief activity, exercise, or brain teaser offered to "energize" the group.

- ✔ **Closers:** Group activity used at the end to bring closure to the session, make commitments, review key points, plan application actions, and celebrate success.

Selecting activities

Okay, you're exhausted just looking at a few of the activity possibilities. How do you know which activities to select? Use two criteria. First think about the learning objective. In which learning category does it fit? Is it *knowledge, skill,* or *attitude*? Match the learning category to the activity. These examples show what I mean. Some of the activities can be used for more than one category of learning. Don't try to perfect this step. This just gets you started.

Strategies for different learning needs

How do you know which type of activity to select? Remember the three categories of learning? Use them as a guide. There will still be some crossover, but it is a place to start.

Different types of learning require different strategies. Match the strategy (type of activity) to the learning objective. Here are a few examples for you.

Knowledge

If you want people to gain knowledge about something, furnish them with information through these activities:

- ✔ Articles
- ✔ Lecturettes
- ✔ Diagrams
- ✔ Audiotapes
- ✔ Buzz group

Skills

If you want people to be able to do something and acquire a new skill, help them experiment by using these activities:

- ✔ Case studies
- ✔ Demonstrations
- ✔ Role playing
- ✔ Videos and practice
- ✔ Exercises
- ✔ Worksheets

Attitude

If you want people to change their values or priorities, assist them to inquire into and observe the old versus the new by using these:

- Instruments
- Role plays
- Debates
- Structured games
- Exercises
- Self-analysis

Considerations for selecting activities

What other questions should you ask when selecting activities?

- **What is the purpose?** Be sure that the design actually accomplishes what the learners need. If they need practice, don't provide a word-match game or a demonstration.

- **How well does the activity assist with accomplishing the learning objective?** Sometimes, a learning objective is broken down into smaller segments. Be sure that the time you invest in activities represents the most critical of objectives as well as covers the most of each.

- **How much time does the activity take? How much time to debrief?** If you don't know how much time, better try it out with a group prior to the training. Don't skimp on time if the knowledge or skill is important. Also, don't try to save time by skipping the debrief. Participants leave an activity without a debrief wondering "What was that all about?" If you do not have time for the debrief, don't do the activity. Also consider how rigid the time restraints may be for the activity and know what you can do if you run short of time.

- **Is the time investment worth the amount of learning that will occur?** Concepts can be taught in many ways. Activities provide a hands-on opportunity for participants to master knowledge or skills that may be harder to master through discussion. Because activities take more time, it is important to be certain that the concepts are related to the most important learning objectives.

- **Will it be fun (or at least stimulating and interesting)?** All activities do not need to be all grins and giggles, but if they are not at least interesting, participants will find something else to do — or at least think about.

- **Do all the participants have the minimum skills to contribute and learn from the experience?** Or are skill levels uneven among participants? Speaks for itself. You may not know about everyone in the session; that's why you're constantly observing and learning about your group. If you suspect that someone will have difficulty, determine how you can offer support without being obvious. It may be in who you pair the person with, what you assign the individual, or how you offer nonchalant sideline coaching. Sometimes, activities can be created in which those with higher skill level are involved by delivering the content in a creative way.

✔ **How comfortable does the group seem with the activity?** Your needs assessment should provide information about what is culturally acceptable in general. In addition, build up to riskier activities as the group is together longer. For example, role plays tend to be accepted later in the training sequence.

✔ **Is the activity appropriate for the size of the group?** Some activities that focus on creativity or mental imagery may seem threatening in small groups. On the other hand, some groups may be too large for certain activities or there may not be enough space to have small groups spread out to complete the activity.

✔ **Does this activity maintain the tone and climate the participants need?** If you're trying to build teamwork, it may not be wise to interject an activity that tears apart what you've built. If you're encouraging participation, you may think twice about an activity that the quieter people may deem threatening.

✔ **Does the activity have enough real-world relevance for this group?** If it doesn't, you may wish to find another or add the relevance that is missing.

✔ **How flexible is the activity?** Mold the activity so the participants are able to easily relate to the situation.

✔ **Will you be able to easily provide clear, succinct directions?** The easier the better. Remember you may have 20, 30, or more participants in your training. If the directions are complex and you still think the activity is worth it, plan for how you can ensure the directions are followed. Here are three ideas. You could have the directions printed on cards for each group. You could have key parts of the directions posted on a flipchart. You could dispense the directions in small doses.

✔ **Will the learning that occurs be straightforward?** If participants end the activity with much to be explained, you will frustrate the learners. Better skip it.

✔ **What is the timing and the sequencing of the activity?** Avoid conducting two similar activities back to back. Think about the time of day, as well. Incorporate activity and movement immediately after lunch. Increase risk as you move through the day.

✔ **How may logistics affect the design?** If you need to travel, you may not want to lug lots of props. It may be difficult to conduct a relay if the room is not large enough. If two trainers are available, you may be able to include demonstrations or role plays. Equipment availability also shapes the activities you select.

✔ **Will the experience and the debrief provide participants with the skill or knowledge they need to acquire from the activity?** Will you be able to easily relate it to the previous as well as the next training module? Finally, how will you evaluate the effectiveness of the activity you chose or designed?

It may seem like a lot of questions. If you're new to design, go through each one. Trust me when I say that eventually this will become second nature to you. You will read a learning objective and immediately have an idea of what activity type will work best.

One last word about activities

Activities can be fun to design and to plan into your training. Remember that balance is the key. To be most successful with activities or games in your session, you must be sure to do the following.

✔ **Have a purpose.** Don't plug a game into a training session just because you have a space. Design it into the session.

✔ **Know the activity.** During the design stage, try out any activities on a small group to see whether they accomplish the purpose for which you have selected the activity.

✔ **Think variety.** As you design the training program, include different types of activities. It is unlikely, for example, that you would use more than one case study in a day when you have so many different activities from which to choose and so many learners with different learning preferences.

  • Reach visual learners through color, charts, pictures, and video clips.

  • Reach auditory learners with debates, group discussions, and stories.

  • Reach kinesthetic learners through role plays, games, and practice.

✔ **Create a consistent theme.** As you design a training program, think of a theme that you could use throughout, or an early event that you could return to, to create consistency. In the "All about icebreakers" section earlier in this chapter, I describe how I have participants introduce themselves using a T-shirt. I continue to use the T-shirts that participants created during the icebreaker throughout the training program. How did I do that?

The group was in the team-formation stage, so I used it as a team-building exercise. Throughout the three days, participants wrote on each others' T-shirts, completing these statements:

- Something I learned about you today is. . . .

- One thing I learned from your presentation is. . . .

- Something I'd like to know about you is. . . .

Finally, I used the T-shirts to bring closure to the session by having participants write on at least two other participants' shirts with a request to "stay in touch" and add their telephone numbers.

Adding Zest with Visuals

I can't imagine facilitating a training session without visuals. They are so useful! Here's what's available:

- ✔ Computer projection systems

- ✔ VCRs, DVD players

- ✔ Overhead projectors

- ✔ 35mm slide projectors

- ✔ Flipchart easels and chart packs

- ✔ Blackboards, whiteboards, and felt boards

- ✔ Electronic white boards

- ✔ SMART Boards

- ✔ Props

Knowing why you need visuals

Why use visuals? The benefits far outweigh the problems they cause and the time it takes to create them. The first bullet is the most important one on the list.

- ✔ Participants grasp the information faster, understand it better, and retain it longer

- ✔ Clarifies a point (a picture is worth a thousand words)

- ✔ Adds variety

- ✔ Communicates message both visually and aurally (through your presentation)

- ✔ Emphasizes a point
- ✔ Makes you more persuasive
- ✔ Helps you be more concise
- ✔ Enhances a transition to change the focus
- ✔ Adds color
- ✔ Keeps you organized and on track (visuals cue you about content and what's next)

You're sold on using visuals. Now what do you need to know during this design stage?

Creating effective visuals

As you design the visuals that will support your training, ensure that you remember what makes them effective. Visuals are most effective when

- ✔ They are relevant to the subject.
- ✔ They are visible and understandable.
- ✔ Page orientation is consistent, using either landscape or portrait.
- ✔ Words are large enough to read.
- ✔ They are oriented to the listener: "Here are four ideas you will. . . ."
- ✔ Color is used appropriately.
- ✔ The typeface varies in boldness and size.
- ✔ The print is in both upper- and lowercase.
- ✔ The typeface enhances the readability (usually a sans serif font).
- ✔ Bullets set off each point.
- ✔ They enhance your performance rather than replace it.
- ✔ The visual becomes an extension of yourself.
- ✔ They are tied together with a common element, for example, sketch, graphic.
- ✔ They are customized for the group.

Designing PowerPoint presentations

Most trainers use PowerPoint as their visual design tool of choice. PowerPoint is an efficient tool, but when overdone can lose its effectiveness.

✔ Keep the limited flexibility in mind because it is not easy to change the slide order or to add content while you present using an LCD projector.

✔ Use a graphic theme and stay with it for the most part; try something other than the canned PowerPoint formats — seeing the same format has become passé.

✔ Use a template that has a fresh look and one that uses a minimum percent of the screen.

✔ Follow the same 8 x 8 rule as for overhead transparencies; 6 x 6 is better for larger groups.

The 8 x 8 (or 6 x 6) rule refers to the number of lines down and words across a visual.

✔ When presenting a list, design it so you can reveal text one line at a time.

✔ To further emphasize the line item you wish to discuss, change the color of the newest item or have the previous items fade subtly.

✔ Headings should be about 44 pt and body 32 pt but no less than 24 pt.

✔ Select one primary transition throughout the content for each module.

✔ Limit colors to two per slide plus black.

✔ Fade to black to signal a new module or if you want to pause for discussion or an activity.

✔ Use a subtle background.

✔ Ensure that there is enough contrast between typeface and background; light on dark is preferred by many.

✔ Use clip art sparingly and don't try to be cute.

✔ If you use animation, select one type and use throughout a module or content section.

✔ Keep sound effects brief, and make sure they add impact.

Designing or selecting film, DVD, and video

A video or film clip adds a surprise element to a training session. To be effective, follow a few guidelines.

✔ Develop program objectives first, and then select.

✔ Media should be proportionate in length to your session.

✔ Show only the portion required to make the point; provide a brief explanation about what happens up to this point.

✔ Provide an introduction that includes the title and tells why you're showing the film.

✔ Preview before showing.

✔ Devise open-ended questions that clarify the objectives of the film and create discussion following it.

Designing overhead transparencies

Although most trainers use PowerPoint and an LCD projector, remember the value and the flexibility that overhead transparencies provide when you keep a few design elements in mind.

✔ Use a variety of colors, but avoid yellow and use red and orange for highlight only.

✔ Add clip art, sketches, and graphics.

✔ Add a frame.

✔ Maximum of eight lines vertically and eight words horizontally.

Some designers advocate a 6 x 6 rule, six lines by six words. This is a good rule if your audience is large, but 8 x 8 works well in a typical training group of fewer than 30 participants.

✔ Proofread text carefully.

✔ Use only data needed to get your message across.

✔ Use headlines.

✔ Use a pencil to number the transparencies in the upper-right-hand corner.

✔ Use overlays to provide dimension and progression to your final message.

Designing flipcharts

Design flipcharts? You've got to be kidding! No, I'm not. Planning an effective flipchart page is just as important as a PowerPoint slide. I usually sketch out the design and words on paper so that when it comes time to actually put the words on the chart paper, I know what I want it to say.

✔ Plan the order of the charts and remember to include blank pages for participant ideas and brainstorming.

✔ Plan for clear and descriptive headings.

✔ Consider using a box, cloud, underline, or other graphic to set off the heading, especially if you may use more than one page for one topic.

✔ Identify the specific words you will use.

✔ Know whether you will want to leave space to add information during the session.

✔ Plan for letters that are 1 to 3 inches high and for ten or fewer lines per page.

✔ Plan sketches ahead.

If you have a model or drawing that you like, but you're not an artist, trace it. Create the flipchart ahead or take a copy to the training setup with you for tracing. If you use a model more than once and participants do not interact or write on the chart, you may wish to have it designed professionally as a poster.

✔ A design that includes bullets can help guide learners.

- Numbers suggest a process, sequence of events, or priority.

- Bullets suggest a list without priority.

- Boxes suggest something that may be checked off after it is complete; for example, learning objectives for the session.

✔ Design the colors of markers; for example, two different colors for every other idea on a list, dark colors for words and bright colors for highlighting.

Inexpensive, clear plastic protector sheets are available for flipchart-sized pages.

Designing handouts or participant books

Participant handouts should not be just a page full of words. You can ensure that handouts and other printed participant materials are effective if you consider these ideas:

✔ Know how the handout will function in terms of note taking, for an exercise, and as a future resource.

✔ Use heads and subheads in a variety of type sizes and degrees of boldness.

✔ Don't mix too many typefaces.

✔ Experts recommend that you use a serif typeface, which makes the letters appear to flow from one to the next.

✔ Use graphics and sketches.

✔ Use bullets, dashes, borders, indentations, and margins for ease of reading.

✔ Number the pages.

Designing a Finale That Brings Closure

It's 4:25 and your session is scheduled to end. Do you just say "That's all folks. Goodbye!"?

Well, of course not. While closing is a small portion of the training session, it is an important one. Just how long is this part of the training? If it is a half-day session, you need at least 15 minutes. If it is a two-or-more-day session, plan on at least 30 minutes. If you test participants before they leave, add time to complete the test. Remember these are just guidelines from my experience. You may have a unique situation.

The conclusion should provide a sense of closure for the learners. It should also create an anticipation for applying what was learned. So what can you include in the design to bring about closure?

✔ Ensure that expectations were met.

✔ Provide a shared group experience.

✔ Evaluate the learning experience.

✔ Request feedback and improvement suggestions.

✔ Summarize the course accomplishments and gain commitment to action.

✔ Send them off with a final encouraging word.

Ensuring that expectations were met

One of the easiest ways to do this is to design time into the agenda to go back to the participants' expectations they shared at the beginning of the session. Did you accomplish all that was expected?

Providing a shared group experience

You may wish to design a closer for your session. It may be used to state a commitment about next steps, review key points of the training, plan for the next actions, or identify how to apply what was learned. It may also be used to celebrate success.

If the group has bonded, you may also wish to do something that helps keep people in touch with each other if they work in different departments, at different locations, or even at different companies. A list of names and e-mails is an easy perk to supply.

I usually design a large group send-off experience. An old favorite goes like this. Have all the participants stand in a circle. Ask them to state what they are going to do as a result of the training within the next ten days. I like this for two reasons. First, each statement gives other participants ideas of other things they could implement. Second, this call to action helps participants bridge the distance back into the real world.

Evaluating the learning experience

You will want to develop an evaluation for the session. Remember that you may need to evaluate at a couple of different levels. Chances are that if you're new to designing training, someone else will assist you with the evaluation for the session. You will find additional information about evaluation in Chapter 13.

Requesting feedback and suggestions

You may also wish to design time into the agenda to obtain verbal feedback and suggestions from the participants about how to improve the session before you offer it again.

Yes, you may ask some of those questions on the paper evaluation that you design. On the other hand, the group discussion often provides more useful ideas because they can be clarified.

Summarizing accomplishments and gaining commitment to action

I usually build this into the shared-group experience in some way. You may wish to use a game, or, if time is critical, you may wish to conduct a brief large-group discussion at the close of the session. Examine the expectations and the learning objectives to ensure they were all accomplished. Then ask for volunteers who could talk about how they intend to implement what they learned back on the job.

In the case of the train-the-trainer presented throughout this chapter, participants wrote a memo to themselves regarding two performance improvements they intend to make. When most people were finished, I asked for volunteers to share one of their improvements with the rest of the group. They placed the memo inside an envelope and addressed it to themselves. I collected them, and one month later, mailed the memos to each trainer.

Sending them off with an encouraging word

One last thing I like to do is to put up a cartoon, a quote, or some inspiring thought that is both rewarding to them and pertinent to the next action they must take. In the case of the train-the-trainer session, I did two things. The first thing I did was to use a mind-teaser.

✔ They were concerned about how they would remember all that they had learned. I have a slide that I put up in cases like this. The slide can be interpreted two ways — with exactly the opposite meanings. Therefore, I ask people to read it out loud as soon as they see it. The slide says: "OPPORTUNITYISNOWHERE"

   • Some read this as "opportunity is nowhere."

   • Others read it as "opportunity is now here."

✔ I explain that just as the letters are the same and can be interpreted two different ways, they are leaving the session with an experience that can be interpreted by them in two ways. They have an opportunity to believe they will be successful or to believe they will not be successful. And no matter what they believe, they will be right. It is really about attitude. The right attitude goes a long way with skills that are maturing.

The second send-off was that I asked them to take their T-shirts with them. I encouraged them to take them home and hang them on their refrigerators. This is a super activity, especially if they have children. Mommy and Daddy are bringing home their school work! It opens discussions at home about what happened in the training. The T-shirt motto is an interesting discussion point, but it is the comments that colleagues wrote on the shirt that is even more interesting to families.

Lastly, stand at the door, shake participants' hands, wish them luck, and say goodbye.

Be sure to design enough time into the plan to include a proper send-off. Nothing is more discouraging than to have the training session fall apart during the last hour because it is behind schedule or that the design is not as tight as the rest of the session.

The schedule for the last 35 minutes of the train-the-trainer looked like this.

✔ **Reviewed expectations on wall chart:** 5 minutes

✔ **Self memo (two performance improvements I will make):** 10 minutes

✔ **Volunteers shared with larger group:** 5 minutes

> ✔ **Evaluated the learning experience:** 10 minutes
>
> ✔ **OPPORTUNITYISNOWHERE:** 2 minutes
>
> ✔ **T-shirts and goodbye:** 3 minutes

Pulling It All Together

At some point you need to capture your design on paper. Most designers use a simple matrix to organize their scheme. Later, a trainer's manual may be written with much more detail. But for now, something simple will serve you well. The design guide that I use has four columns like the one you see in Table 5-1. Think of the design guide as a blueprint if you were building a house. Use it to capture your plans. You see that it has just enough information so that you can capture the flow of content from a big-picture perspective. You identify the knowledge or skill and the activity or method you intend to use. List also the support materials (participant handout, media or visual, prop) required and how long each item will take. If you're like most trainers, you have too much in your initial design. You may have 7 hours of available face-to-face time with your learners, and your design is 12 hours long. Trust me, that's normal.

Table 5-1		**Design Guide**	
Module_____		Time _____	
Learning Objectives:			
✔			
✔			
✔			
Time	**Knowledge or Skill**	**Activity or Learning Method**	**Support Materials and Media**

Before you begin filling the blanks, think about the factors that affect your design and the strategies you may consider. The next two sections in this chapter present you with these considerations.

Factors that affect a design

Every training design you create will be different. That, of course, doesn't mean that you cannot use aspects of a design or modify a design for two different purposes. You can. If you design often, take care that you do not fall into a rut of doing the same things over and over. Try something new. It keeps your designs fresh and keeps you inspired and interested.

Think of these factors as the big-picture items you should think about before putting design pen (or keystroke) to paper.

- ✔ **Content:** How do you determine content? Content should be a natural offshoot of the learning objectives. Include what the participants need to know — not what would be nice to know. If you're a subject matter expert (SME in trainer jargon), you may have most of the information you need. However, if not, or if you need additional facts, you can start here.

  - **Research:** Start with the Internet or your organization's library.

  - **Brainstorm:** Get a group of people from your department together to identify resources and materials that may already be available.

  - **SME:** Identify the subject matter expert and ask what you need to include. Be sure that the SME understands who the target audience is and their skill and knowledge level.

- ✔ **Time available:** How much time will be allowed for the training? The amount of time available for training has been decreasing as organizations find they cannot spare people away from the worksite.

- ✔ **Participants:** If you did not gather this information during the Needs Assessment stage, find out now the number of participants, how familiar they will be with each other, their level in the organization, and their knowledge level of the content.

- ✔ **Culture:** Determine anything unique about the culture of the organization or the department that may be a concern as you develop the materials.

- ✔ **Cost:** Find out how much money has been budgeted for the design and development.

- ✔ **Trainer's experience and expertise:** Assess your skills and knowledge. Do you have the ability to develop your own activities and participant handouts? Perhaps you need to rely on purchased off-the-shelf materials. Chapter 6 provides you with a way to evaluate the usefulness of off-the-shelf materials.

Strategies for a good design

Of course you want to design the best darn training possible. The following guidelines help you determine how to do just that.

- ✔ **Variation:** Use as many different methods and types of activities as possible.
- ✔ **Timing:** Plan for a high level of activity after lunch, decide on the best time for breaks, increase risk slowly, and so on.
- ✔ **Participation:** Design activities to keep participants involved and engaged.
- ✔ **Sequence:** Content should build on itself.
- ✔ **Application:** Design activities that relate directly to the learner's real-world needs.
- ✔ **Lecturettes:** Remember, lecture when you must, but keep it short and involve the participants.

Table 5-2 is a sample of the completed Design Guide I developed for the train-the-trainer session you read about in this chapter. I must admit that it is much more complete than the actual guide I completed. As you acquire more design experience, you, too, can begin to take shortcuts.

Table 5-2	Sample Completed Design Guide

Module ___Facilitation Skills___ Time ___155 minutes___

Learning Objectives:

✔ Participants will list ten ways they will prepare to facilitate a group.

✔ Participants will identify their preferred training style using a self-assessment.

✔ Participants will provide feedback to another facilitator, identifying what went well and what could be improved.

Time	Knowledge or Skill	Activity or Learning Method	Support Materials and Media
30 min	Preparation for facilitation	Intro with ten-minute interactive discussion: "what ifs." Small group guided discussion (find someone on the other side of the room you have not worked with yet — groups of five).	PowerPoint Worksheet

(continued)

Table 5-2 *(continued)*

Time	Knowledge or Skill	Activity or Learning Method	Support Materials and Media
45 min	Identify training style	Complete self-assessment. Share in pairs to identify personal strengths and weaknesses.	Training style instrument Assessment sheet
60 min	Co-facilitating skills Note: critical new skill	Role play with observers. Three rounds with different person as observer each time. Role plays get progressively more difficult. Summarize in large group: what worked, what didn't?	Role play card Observation sheets Team trainer checklist
20 min	Apply co-facilitating skills to personal situation	Write memo to co-facilitator: more of, less of, continue doing	Handout: memo

As you examine the sample guide can you see some of the strategies I planned into the design?

- ✔ Sequencing of topics to build on each other as well as difficulty within the role play
- ✔ Variation in types of methods
- ✔ Variation in pace from moving around to sitting alone for self-assessment
- ✔ Variation in grouping size: pairs, five, self, large group
- ✔ High level of participation
- ✔ Variety in who learners are learning with
- ✔ Critical skill receives more time
- ✔ Minimal amount of time spent "telling"

Developing materials

Materials support the training you have designed. You either develop or purchase these materials, which supplement and support each learning experience. Materials may include some or all of these:

✔ Participant material that includes at least the handouts and/or manual with information and note-taking space.

✔ Media or visual support such as a PowerPoint presentation to guide a mini-lecturette.

✔ Activity support that the participants may need for the activities such as role-play cards, self-assessment instruments, or checklists.

✔ A trainer's manual to guide your facilitation or for others who may facilitate the session.

✔ Administrative support that you use in order to keep yourself organized or to complete the administrative requirements of the session. It may include an agenda, roster, supply checklist, certificates, and evaluations.

When developing the participant materials, don't try to include everything on paper. The activities you design tap into the knowledge, experience, and expertise of the participants. Participants should have a place to capture ideas they may want to use after the session. Allow space for note taking.

Do consider job aids, checklists, reference cards, and other guides that can be used after the completion of the session. Investing time to develop these materials, especially for tasks that are done infrequently or for complicated tasks, is a good decision. You still include these tasks in the design, but you free up some classroom time instead of increasing the amount of practice time for tasks that may not be completed very often.

Essential components

Desktop publishing has taken most of the pain out of creating participant materials. As you design them, begin by knowing what content you will include and how participants will use them. Will they be assigned reading prior to the session? Read during the session? Basis for an exercise? Backdrop for taking notes? Future resource? What else should you remember?

✔ Make it easy to read and quick to find information by breaking up the text with heads and subheads in a variety of type sizes and degrees of boldness.

✔ Use short paragraphs and wide margins, leaving space for taking notes.

✔ Use bullets, dashes, borders, indentations, and margins to enhance each page.

✔ Write in a conversational tone.

✔ Use graphics and sketches, even just lines and boxes, to set off key concepts and to add interest.

✔ Number the pages.

How about a trainer's manual?

Your trainer's manual may be anything from your notes written on the participant handouts to a complete manual with references to the training plan, facilitation tips, time use, media and visual list, and masters for the participant materials. A well-designed trainer's manual:

- ✔ Uses icons.

- ✔ Has plenty of room for writing notes.

- ✔ Identifies everything you need to know at a glance (what visual you're using, what page participants should be on, what materials you require, and so on).

- ✔ Provides you with either a lead-in statement, a transition statement, or both.

For now, I suggest that you allow someone else to worry about writing a trainer's manual. The preparation chapter provides a few ideas for what you can do to personalize your manual.

Whew! That's all, folks! As you can see, the design and development stage of The Training Cycle requires lots of work. You may decide to purchase off-the-shelf materials instead of designing them yourself. However, you most likely still want to customize them for your organization. In that case, most of this chapter can help you with that task. Chapter 6 is all about selecting off-the-shelf programs.

The design and development of training is a big job, but don't forget to have fun and to build fun into your design. You can do it. I pass on Henry Ford's advice: "Whether you believe you can or you can't, you will prove yourself correct."

Chapter 6

Using Off-the-Shelf Training

In This Chapter

▶ Selecting off-the-shelf training

▶ Customizing and adapting off-the-shelf training

▶ Adding creativity to your training

*N*o time to design? An off-the-shelf product may be your answer.

You may just not have time to custom design a training program, especially when the training must be given immediately. In addition, some basic training principles are so universal that creating something new isn't necessary. Some examples include topics like supervisory basics, time management, meeting management, and stress management.

At times like these, trainers turn to vendors who create off-the-shelf training programs for a living. To maximize these products, you can spend a little time creatively customizing the off-the-shelf programs for your organization.

This chapter explores how to be savvy about selecting off-the-shelf materials and how to customize them after your decide to use them.

The Art of Selecting Off-the-Shelf Training

At first glance, purchasing materials that have already been designed and are packaged, tested, and ready to implement may appear to be a perfect solution. What are some of the possibilities for pre-packaged training?

✔ Presenters and speakers from consulting firms, speakers bureaus, and universities.

✔ Films and video on almost any training topic.

✔ Public seminars offered regularly by training and consulting firms; some are on a regular travel schedule presenting in most large cities.

✔ Packaged training programs that come ready to unwrap including the participants' materials, a trainer's guide, media and visual support, computer support and programs, and even the job aids, the "cheat sheets" that participants take back to the workplace to remind them of what they learned.

✔ Customized training packages designed by training and consulting firms but created to your specifications; most start with a needs assessment (see Chapter 4).

Make or buy? That's the question!

With so many opportunities to purchase training off-the-shelf, is there ever a reason to actually go through all the trouble of designing your own training? Well, yes, there is, especially when you need to make some changes to the off-the-shelf training, as many organizations do. Examine the pros and cons of off-the-shelf training in Table 6-1.

Table 6-1	Pros and Cons of Off-the-Shelf Training
Pros	**Cons**
Can be acquired and delivered quickly.	May be difficult to customize easily.
Initially cost effective.	May be difficult to find one program that meets all your needs.
Eliminates the need to reinvent the wheel.	Customizing the program may reduce the effectiveness.
Can be adapted to meet different needs of different levels of employees and managers.	Customization may take so long that it defeats the original cost/time benefit.
Can obtain evaluation data from organizations that have used it.	May be difficult to customize media.
Usually has solid research to support the design.	May have copyright issues to address if you make changes.
Provides deliverable when subject matter expert doesn't reside inside the organization.	After you start, you may be forever reliant on the vendor for supplies.

What should you know before you buy?

If you've decided to buy an off-the-shelf program, find out the following about the package and the company before you buy:

- ✔ **What's the track record of the company?** What is its reputation with other vendors? Ask to see its client list.

  Ask whether you can speak with clients who have used the product you're considering. Most people ask for a couple of names, and most consultants give you the names of their most satisfied customers. Instead of doing this, I suggest you ask for the entire client list and select from it.

- ✔ **What kind of support will you receive from the company?** Will it provide a pilot program? Does it provide train-the-trainer sessions? What other startup support can you expect? Who, specifically, will be working with your organization? Keep in mind that the salesperson is rarely the trainer or the designer.

- ✔ **Who is responsible for getting the work completed?** Have this person's name in writing. Find out what you're responsible for and what your contact person is going to do.

- ✔ **What's the timeline for completing the project?** If you're speaking to a salesperson, find out when the development staff will start to work with you.

- ✔ **What, exactly, are you purchasing?** Participant materials? Trainer's guides? Media support? Do you actually own the materials, or are you buying the rights to use the materials one time? Can you deliver the program to other employees later? Or will you always need to rely on someone from the company to conduct future sessions?

- ✔ **What's the quality of the materials?** Are they written in terms consistent with your industry? Does a version exist that is specific to your industry? Do the examples match the situations your employees face? If not, can they easily be changed?

- ✔ **Does the program include a trainer's manual?** How complete is it? How easy to use?

- ✔ **Do you know how much you're paying?** The absolute bottom line without any hidden costs, for example, travel or supplemental material that isn't included in the cost.

- ✔ **Do you believe that the company knows enough about your situation to recommend the training program that you're considering?** Why? What makes you think that?

✔ **How consistent are the objectives of the program with the needs of your organization?** In fact, are the outcomes presented as learning objectives or vague results? Does the program offer an ample amount of hands-on practice?

✔ **Is the program rich in content?** Is it based on adult learning principles? Is it interesting, engaging? Does it offer a unique twist?

✔ **How will your most critical participants view the program?** Will they see relevance to the organization? How will your typical participant's experience and expertise match the program?

✔ **How well does the design match your organization's culture?** How well does the design match your organization's training philosophy? What percent of the program is dedicated to theory? What percentage to real-world examples? What about hands-on practice and role plays? Are a variety of activities introduced? Does the program have backup activities? Is the time used efficiently?

✔ **What about the logistics?** Where will the training occur? How many trainers will you pay for? Who supplies the equipment? What if the trainer is ill the day of the training? What's the backup plan?

Vendors are interested in selling you a product. Be sure that you have all of your concerns and questions identified prior to meeting with them. Don't buy until you have all questions answered to your satisfaction.

How can you make sure off-the-shelf training meets your needs?

You've completed your analysis, and you have decided that an off-the-shelf program will meet your needs this time. What can ensure a wise buy?

✔ **Know your objectives.** Before reviewing an off-the-shelf training program, make sure you have clearly stated the learning objectives the program must accomplish. Look for the off-the-shelf program that most clearly fits the needs of your stated objectives.

✔ **Make sure it's the best fit.** Look for a program that is designed for your industry (participants in manufacturing will not be very interested in a program geared to retailing, for example).

✔ **Consider buying from a vendor who is willing to customize for you.** These folks have the "core" topics for any program but are willing to adapt them to fit your specific training needs.

Molding It to Meet Your Needs

After you've selected the packaged program you desire, customize the materials to make them truly yours.

Adapting the design

Buying a training program isn't always as easy as it sounds. To ensure that the design achieves what it needs to, you will most likely need to adapt the design to your organization.

- Circulate the off-the-shelf program to key managers and participants. Ask for their suggestions to make it a perfect match for your organization.

- Review the program well in advance of the training. Make notes in the margins using company examples, anecdotes, policies, and so on that bring the topic home.

- Weave your organization's core themes and philosophies into every part of the program. The skills and behaviors taught may be generic, but the way your organization applies them is not.

- If a technical process or procedure is being taught, add or delete steps to be consistent with the way the process is performed in your organization.

- If a behavioral skill is being taught, add comments that reflect your organization's management beliefs and philosophy regarding the behavior.

Off the shelf, out of the can

When the training is in your hands, you can take a few steps to make it look less like a canned program and more like yours.

- Give the program a new title that reflects the essence of your organization and what it is facing.

- Consider including an "extra" something (posters, wallet cards, job aids) that is specifically customized to reflect the policies and principles of your organization.

- Massage the media. Can the handouts, overhead projection visuals, and PowerPoint presentations be slightly reworked to reflect your company's personality? For example, can you add your logo, change department names to actual departments in your organization, change job titles to actual jobs?

✔ Review models, case studies, role plays, and group activities. Can you change the issues being discussed, modeled, or worked through to reflect current issues at your organization?

✔ Consider putting the training materials in your organization's own binder.

✔ Delete portions of the package that are not pertinent to your organization. For example, if the material discusses dealing with field offices and your company has only a headquarters office, delete the section for working with the field.

✔ Add portions to the package that are pertinent to your organization but are not a part of the packaged program. For example, if your organization has a values statement, add it to the package and adapt the package accordingly.

Adding Creativity to Training

Creativity is an important aspect of all training, whether you've designed it yourself or you are adapting an off-the-shelf program for your organization.

✔ Promote your next training session in a unique way, for example, by sending the invitation in a paper bag.

✔ Title your next training session in a creative way, such as "Bag That Problem."

✔ Hold your next training session in a unique location.

✔ Introduce new ways to think about the training topic.

✔ Use themes to energize a session, for example, paper bags, crayons, seeds, hats, maps, airplanes, tools, puzzles, T-shirts.

✔ Use at least three different training techniques or methods per hour of instruction.

✔ Use cartoons with the names of managers in your organization.

✔ Look for double meanings in the words and topics of your training, and then play with those double meanings. For example, trainers often claim to have a "bag of tricks." You could play off of the "bag" theme or the "tricks" theme. Use a "bag your problem" activity or use magic tricks as an analogy to some of the knowledge you are training.

✔ Encourage participants' creativity; engage them in brainstorming.

✔ Present your participants with challenges, puzzles, and brain teasers.

✔ Keep a creativity file that you can refer to when you develop your training programs.

✔ Use energizers often. Be sure they are short, quick, and, of course, energizing! An energizer is a brief activity, exercise, or brain teaser offered to re-ignite the group's energy.

✔ Add planned humor to your next training session. Be sure to use your funny experience as an example.

✔ End your training session with a story, poem, quote, picture, or gimmick. For example, thrusting a straw through a raw potato to demonstrate the importance of seeing success and following through.

✔ Read as many articles and books about creativity as you can.

✔ Shop in toy stores, dollar stores, and children's bookstores for ideas.

✔ Ask participants to evaluate your training program with a limerick.

✔ Take more risks; try things that you have been reluctant to try. For example, I avoided using debates in the classroom for too many years because I was afraid to take the risk. When I did finally use a debate, I was pleasantly surprised about participants' willingness to get involved, as well as the richness of the follow-up discussion.

✔ Trouble getting folks to return after a break? That's probably a good sign that they are communicating during the break. But you do need to start again. Use a cartoon or flick the lights. You may also signal with a noise maker, like a train whistle, kazoo, cow bell, chime, or sleigh bells. Try to vary your approach from one break to the next.

Another way to get participants' attention is to snap your fingers. I begin snapping my fingers and quietly say, "If you can hear me, snap your fingers." Participants in the front can hear it the first time. I repeat myself and eventually the snapping works its way to the back of the room.

✔ Study other presentations you see and identify new approaches to use during your next training.

Caution: Stick-in-the-muds ahead

No matter what you add to your training design to make it fun and interesting, you must continue to keep the learning objectives in front of you. I purposefully do not call active learning methodologies "games." Using that term implies, unfortunately, that the training session is all about having fun, not about learning.

Even though you and I know that people do learn and remember when they are having fun, be cautious about the label you use. "Learning activity" just sounds better outside the session to people who weren't there to see all the learning that occurred.

Take a list of key concepts for your next training session with you to your local dollar store. Compare the concepts and the merchandise in the store to identify themes for your next training session. For example, you can use play money for investing in your future, your health, or your team; puzzles for finding the right fit or everyone has a role; a compass for finding your way or determining a new direction; rulers for measuring potential, setting goals, or determining growth; or hundreds of other ideas.

Adding creativity to your training session adds to the entire learning experience and creates an adventure for your participants. As Helen Keller said, "Life is either a daring adventure or nothing."

Chapter 7

Be Prepared to Succeed

- -

In This Chapter

▶ Preparing your training environment

▶ Preparing your participants

▶ Preparing yourself for facilitating

▶ Understanding training styles

- -

"**P**roper preparation and practice prevent poor performance." As a new trainer in the early '80s, this is one of the first messages my colleagues shared with me. I later leaned that Bob Pike coined and published this statement that he calls the six Ps of an effective presentation. Bob believes that 80 percent of being a good trainer and getting people involved depends upon adequate preparation.

A training session may at times seem like the proverbial iceberg: Participants see only the top 10 percent. And I think that's the way most trainers want to keep it.

In this chapter, you discover how to address the other 90 percent that's below the surface: How do you prepare the environment, the participants, and yourself before the training experience? You know you need to be prepared to succeed, and this chapter gets you there.

Preparing Your Training Environment

When your participants walk into the training session, what do you want them to see? Empty boxes turned on end? Chairs awry? Technicians scurrying about trying to get your PowerPoint up and running? Facilities people moving the refreshment table to the back of the room and bringing extra chairs? You running to and fro trying to find missing materials? Of course not. You're letting them see the other part of the iceberg.

Establishing an environment conducive to learning is a critical aspect of starting a training session off on the right foot. You can ensure that participants walk in to a relaxed atmosphere and an environment that is welcoming and ready. The room says you took the time to get ready for them. You have time to greet them and welcome them to a great training session.

After reading this section you may be amazed at how much time you will spend preparing the environment for your participants. Believe me it is worth every minute. The more time you spend in the room, the more comfortable you will be during the training session. Make the room yours so that when participants arrive it will feel as if you're welcoming them to your space.

Know when, where, what, who

It seems logical that you would know the logistics of a training site, yet every trainer I've met has encountered at least one training nightmare. Some (not all) of these could be prevented by additional preparation. These questions may help you obtain the right information, but it will do you little good if you don't write the answers in a safe place.

- ✔ **When:** When is the training? Day? Date? Time? Also, do you have enough time to prepare? Is the amount of allotted time for the amount of content adequate?

- ✔ **Where:** Where is the session? On-site or off? If off-site, is it easy to travel to the location? How do you get there? What's the address? Telephone number? Will you need to make travel arrangements? Is public transportation available? How do you get materials to the site?

- ✔ **What:** What kind of training is being expected? What resources are required? What kind of facilities are available? What will you need?

- ✔ **Who:** Who is the key planner? Who are the participants? How many? What's their background? Why were you chosen to deliver the training? Who is the contact person at the training site? How do you reach that person on-site and off?

Lots of answers. Write them down.

Room arrangements

Your room may have significant impact on your training session. Arrange the room to support the learning objectives and the amount of participation you will desire.

Typically you will not have the opportunity to select a room. However, if you do, consider the attributes that will create the best learning environment for your participants.

- ✔ **Size:** Arrange for a room to accommodate the number of participants. Remember that a room that is too large can be as bad as one that may be too small.

- ✔ **Training requirements:** If the training session entails many small group activities, determine if there is enough space in the room. If not, arrange for additional breakout rooms to accommodate your needs.

- ✔ **Accessibility:** Ensure that the room is accessible to all, including those who have limited mobility.

- ✔ **Location:** If participants need to travel (either by foot or vehicle) to the session, the location should not pose a hardship, for example, walking in rain, or parking difficulty.

- ✔ **Convenience:** Readily accessible restrooms, telephones, snacks, lunch accommodations, and so on help ensure that participants return on time following breaks or lunch.

- ✔ **Distractions:** Select a room that is free of distractions and noise. Thin walls with a sales convention next door may not create the environment you're trying to establish for learning.

If you're in a room with a telephone, turn the ringer off and provide an alternate number for participants who need to be available for messages. Set a message center up outside the room; sticky-back notes available for leaving messages may be adequate.

- ✔ **Obstructions:** Select a room that is free of structures such as posts or pillars that may obstruct participants' views.

- ✔ **Seating:** Select a location that provides comfortable, moveable chairs. Seating arrangements should further enhance the learning environment you wish to establish. Determine what's most important for the learner. There are probably two dozen ways you could set up the training room. The seven seating arrangements in Figure 7-1 are typical. Consider the advantages to your participants for each arrangement. Table 7-1 provides guidance about why you may select each.

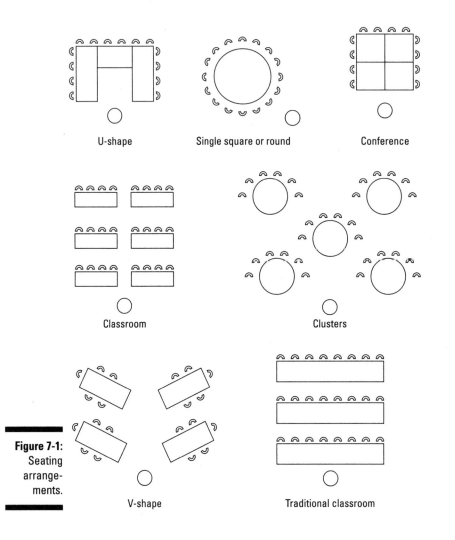

Figure 7-1: Seating arrangements.

Table 7-1		Seating Arrangements	
Seating Style	*Number*	*Benefits*	*Drawbacks*
U-shape	Best for groups of 12 to 22	Encourages large group discussion Can push back to form small groups Close contact between facilitator and participants	Difficult to form small groups with those on other side Eye contact between some participants is difficult due to the linear layout

Seating Style	Number	Benefits	Drawbacks
Single square or round	Best for groups of 8 to 12	Facilitates problem solving Smaller size increases total group involvement Easy for facilitator to step out of the action	Media and visual use is difficult Limited group size
Conference	Best for groups of 8 to 12	Moderate communication among group	Maintains trainer as "lead" Sense of formality
V-shape (with V pointing to front)	Best for teams of 4 or 5 and groups of 16 to 25	Easy to work in teams at each table No one has back totally to the front of room	Some difficulty to promote teamwork among entire group
Clusters	Best for groups of 16 to 40	Promotes teamwork in each cluster If chairs are placed on only one side of the table, everyone will face the front of the room	Difficult to get those whose backs are to front to participate Some participants may need to turn chairs to face the front of the room
Classroom	For groups of any size	Traditional; may be expected by learners Trainer controls Participants can view visuals	Low involvement One-way communication Difficult to form small groups
Traditional classroom	Best reserved for groups over 40	Traditional; may be expected by learners Trainer controls	Low involvement One-way communication Difficult to form small groups

✔ **Furniture:** In addition to decisions about the seating arrangements and the kind of tables you prefer, you will want a table in front of the room for your supplies and equipment. Don't allow too much space between the table from which you will present and the front participant row. I usually allow just enough room for me to squeeze through when I move from the table to roam about the group. Reducing the amount of space between you and the learners increases the affect level in the room. It closes the distance between you and the trainees both physically and emotionally. The participants feel better about you, themselves, and the training session.

You may also want to consider positioning a table for refreshments in the back of the room. Located there, it can be easily serviced throughout the day. One more thing. Don't forget the wastebasket! In my experience neither training rooms nor hotel conference rooms have wastebaskets. Remember to ask for one.

✔ **Lighting:** Lighting should be adequate. Dimly lit ballroom ambiance will not promote energy in a training session. Is the lighting bright enough? Is it natural lighting? If the room has windows, which direction are they facing? Can windows be darkened, if necessary? A morning sun coming up behind your projection screen will blind the participants and wash out the image on the screen. Know where light switches are located so that you can brighten or darken the room as needed.

✔ **Workable walls:** Most trainers hang flipchart pages on the walls: the session objectives, small group work, and so on. Is wall space available or do windows surround the room? Does art cover the walls or are they open? Usually the front of the training room should be opposite the entrance to avoid distractions when folks come and go. Is that possible in the room you're considering?

Use markers that absolutely do not bleed through so there is no danger of ruining walls. The only brand that I know lives up to this expectation is Mr. Sketch. Not only that, but they smell good as well — scented like cherry, mint, orange, licorice, and blueberry!

✔ **Climate control:** You will never be able to please everyone in your session. However, if you have the ability to adjust it yourself, you can try. Determine where the thermostat is located and whether you have any control over it. Experiment with it while you set up the room. Does it respond quickly or slowly? Do you need to contact someone to make adjustments?

When adjusting thermostats, make changes one degree at a time and give the equipment time to work. Large changes in the thermostat will cause a once too-cool room to become too warm.

✔ **Microphone:** If you have a large room or a large group or the room has poor acoustics or you have a tiny voice, you may need a microphone. Check the room to ensure it is wired for a microphone.

Equipment and visuals

It seems that if anything goes wrong that interferes with conducting the training session, it will have something to do with the equipment.

How does your training chair stack up?

Have you ever attended a full-day training session sitting on a hard chair that was not adjustable? Most people have, and that's why trainers are interested in providing the most comfort possible to learners. Providing the right chair is critical. If the chair is too small and uncomfortable, participants fidget and get irritable. If the chair is too comfortable, participants may fall asleep.

The chair that you use should allow participants to sit comfortably for six hours. What is the perfect training chair? The ideal training chair should include these features:

✔ Has a back.

✔ Is adjustable in terms of height.

✔ Has adjustable arms to relieve body fatigue by supporting some of the weight. The forearm should be positioned at a 90-degree angle from the upper arm.

✔ Is upholstered in fabric (not vinyl).

✔ Has wheels so participants can move chairs to small groups easily.

✔ Swivels so participants can easily move with the conversation of the large group.

✔ Is at least 20 inches long and 20 inches wide.

Stacking chairs, most often used in training rooms, meet very few of these standards.

Your media and visual equipment — LCD, VCR, overhead projector, flipcharts — all help participants understand the message faster and easier. But when something goes awry, it can spell disaster. Preparation can prevent some potential headaches.

Preview one week before the event

✔ Set up the machines and go through all visuals.

✔ Practice with PowerPoint and overhead slides to ensure they are in order.

✔ Experiment with dissolve enhancements, animation, and sound effects.

✔ Practice with the equipment you will use, even the flipcharts require you to practice your flipping, ripping, and hanging techniques.

Set up the day before the event

The best thing you can do to be prepared for a training is to set up the day before the training is scheduled. If anything is missing, or if anything goes wrong, you will be happy to have learned about it a day early.

✔ Be certain the equipment works.

✔ Focus all equipment and set the volume level where needed.

✔ Check volume control and know how to adjust it.

If playing a DVD off a computer, be sure to check the quality of the sound because the speakers on the computer may not be as good as they need to be.

- ✔ Make sure that the projector has the right lens and that it is clean.
- ✔ Clean the light source and the glass of the overhead projector.
- ✔ Mark the projection table placement with masking tape on the floor.
- ✔ Check that the screen is large enough and placed where you want it.

How large of a screen do you need? The distance from the participants should be six times the width of the screen.

- ✔ Tilt the screen forward at the top to avoid keystoning (the image distortion caused when the projector beam doesn't meet the screen at a 90-degree angle).
- ✔ Check the seats (sit in them) to make sure everyone can see.
- ✔ Decide whether you need to dim the lights; do so only if you must.
- ✔ Cue up the VCR.
- ✔ Plan ahead to know where you will be standing.

Prepare for an emergency

Although you can't be prepared for every emergency, you can prepare using these suggestions:

- ✔ Bring an extra bulb to the session.
- ✔ Know how to change bulbs.
- ✔ Learn a few troubleshooting tricks for the equipment you use most often.
- ✔ Pack an adaptor plug and perhaps an extension cord.
- ✔ Pack a roll of duct tape to tape down stray cords.
- ✔ Have an alternative plan if the electricity fails — that may mean markers and a flipchart.

Special computer considerations

If you're teaching a computer class or using computers during the training session, take special precautions. Unless you're a computer troubleshooting whiz, have someone who is available when you set up and as you begin the session. Check out a few other things prior to the session.

- ✔ Make sure that you have the name and contact number, including cell-phone number of the person who will assist if you have difficulty.
- ✔ Ensure that the computers have the correct software and version installed.

✔ Make sure that you have been informed of the log-in ID and password required to access the computers.

✔ Determine who is responsible for providing discs or other special computer supplies.

✔ Supplies you may want to add to the training kits described elsewhere in this chapter include a long telephone cord, power strip, remote mouse with extra battery, and a screwdriver (if you're traveling by air, you'll need to place it in checked luggage).

✔ Bring electrical tape if you will work in a makeshift lab to tape computer cables and other cords out of the participants' way.

Setup tricks for flipcharts

When your flipcharts are prepared, you will feel more organized and ready to conduct the session.

✔ Use a design you create on paper to guide your writing.

✔ Write on every other page (so you can't see through to the next page).

✔ Use a variety of dark colors; use red for emphasis only.

✔ Use numbers, bullets, boxes, and underlining.

✔ Some trainers like to use two different marker colors for every other idea on a list.

✔ Letters should be 1 to 3 inches high.

✔ Pencil cues in the margin.

✔ Print; do not use cursive writing.

✔ No more than ten lines per page.

✔ A misspelled word can be cut out with a razor blade; tape clean paper to the back and rewrite the word.

✔ Bend corners or use tape tabs to find and turn pages more easily.

✔ Adjust the easel to a comfortable height.

✔ Position the easel where you want to use it.

Plan flipchart placement so that your back is to the least number of participants. As you face the audience, the chart should be to your non-dominant side if you use it mostly for writing. It should be to your dominant side if you use it mostly for pointing to content. I usually have two charts, one for each purpose, and more if the participants will use them for listing ideas or decisions in small group activities.

✔ Make sure the easel is securely locked and balanced and that the pad is firmly anchored on the easel.

All this equipment preparation may seem like a great deal of work. The first time something goes wrong, however, you will appreciate the attention to details.

Preparing Your Participants

Preparing your participants is tricky. What you think will work to get them involved in the session probably won't. And what you think may be minimal preparation is perhaps the best thing you can do. Imagine that! As you peruse some of these ideas, remember you're working with adult learners. You will see Malcolm Knowles' adult-learning principles are alive and well.

Preparing participants: What works?

How do you help prepare your participants before the session begins? I have found all of these to work:

- Connect with them before the session. Let them know what's in it for them (Bob Pike calls this radio station WII-FM) by relating it to their job. Will the session make their job easier? Will it enhance relationships? Will it show them how to manage time better? Tell them about it.

- Send a welcome letter stating the objectives of the class. Provide an e-mail address or phone number and welcome them to contact you if they have any questions.

- Send the agenda.

- Send a handwritten note introducing yourself and stating why you're looking forward to working with this group.

- Send a puzzle or brain teaser that arouses their curiosity.

- Send a provocative statement or question that makes them wonder what you're up to.

- Send a cartoon that is pertinent to the session.

- Send the welcome letter in a unique way. One example is to send it in a paper bag. I then used the paper bag as a theme throughout the session; for example, participants were encouraged to write an issue on an index card and place the card in a provided paper bag, thus "bagging" their issue until later.

- Send participants a roster of who will attend the session.

✔ Send them specific logistic information. Where is the training site? What room? Where can they eat lunch? What time will lunch be held? What's the phone number at the site? Will they be able to check their e-mails? Where can they park their cars? What's the closest metro station?

✔ Get them involved early by sending them a questionnaire and using their responses to tweak the agenda and incorporate their needs.

✔ Provide participants' supervisors with a discussion sheet to review. Ask the supervisors to discuss what they hope the participant brings back to the workplace.

Preparing participants: What doesn't work?

Through many years of experience, I have also found things that do not work. Don't bother with these!

✔ **Don't send lengthy preread material.** It will only be read by two people and they will complain.

✔ **Don't send short preread material.** It will be read by 30 percent, ignored by 30 percent, and lost by 40 percent.

✔ **Don't ask them to write more than a half a page of anything in preparation.**

✔ **Be sure you have management support.** If participants sense that management is not behind the training, you will expend a great deal of energy on the issue during the session. Participants may be discouraged when they walk into the session,

✔ **Don't send more than one e-mail.** If you must send an e-mail, be sure that you have included everything and that everything is correct, so that you don't need to send a second e-mail to correct the first!

✔ **Don't do nothing.** That's right. Nothing doesn't work, either. Make at least one contact with participants prior to the session.

Preparing Yourself

While everything in this chapter is in one way or another preparing you, this section truly focuses on things you can specifically do, from thinking through crises that may occur, to practicing your activities, to keeping yourself organized. The better you're prepared, the smoother the session will go.

Prepare to avoid crises

The key to handling crises in the classroom, those unexpected events that crop up at the most inopportune moments, is prevention. The experienced trainer is a close friend of Murphy and his laws of random perversity. A trainer knows that "If something can go wrong, it will." As a result, experienced trainers will take every possible step to ensure a problem can be prevented. Furthermore, they have some contingency plans ready if something actually does go wrong. These pointers will help you prevent catastrophes during the training session.

✔ Go through your presentation thoroughly. List every single logistic detail as you come to it. After you have done this for the entire program, create a checklist for yourself. Review this checklist one week before the program, three days before the program, the day before the program and the morning of the program. This ensures that you have thought of every detail on time.

✔ Have your handouts and visual aids prepared early enough so that they can be thoroughly proofread and checked to see whether they are in the proper order. If something is wrong, you will have time to correct it.

✔ Don't assume that, just because you reserved a room, it will be there waiting for you. Reservations and room schedules have a unique way of canceling themselves. If you're making a reservation at an outside facility, write down the date and time you made the reservation, the name of the person who took your reservation and the confirmation number. If you're scheduling a room internally, write down the date and time you made the reservation and the name of the person who scheduled the room.

✔ One week before the program call to ensure the room is still being held. Do the same thing the day before the program.

✔ Even if the room is available, don't assume it will be set up as you requested. To help the facilities people arrange the room, you should provide them with a detailed diagram of how you want the room.

✔ The day before the program, you should call to remind them that you want the room set up that day. If that is not possible, get their commitment to have it set up at least two hours before the program is scheduled to begin.

✔ Get the name of a contact person who will be at the training site on the day of the training. That person can help you locate any missing materials or fix (or replace) any broken equipment.

✔ Arrive at least one hour early on the day of training. This gives you time to set up your own materials as well as time to tend to any last-minute crises. You may be the one who actually tidies the room, arranges (or rearranges) furniture, sets up and tests the equipment, and makes last-minute arrangements.

Check your room

Even if someone else is responsible to set the room up, check it out. Theoretically, the room should be set up exactly as you requested. Practically, it will not be. Some folks like to make changes because they think they are doing you a favor. For example, I have found that most hotels like to set up the room with extra seats "just in case." Setting up a room for 26 when no more than 20 are expected causes a problem in two ways.

✔ First, the empty seats make it appear that there are no shows, and participants will wonder why that occurred.

✔ Second, the additional chairs mean that people will be farther away from each other

and/or that there may be empty chairs between participants, making it more difficult to encourage interaction and participation.

You may need to do more than just put the extra chairs away. When presenting at a hotel (even when I have had personal discussions and provided detailed drawings), I have had to tear down the table arrangement and redo it. I will call facilities, but they are usually delayed, because of course they think they have completed this job and are off on another. On some occasions I learn when the set up will occur and I try to be present, using the time to complete other setup myself.

✔ Know how to change the light bulb for any projection equipment and make sure there is a spare available.

✔ Because of the possibility of last-minute crises, have your presentation completely prepared and rehearsed *before* you arrive at the training site. If you plan to do it when you arrive, you may get distracted. Then, when it's time to begin, you will not be prepared.

✔ If you're flying to the training program, either send the materials (insured) well in advance or carry them on the plane with you. This will prevent you from having to worry about them getting lost en route.

When I travel to a site, I pack one master set of participant material in my carry-on luggage. If the participant materials are not there for any reason, I can at least have copies made to get the session started.

Of course, no amount of preparation can ensure that your program will go off without a hitch. Use these tips to deal with catastrophes during the presentation.

✔ If equipment fails, calmly look at the equipment and check for obvious problems (accidentally turned off, became unplugged, and so on).

✔ If you're uncertain about how to fix it, ask for volunteers from the participants. There are usually one or two handy people in every program.

✔ If no one can pinpoint the problem, give the group a five-minute break while you find help.

✔ If help cannot be found or if the problem is not fixable, rearrange your agenda to delete the activity or to have it at a later time when the equipment is fixed or replaced. This requires that you're absolutely prepared, know your program forward and backward, and are flexible enough to see new linkages and sequences.

✔ Use group problem solving or brainstorming to come up with alternatives to any problem (for example, overcrowded room, broken air conditioning, missing handouts).

✔ Be prepared for any type of participant response. You may have a group that refuses to participate, or you may have one where all the individuals talk at once. Have a plan for facilitating any type of group.

✔ Use humor to defuse unexpected situations. Check some of the ways to add humor listed at the end of this book.

✔ Most importantly, keep your cool. A crisis situation only becomes a crisis when you treat it that way. If you maintain your composure under any circumstance, your participants will assume everything is under control.

Identifying your training style

Even if you have never trained a day in your life, you have already developed a training style. Like everyone, you have developed preferences in life. How you give directions to strangers. How you explain a task to colleagues. How you clarify information for your spouse. You have developed a preferred way to do each of these and they provide clues about your training style.

Several instruments exist to assist you to identify your training style. You may wish to complete one to determine your style. Most suggest that there are four styles. You may have learned about your communication style, managerial style, or leadership style in the past. The most important correlation between training style theory and other style theories is that all styles are appropriate for different situations. There is no right or wrong style.

What is most important to know about training styles? Consider these elements as you prepare for your training session. Chapter 11 discusses training style in more depth.

✔ Everyone has a preferred training style that has been developing over the years.

✔ All styles are appropriate for various situations.

✔ Each style has advantages and disadvantages.

> ✓ Learners each have preferred learning styles, and each of the training styles affects each of the learning styles in different ways, some helpful and some less so.
>
> ✓ The most successful trainers will be those who are flexible, that is, they can adapt their training style to that of the learner.

When you consider all the information based on the research about training style, one concept remains at the focal point. Trainers must be learner-focused. They must view themselves as facilitators of learning and guides to the learners. The learners are central to the training experience. Table 7-2 clarifies the differences between being learner focused and training focused. Keep these in mind as you move forward in your growth as a trainer.

Table 7-2	**Trainer Focuses**
Learner-Focused	*Training-Focused*
Facilitator, guide, coach	Instructor, expert, directive
Learning objectives are flexible	Learning objectives established
Learners influence pace and timing	Trainer follows agenda
Learn by practicing skills	Learn by listening
Elicit examples and ideas from participants	Provide examples and ideas
Assume learners are experienced and knowledgeable	Assume learners are inexperienced and not knowledgeable
Ask more questions	Make more statements
Learners are primary resource for information; gleans concepts from learners	Trainer is primary resource for information; explains, demonstrates
Activities are primary methodology; learner is active participant	Lectures and discussion are primary methodology; learner is passive, absorbing information
Facilitator uses mini-evaluations throughout training session	One final evaluation used

As you continue to read this book, you will find that most research and common opinion favors a learner-focused approach to training. There is even a movement afoot to change the name of the training profession to include the noun "learner." This is a part of the growing pains the profession is experiencing.

What you call yourself is less important than what you do. And what you do as a trainer is to ensure that learning takes place and that the learning is transferred to the workplace, where performance improves.

Find out who's in your session

You will want to learn as much as you can about the individuals who will attend your session. You may have already obtained this information when you conducted the needs assessment. And you designed the session based on that information. Now you may want more specifics.

Obtain a roster as soon as it is available and then identify those factors that will help you plan the level, pace, and focus of your session.

- Their jobs in the organization
- Their levels of responsibility and authority in the organization
- Their understanding of the subject matter, any definitions you may need to clear with them early
- The reason they are attending this training: lack of performance, new skills, new employee. Is their attendance voluntary or mandatory?
- Their opinions about the training session
- Unique personalities that may include informal leaders, outspoken employees, decision makers, experts
- Baggage they may bring with them
- Negative concerns: hot buttons, corporate issues, negative experiences

Learn what you can about the participants' schedules. Find out what the group will be doing just before the training and immediately following the training. If the session starts early or runs late, determine whether anyone is in a car pool or on flex-time that will affect their attendance. If the session is off-site, learn what you can about traffic or parking concerns and the ease of locating the site and room.

Practice, practice, practice

Master the content of your training session better than you ever imagined. If you were lucky enough to design and develop the session, you have a head start. You were involved in the research and discussions so you have experienced the design and the decisions as to what needed to be included. You have read the background information. You know more about the subject than what is included in the training session.

✔ You may still want to practice some portions of the session. You may want to practice the activities with a small group to determine timing or whether the results are as you anticipated. This is a good test to find out whether the directions are as clear as they need to be. Perhaps questions arise that you cannot answer. This may still happen during your training session; you can't control that. However, a practice run will still uncover critical flaws or omissions.

✔ Practice the mechanics of the presentation. If you're revealing something to the participants, determine the best time to provide the handout or show the picture or whatever to maintain the surprise element.

✔ Practice the theatrics. If you're telling a joke or a story with a punch line, practice it out loud. If you need to show emphasis through pronunciation, with pauses, or through inflection, practice out loud. If you need to demonstrate something or use gestures to explain something, get feedback from someone.

✔ Practice in the room where you will actually conduct the training. This helps to make the room feel like home.

✔ Videotape yourself conducting some of the activities or delivering the lecturettes. Review the videotape and decide what you still need to polish.

✔ Identify questions you will want to ask at specific points of your presentation to elicit another perspective, to check for understanding, or to generate audience participation.

✔ Anticipate questions the participants may ask. Plan your answers to these questions. No, you will not think of everything, but you will think of some, and this is a good exercise.

Practice is important and you will want to invest time in practicing. However, what you put in your head is more important than what you put into practice. In other words, know your material. Read as much as you can about the subject. Tap into your subject matter expert (SME) for extra tips. Observe the process. Do the process yourself. Know your material.

Tips for staying organized

Your participants will notice how organized you are. It is a sign of professionalism. Get organized. Stay organized.

Be organized before the session

Create a packing list. I use a generic packing list like the one that follows. This serves as my guide and keeps me organized when I prepare for almost any training session. It is generic enough to use for most sessions. As soon as a date has been established, I begin to complete the information. It is copied on a brightly colored sheet of paper (lime green) so that it is easy to spot among an avalanche of white paper.

Facilitation Training Packing List

General materials:

- ❑ Trainer's manual
- ❑ Trainer's kit
- ❑ Markers for trainer
- ❑ Masking tape
- ❑ Strapping tape
- ❑ Blank transparencies and pens
- ❑ Prepared overhead transparencies
- ❑ Bag of creativity goodies
- ❑ White index cards _____
- ❑ Index cards: colors _____ sizes _____
- ❑ PowerPoint presentation
- ❑ Computer
- ❑ Wireless remote
- ❑ Resources
- ❑
- ❑

For each table:

- ❑ Markers for table tents
- ❑ Sticky-back notes : colors _____ sizes _____
- ❑ Tactile items
- ❑ Prizes
- ❑ Play Doh
- ❑ Crayons
- ❑ Team cards
- ❑ Paper: colors _____ sizes _____
- ❑
- ❑

For each participant:

- ❑ Table tents
- ❑ Participant manuals
- ❑ Envelopes
- ❑ Infolines
- ❑ Handouts
- ❑ Evaluations
- ❑ Certificates
- ❑
- ❑

Contact information:

Contact person:	Company:
Telephone (o):	Telephone (c):
Date: Time:	Number of participants:
Training location:	Building: Room:
Equipment ordered:	
Travel arrangements:	

Stay organized during the session

The agenda you provide for your participants helps them stay focused on the big picture, the learning objectives, and the sequence of learning events. Your agenda, like the one described in the following section, will be different in a number of ways. The suggestions provided here work for me. You may have other ways for how the agenda will help you stay organized.

- ✔ Add times so that you can tell whether you're ahead, behind, or on time.
- ✔ Print it on bright paper; I use astro yellow so that if it becomes lost among other notes on the table, I can easily spot it.
- ✔ For cues, have <u>Activity</u> underlined, PROPS in all caps.
- ✔ Add corresponding page numbers in participant materials.

Use your trainer's manual or training notes to stay organized. Underline key words and highlight key concepts.

Bring a small travel clock to help you stay on schedule. Even if you wear a watch, get in the habit of looking at the clock on the table. Looking at your watch leads participants to do the same thing. If you glance at it too often, they may begin to get nervous about whether you're still on time. It's not a big deal. It's one of those small things between being a trainer and being a professional trainer.

Train-the-Trainer Program: Training Agenda

Monday, June 30, 9:00 a.m. to 5:00 p.m.

Overview

9:00   Icebreaker HO <u>Exercise</u> PROPS (your motto); mini-needs assessment (time/experience)

9:30   What We Expect of Each Other <u>Exercise</u>; me/each other/HOPES on FC; ground rules

9:45   Your Greatest Need: "Bag Your Problem" <u>Exercise</u>

9:55   Training Skills Inventory pp 1–4 <u>Exercise</u>; FC example

10:15   Characteristics and Skills of Effective Trainers pp 5–6

         Note: Write directions for eating pie before break

10:30   Break

10:45   Do You Have What It Takes? pp 7–8 (someone don't know well)

11:00   Overview of the Training Cycle pp 9–11

Needs Analysis

11:15   Training Needs: The Whats, Whos, and Hows pp 12–15 <u>Exercise</u>

         Write directions for eating pie <u>Exercise</u>

Lunch   Prepare for creativity activity; put crayons on table

Needs Analysis (continued)

1:00   Task Analysis (pie demonstration) p 16

1:20   Developing Learning Objectives p 17

Development and Design

1:30   Adult Learning Theory pp 18–22 <u>Exercise</u>

2:15   Break (candy out)

2:30   Customizing and Tailoring Off-the-Shelf pp 23–24

2:40   Presentation and Activities pp 25–29

3:00   Add Creativity to Your Training pp 30–32 PROPS

3:45   Break

4:00   Creative Activity p 33 <u>Exercise</u>

4:50   Designing Smooth Transitions pp 34–35 FC

5:00   Wrap: Rate 1–7 and why

End of Day:

Change room arrangement

Infolines out

Play Doh out

Summarize and post evals on FC

Plan for how and when you will distribute materials. This may not be a problem for a group of 20, but it is for a group of 50, and can be a logistical nightmare for over one hundred.

Packing a trainer's kit

The well-packed trainer's kit includes the following items:

✔ Training supplies

❑ Masking tape

❑ Overhead projector pens

❑ Watercolor markers in assorted colors

❑ Ten sticky-back pads, various sizes

❑ Push pins

❑ 3 x 5 note cards

❑ Blank name tags

❑ Table tents

❑ Invisible tape

❑ Glue stick

❑ Small stapler and staples

❑ Resealable plastic bags

❑ Small scissors

❑ Stir sticks to use as pointer for transparencies

❑ Self-adhesive (1-inch wide) correction tape for flipcharts

❑ Rubber bands

❑ Paper clips

❑ Blank transparencies

✔ Emergency items

    ❑ Band-Aids

    ❑ Tissue

    ❑ Sewing kit

    ❑ Lip balm

    ❑ Cough drops

    ❑ Aspirin

Prepare your body and brain

Learn to relax your body. Use whatever technique works for you. Some trainers see a mental image of relaxing each body part from the top of their heads to their toes.

Learn breathing techniques. Slow, deep breathing lowers your heart rate and increases the amount of oxygen flowing to your brain.

Be prepared to give yourself a rousing pep talk. You know ten times more than any other person in the room. You're well prepared. You have memorized your introduction, and your media and visuals are well designed. Your participants are looking forward to being in this session with you. So go out there and let 'em have it!

Prepare yourself by knowing what you will drink before and during the training session.

✔ Avoid coffee. If you're new to training, your nervousness may prevent you from counting how many cups you're drinking. Adding caffeine to your presentation anxiety may create a bodacious buzz!

✔ Avoid dairy products — for example, milk, yogurt — to prevent mucus build-up requiring you to clear your throat.

✔ Avoid sugary liquids such as fruit juices and sodas; they coat your vocal cords.

✔ Avoid icy beverages because they constrict your vocal cords.

Okay! What's left? Room-temperature or cool water, warm water with lemon, herbal teas, and decaffeinated teas or coffee. Remember, this is just to get you through the first few hours. Later, when your nerves have calmed down, you can switch to one of your favorite drinks (nonalcoholic, of course!).

Travel if you must

Travel can be fun and exhilarating or it can be painful and exhausting. This list of tips for preparation will assist the trainer who travels to training sites.

- ✔ **Buy wheels.** You will need to schlep lots of things. Make it easy on yourself and purchase luggage on wheels.
- ✔ **Pack your carry-on luggage as if the rest will not arrive.**
  - The clothes you intend to wear the first day.
  - Personal hygiene supplies.
  - A master of the participant materials and all support supplies.
  - Your PowerPoint presentation and overhead transparencies.
  - Your trainer's manual or notes.
  - A mini set of the supplies you depend on: couple of markers, pack of index cards, and sticky notes packed in a resealable plastic bag.
- ✔ **Send participant materials and supplies ahead if you can.** Call several days ahead to ensure that they arrived.
- ✔ **Personally talk to the contact person for directions** to your hotel and from the hotel to the training site. E-mail a copy of your flight and hotel information to the person.
- ✔ **Exchange home and cell phone numbers with the contact person,** especially if you're flying in on a Sunday for a Monday training session.

The procrastinator's checklist

Are you a procrastinator like me? Don't have time to read this entire chapter? Here's a quick and dirty checklist of what you need to do when. The following list is particularly good if this is the first time you present. On the other hand, if possible, this is the list I prefer to use each time.

One week before

- ❏ Practice your session in front of a colleague, asking for input, feedback, and ideas.
- ❏ Know your subject cold. Your confidence will grow if you're assured about your knowledge.
- ❏ Memorize the words you intend to use during the first five minutes. The first few minutes of a training are usually the most nerve-wracking for a trainer.

❑ Make a list of things you will want to remember to do or pack for the session: equipment, supplies, how to set up the room, what you will place at the participants' seats, and names and phone numbers of people who will support the session in any way, for example, the person who has the key to the training room.

❑ If you asked participants to complete a survey or other pre-work, check to be sure you have all the responses.

❑ Confirm all room arrangements, refreshments, equipment, and supplies for the session.

One day before

❑ Run through the entire session, practicing with visuals.

❑ Confirm that you have enough participant materials and all your supplies.

❑ Check that you have your trainer's guide or notes and keep them with you to take to the session.

❑ Check on everything you need regarding the training site including location of restrooms, refreshments, support staff, and so on.

❑ Set up the training room, placing tables and chairs to encourage participation.

❑ Observe the room's mechanicals. Will lighting cause any problems? Windows facing east or west? Determine where the light switches are located. Figure out where the thermostat is located and whether you have any control over it.

❑ Set up your equipment, marking placement of the projection table with masking tape on the floor.

❑ Test the equipment. Run through PowerPoint slides or overhead transparencies one last time to ensure they are in order. Practice with the actual equipment. Do you know how to use the wireless remote control? Where is the reverse button? Can you roll the pages on the flipchart smoothly? Is the VCR cued to the correct place?

❑ Arrange the participants' materials on their tables. Place their training manuals, pens, agendas, table tents, markers, and anything else each participant needs neatly at each seat.

❑ Place shared materials participants need for small group activities or exercises in the center of round tables or equally spaced around a U or other linear placement. These items may include sticky notes, index cards, handouts, or paper.

❑ Take one last look around. Empty boxes in the front of the room? Get rid of them. Don't depend on the cleanup crew to discard them for you.

❑ Get a good night's sleep.

One hour before

- ❑ Arrive at the training site at least one hour before start time.
- ❑ Complete last-minute setup.
- ❑ Organize the space from which you will train. Tools and supplies are where you want them: markers are on the flipchart tray, pencil near your notes, sticky notes and index cards at the side, pointer on the overhead transparency tray, completed table tent at the front of the table.
- ❑ Ensure that your notes are in order, turned to the first page, placed where you can stay organized. Check that your visual support is in order and placed where you want it.
- ❑ Prepare for emergencies. Fill a glass with water. Find a few paper towels for an emergency.
- ❑ Ensure cords are covered or taped down.
- ❑ Check that media equipment placement is correct, test it, set to first slide.
- ❑ Make yourself comfortable: Use the restroom, get a drink of water.
- ❑ Move around the room and greet people as they arrive up until two to five minutes before start time.

One minute before

- ❑ Take one more peek at your opening line.
- ❑ Take a deep breath.
- ❑ Tell yourself how phenomenal this is going to be.
- ❑ Find a friendly face.
- ❑ Smile.
- ❑ Go for it!

Being prepared to succeed

There you have it, the long and the short of preparation — list that is. As a trainer you will find that practice and preparation can make your training session all that you had hoped it would be. And that's something that you knew before you read this chapter.

To paraphrase Bob Pike from the beginning of this chapter, Publius Ovidus (43B.C.–17A.D.) said, "Practice is the best of all instructors."

Part III

Showtime: Delivering a Dynamic Training Session

The 5th Wave   By Rich Tennant

"GET READY, I THINK THEY'RE STARTING TO DRIFT."

In this part . . .

You were made to be a trainer, and you want to do it well. How do you ensure that doing what you love is the best for the participants? What's your training style and how can you make it work for you? What do you need to know about audiovisuals? How do you address group dynamics? How do you overcome nervousness? And how do you deal with those pesky problem participants?

Chapter 8

Implementing Training Designs: Your Job as a Facilitator

- -

In This Chapter

▶ Clarifying the terms: trainer, presenter, and facilitator

▶ Identifying facilitation techniques effective trainers use when presenting information

▶ Introducing, supporting, and processing activities

▶ Determining how to increase participation

- -

*I*f you read the latest adult training, learning, and development journals, you will see a subtle semantics battle brewing.

Building on the definitions presented in Chapter 2, I want to further clarify so that you do not become wrapped up in someone else's cognitive conflict. I believe this is really about what you do, not what you call yourself. So whether you call yourself a trainer, a facilitative trainer, a facilitator, a facilitative presenter, or a performance technologist (which is really a role that expands beyond "implementing training"), the title doesn't matter as long as you are all clear about what this person does to ensure that learning occurs.

I continue to use the term "trainer," and ask, "What does a trainer do?" "What skills make a great trainer?" "What's important about conducting an activity?" "And if participation is so important, how does a trainer increase it?"

This chapter answers these questions.

Training, Facilitation, and Presentation: What's the Difference?

I recently conducted a training session with a co-trainer, who was upset that I was calling him a trainer. He considered himself a facilitator. Funny thing though; he did the same thing I did: presented information in small doses, facilitated discussion, encouraged participation, conducted small and large group activities, and ensured that participants gained the knowledge and learned the skills the client expected.

You will run into people, like this gentleman, who get wrapped up in words and labels rather than just a clear definition of the actual role. The meanings of words are in people, not in dictionaries. Therefore, I take a pragmatic view of the definitions and begin to make some sense of them.

Note that this chapter focuses specifically on the trainer's role of facilitator.

Are you a trainer or a facilitator?

New trainers sometimes question the difference between the training and facilitating roles when implementing the training design. In *The Winning Trainer,* Julius E. Eitington defines them as follows:

- ✔ **Trainer:** Term used to describe a learner-centered conductor of a course or program. See also Facilitator.

- ✔ **Facilitator:** A trainer who functions in a way to allow participants to assume responsibility for their own learning. The term is in contrast to the more didactic instructor, teacher, lecturer, presenter, and so on.

As you can see, Eitington, for one, believes that the words are interchangeable because the roles are identical. I do as well. In this section, I continue to explore the two terms so that you can understand why label confusion may exist.

Some folks are not aware that the term training brings with it a definition that encompasses adult-learning theory. It assumes that an effective trainer has acquired a certain amount of knowledge and a specific skill set. A manager is a manager. No one tries to tag on another title (well aloud, anyway) that differentiates effective managers from ineffective managers.

There may have been a time when trainers were "tellers" of information, using a didactic model with learners. This was before Malcolm Knowles started to promote the concept of andragogy in the 1960s. To add further confusion, some confuse college instruction with training. While it may be true that college professors should base more of their delivery on adult-learning principles, some trainers remember their experiences and want to disassociate themselves from it. Therefore, they give themselves a differentiating title of "facilitator" or "facilitative trainer." A trainer *is* a facilitator. Let me correct that: An *effective* trainer is a facilitator.

Now I add one more dimension: presenter. The definition provided in Chapter 2 states the following definition:

✔ **Presenters:** Title given adults who deliver speeches at conferences or to larger groups; minimal emphasis on two-way communication.

Sounds like an ineffective trainer. Wait a minute. Trainers present. They have to present new information in some way, or what would there be to learn? Do trainers only facilitate? No.

Trainers certainly facilitate activities. In addition, they also present information. An effective trainer makes certain that he or she presents this information in a facilitative way. Trainers who are delivering or implementing the training design (sometimes called *stand-up trainers*) must master two key skill sets when they conduct training sessions.

✔ They facilitate small-group activities, large-group discussions, and learning in general.

✔ They present new information, data, and knowledge.

Both of these skill sets are requirements for the job.

Mystery solved. A trainer is a facilitator *and* a presenter. An effective trainer understands both roles and the skills associated with each. An effective trainer implements both roles when delivering training.

If you, as a trainer, believe that

✔ Adult learning theory has merit.

✔ Adults learn best when they are active rather than passive.

✔ Adults learn best when challenged rather than talked at.

✔ Adults learn best when involved rather than observing.

Then you probably embrace a participative training method, and make an effort to be an effective trainer who models both facilitation and presentation skills. You're an effective trainer.

Use facilitative skills when you present

At some point, trainers need to *present* information. Sometimes, "presenting" is nothing more than having participants learn by reading from a handout. The trainer has *presented* the activity to the learner. Good trainers require good presentation skills. Specific presentation skills such as eye contact, verbal ability, physical control, and others, will be addressed in the next chapter. But for now, think of the one most didactic learning activity you can imagine. Did you think "lecture?" Right!

How can a trainer use a facilitative trainer style to present a lecture? Well, first of all by not calling it a lecture. Try calling it a lecturette. You may think this is a minor point, but it will help you stay focused on "brief," which is what a lecturette should be.

Besides being brief, you can use facilitative methods to obtain a high level of participation during lecturettes. Try these suggestions:

✔ Ask questions during the presentation.

> You probably know that you encourage more dialogue with open-ended questions than closed. However, examine your questions. "Can you iden-tify ideas for how to move forward?" may at first blush sound like an open-ended question, but it really is not. It would be better stated as "What ideas do you have to move forward?"

✔ Answer questions throughout the presentation.

✔ Call on individuals for ideas or predictions of what occurs next.

✔ Conduct round robins to get opinions, ideas, concerns, or questions.

✔ Form small groups to discuss the information presented.

✔ Pause and check for understanding from everyone by creating a conversation.

✔ Use humor in the words you use, the examples, or the visuals.

✔ Involve participants in deciding what they need to learn.

✔ Pull ideas together from different participants.

✔ Compare or contrast participants' ideas.

✔ Use a parking lot for questions yet to be addressed.

Create a "parking lot" or place for participants to "park" their questions until adequate information is available to answer them with ease. One idea is to post a flipchart page with a sketch of a parked car on an easel or on the wall. Participants can write their questions on sticky notes and hang them on the page.

✔ Form buzz groups (two or three people who "buzz" for two minutes in response to a question) to identify one concern.

✔ Stop midlecture to ask whether everyone is with you.

✔ Reinforce those who ask questions or provide answers.

✔ Integrate quizzes (bingo, crossword puzzles, word completion) within the context of the presentation.

✔ Create a conversation between trainer and participants instead of deliv-ering a presentation.

✔ Intersperse tasks or demonstrations throughout the presentation.

> ✔ Develop a handout to follow the presentation with key words from the presentation; allow room to take notes.
>
> ✔ Design visuals to support the lecturette so that participants can follow your words visually.

As you can see, there are many ways to make a lecturette interesting and interactive when delivering information through a presentation.

Sooner or later trainers need to present information. You will be better equipped to "facilitate" that lecturette if you have mastered both the basic presentation skills as well as basic facilitation skills.

Facilitating Successful Training

Trainers walk a fine line between being proactive and responsive, between being flexible and sticking to the agenda, and between presenting content and facilitating discussion. They must be adaptive to the many learning styles in the room and supportive of the various requirements of all the participants. How do they do all this, act as a role model for the participants, and ensure that the learners have learned all they need to learn?

 The 2004 American Society for Training and Development (ASTD) Competency Study identifies *facilitating learning* as one of the key actions required to deliver training. It is described as "adjusting delivery and curriculum to adapt to the audience and the needs of the learners."

Throughout this book I have tried to emphasize that training is really all about the learner. Trainers must provide opportunities for actively involving participants in their learning. Of course the goal is not just activity and participation. The goal is to ensure that the participants gain knowledge or learn skills to improve performance. Active learning may be incorporated in hundreds of methods (some found in the design chapter) such as role plays, simulations, games, and so on.

It is not enough for a trainer to cover all the content and ensure that the learners are involved. A trainer must ensure that learners practiced the skills, that learning occurred, and that the learners are prepared to perform the skill or use the knowledge when they return to the workplace. Learners must transfer the learning to the workplace.

The experiential learning process is often used by facilitators to ensure that learning occurs and that learners are ready to perform on the job. Participants learn inductively, that is, they discover for themselves by experiencing the activity. Other names you may hear used are interactive learning, experience-based learning, action learning, and discovery learning.

Real secrets of successful facilitation

by Sivasailam "Thiagi" Thiagarajan

Twenty-five years ago, I had this get-rich scheme: I will videotape brilliant instructional facilitators in action. I will find common patterns of behaviors and create a training package based on these consistent techniques. Then I will retire to some island in the sun.

I implemented the project by lugging around a heavy video camera and recording ten different facilitators. They were definitely brilliant, but my behavioral analysis was disappointing. I found no consistent common behaviors among these facilitators. To make matters worse, even the same facilitator conducting the same training activity employed different behaviors from one session to the next. To cut the long story short, I did not become a millionaire, but I discovered the real secret of effective presentation: Be inconsistent. In more positive terms, here is the secret: I f you want to be an effective facilitator, be flexible, adaptive, and responsive.

To understand this secret, you should understand seven dimensions of facilitation that enhance or destroy a facilitated activity. Because each dimension has two undesirable extremes, I call them the seven facilitation *tensions*. Here they are with their extreme poles.

PACE: Too slow . . . Too fast

INTERACTION: Too cooperative . . . Too competitive

TONE: Too serious . . . Too playful

IMPLEMENTATION: Too rigid . . . Too loose

SHARING: Too intrusive into personal feelings . . . Too protective of personal feelings

FOCUS: Too much focus on results . . . Too much focus on the process

CONCERN: Excessive concern for the individual . . . Excessive concern for the group

Effective facilitation is a balancing act. When an aspiring facilitator asks me, "Should I conduct the activity at a fast pace or a slow one?" I simply answer, "Yes." The appropriate location of an activity along the seven tensions depends on several factors, including the number and types of participants and the structure and purpose of the activity. The secret of effective facilitation is to make these tensions transparent by maintaining a balance between the two extremes. However, "balance" resides in the perception of participants. Thus, the balance along the cooperation-competition dimension may differ drastically between a group from an ashram in South India and a group from a brokerage firm in New York.

How to prevent tension headaches. You can use a variety of common-sense tactics to increase or decrease each tension. For example, to speed up the pace, begin the activity promptly and get it rolling fast. Also announce and implement tight time limits. To slow down the pace, avoid time limits. If a team finishes the task ahead of others, insist on review and revision. Introduce a quality-control rule that punishes teams for sloppy work.

You can figure out your own techniques for increasing or lowering the tensions among the other six dimensions. To implement these secrets in your next facilitation session, begin your activity with confidence. As your participants work through the activity, continuously monitor the levels along various dimensions. If the seven tensions are at optimum levels, do not interfere with the flow of the activity. If some tension becomes noticeable, intervene with appropriate adjustments. Do this as quickly and as unobtrusively as possible. Continue monitoring the group and adjusting the activity as required.

Do you think I could make my millions by selling this flaky, but powerful, advice?

Sivasailam Thiagarajan, most often known as Thiagi, is well known in the training world as the man who gave games respect in the training room! He considers himself the resident mad scientist at the Thiagi Group. Those of us in the training field have him to thank for designing hundreds of games and sharing both the games and his facilitator concepts in about a dozen books. Thiagi encourages all facilitators to constantly monitor participant reactions and switch between the passive and active facilitator roles.

Experience is the best teacher

Experiential learning occurs when a learner participates in an activity, reviews the activity, identifies useful knowledge or skills that were gained, and transfers the result to the workplace. An American baseball player, Vernon Sanders Law, stated that "Experience is a hard teacher because she gives the test first, the lesson after." This is the learning process you go through in your day-to-day life—your *life experience.*

Experiential learning activities attempt to duplicate life experience. Participants "experience" what they are to learn before they discuss it.

Experiential learning activities (ELAs) are based on several characteristics.

- ✔ They are directed toward a specific learning goal.
- ✔ They are structured; that is, they have specific steps and a process that must be followed to ensure results.
- ✔ There is a high degree of participant involvement.
- ✔ They generate data and information for participant analysis.
- ✔ They require processing or debriefing for maximum learning.

The steps in Pfeiffer and Jones' experiential learning cycle explain what must occur during an activity to ensure maximum learning occurs. The five steps are experiencing, publishing, processing, generalizing, and applying.

Step 1, Experiencing: Do something

This is the step that is associated with the "game" or fun or the experience. Participants are involved in completing a defined task. If the process ends here, all learning is left to chance and the trainer has not completed the task.

Step 2, Publishing: Share observations

The second step of the cycle gives the learners a chance to share what they saw, how they felt, and what they experienced. The trainer can facilitate this in several ways: record data in the large group, have participants share or interview in subgroups, or lead a variation of a round robin. Questions the facilitator may ask are:

- What happened? What did you observe?
- What occurred during the activity?
- How did you feel about this?

The facilitator typically begins with a broad question and then focuses on more specific questions. The facilitator may probe for turning points or decisions that affected the outcome. This stage is important because it allows the participants to vent or express strong emotions and it allows the facilitator to gather data.

Step 3, Processing: Interpret dynamics or concepts

This step gives the participants a chance to discuss the patterns and dynamics they observed during the activity. Observers may be used to discuss this step. Questions the facilitator may ask are:

- Why do you think that may have occurred?
- What did you learn about yourself?
- What did you learn?
- What theories or principles may be true based on your experience?

The facilitator will again begin with broad questions and then home in on more specific questions. This stage allows participants to test hypotheses, preparing them to apply what they learned. This stage allows the facilitator a way to observe how much participants learned from the experience.

Step 4, Generalizing: Connect to real life

The key question in this step is "So what?" Participants are led to focus their awareness on situations that are similar to what they have experienced. This step makes the activity practical. Facilitators may ask:

- How does this relate to . . . ?
- What did you learn about yourself?
- What does this suggest to you about . . . ?
- How does this experience help you understand . . . ?
- What if . . . ?

This stage ensures that the participants grasp the learning that was intended. The "what if" question becomes a bridge to the last step, which is application.

Step 5, Applying: Plan effective change

The last step presents the reason the activity was conducted: "Now what?" The facilitator helps participants apply generalizations to actual situations in which they are involved. The group may establish goals, contract for change, make promises, identify potential workplace changes, or initiate any other actions that result from the experience. The questions that are asked are:

- What will you do differently as a result of this experience?
- How will you transfer this learning to the workplace?
- How and when will you apply your learning?
- How may this help you in the future?
- What's next?

Participants frequently follow this step with an action plan or at least spend some time noting their thoughts about how life may be different as a result of the ELA.

The ELA is a powerful tool available to facilitators. It is time-consuming and, therefore, is used sparingly. If you decide to facilitate an ELA, don't take any shortcuts. The value is truly in the process.

Tips for facilitating activities

Activities are potent learning tools for participants as long as the facilitator is prepared and follows a few suggestions for conducting them. These tips for introducing, supporting, and processing activities will help you think through all the nuances of facilitating activities.

Introducing activities

Ensuring that each activity gets started efficiently is critical. Use these steps to ensure that happens. Note that this is prior to the group's starting an activity or an ELA.

- Provide brief, general instructions including whether they will need materials, pens, and so on.
- Establish a clear objective that positions the activity within the context of the training module or session.

✔ Don't provide too much information if the intent is for the participants to discover an AHA!

✔ Use a process to help participants form small groups. Do this now before you provide more specific instructions. Otherwise, participants will forget what you told them in the first place!

✔ After participants are settled in their working groups, ascertain that you have everyone's attention. Then provide more specific direction.

✔ Tell participants how much involvement is expected of them. Depending on the activity, you may also wish to tell them what will happen after. Will they be expected to share scores with the larger group? Will they be working in the same group? Will there be a large-group discussion?

✔ Distribute additional materials that may be required and demonstrate any processes that are necessary.

✔ Announce the amount of time the activity will require. It is a good idea to post the time on a flipchart so that it is visible to all. If the activity has steps within the process, you may wish to post a schedule of how much time should be spent on each step. Suggest any roles that may make the activity move smoothly: timekeeper, recorder, or a spokesperson.

✔ Ensure that everyone knows what to do; ask if anyone has any questions.

✔ Circulate among the groups to ensure that everyone understands the activity.

Supporting activities

Facilitators can be quiet guides to ensure that participants are successful with their activities. Facilitators will walk among the groups to ensure that everyone understands the task, stays on track, and reaches the end. Note that this would actually occur during the activity or step 1 of an ELA.

✔ During the activity, remind participants of the rules, if necessary.

✔ Give a "time is half up" signal and a "5 minutes left" or a "1 minute left" signal. Abrupt commands of "stop" or "time is up" may prevent participants from achieving the goal.

✔ You may need to make suggestions about the process. Take care, however, that you do not give away the answer. Suggesting, rather than commanding, allows participants to maintain control of the situation.

✔ Walk among participants to identify confusion, problems, questions, and time needed to complete the task.

✔ Adjust time, if necessary, and announce to the group, but only if all the groups need more or less time. Allowing some groups to have more time when others finished within the time limit will be perceived as unfair.

✔ Be sure to debrief the activity at its conclusion.

Processing activities

This is probably the most important part of the activity. If you were conducting an ELA, then you would be addressing the questions and working through the process included in steps 2, 3, 4, and 5. Otherwise, you will want to assist the learners to understand the implications of what they just experienced or completed. Help them address the importance and the relevance of the activity to themselves personally. Use these suggestions:

✔ Relate the activity to previous as well as future training modules.

✔ Maintain a facilitative role without one-upping participants' experiences. Add information if it is a tip or a technique that will be useful for participants to understand the content or to improve a skill. However, if you can add that information at another time, save it until then.

✔ Share pertinent observations you made during the exercise.

✔ Avoid teaching, preaching, or lecturing.

✔ Stress practical application.

✔ Correct only when participants have obviously come to incorrect solutions, and then use either a questioning technique or participation from other groups to make the correction.

✔ Debriefing is required so that learning outcomes can be discussed. You may wish to record comments on a flipchart.

✔ You may use representatives from each group to conduct the debrief.

✔ Even if participants disagree on the outcome, ensure a common understanding among the group of what occurred before moving on.

Designing your own experiential learning activity

Each year, over one hundred trainers and consultants submit experiential learning activities (ELAs) for publication in the Pfeiffer *Annuals* (one for trainers, one for consultants). You, too, can design activities that are customized for your participants.

Use Table 8-1 to plan your activity. If you wish to submit the activity to the Pfeiffer *Annuals*, contact Pfeifferannual@aol.com for submission guidelines.

Table 8-1	Experiential Learning Activity Worksheet

Learning objective _____

_____

Group size _____ Time required _____

Materials/supplies _____

Handouts _____

Physical setting _____ Risk level _____

Process/directions _____

_____

_____

_____

Trainer notes:

    Introducing_____

    Conducting_____

    Processing_____

Participation Prescription: Continue to Increase the Dosage

Participation has been mentioned so often that it may seem as if I am pre-scribing it as the cure-all for learning. Well maybe so. While a participant may overdose on too much participation, it isn't too likely.

Gotta play the game to perform

In Chapter 2, I asked you to remember something you learned in the past 60 days and *why* you learned it. Now think about *how* you learned what you did. Suppose you selected a game or a sport. Did you select tennis, for example? Perhaps some of these learning activities occurred that resulted in learning.

✔ Someone may have presented you with information and you learned:

- Rules of tennis
- How to keep score
- Best kind of racquet to purchase

✔ You read a book about tennis and you learned:

- History of the game
- Where the big tournaments are held
- Simple technique to get started

✔ Someone demonstrated techniques and you learned how to:

- Properly grip the racquet
- Serve
- Volley

✔ You observed several matches and you learned:

- What the courts look like
- Where the players stand to serve

✔ You practiced by hitting the ball against a practice wall and you learned:

- Eye-hand coordination
- How to direct the ball
- How to position your feet and body

Well, you get the idea. You have learned information and skills, but knowing the rules and hitting a tennis ball against a practice wall doesn't mean you can play tennis. You need to participate in a game with another tennis player. You need to serve the ball over the net and experience a returned hit. You need to play in a real match with other people to practice what you learned. You've gotta play the game to perform.

Learners need to participate to increase their performance. They need to be involved with the other participants to get feedback on what they think they know. In almost all cases, learners need to be in the game, participating to learn.

Participants' expectations of participation

Initially, participants expect you to take the lead in the training session. You will begin to shift the focus away from your role as the leader and to your role as the facilitator as quickly as you can. This will be dependent upon the experience and the communication skill level of individuals in your group. In most cases you will have a mix that includes at least three participant types.

- ✔ Some people will be good listeners, use no more than their fair share of talk time, and contribute when they have something new to contribute. They will be a joy in your session.

- ✔ Others will speak often and long, sometimes repeating what was just said by someone else. You may wonder if they are speaking just to hear them-selves talk. Actually they may just be unfamiliar with having airtime in front of a group, or it may be their rambling style. Whatever it is, you may need to use your facilitator skills to cut them off or to keep them focused.

- ✔ The third group will be quiet, cautious about volunteering and getting involved. I generally hold back a bit with these folks. I plan activities that allow them time to reach their participation comfort zone. I push just a bit more each time.

Increasing participation — or why are they called "participants"?

Throughout this book, I use two terms to discuss the individuals in your training session: "learners" and "participants." They are interchangeable, and you will most likely use a term that is most comfortable to you or that is cul-turally acceptable in your organization.

Though the learner/participant label has switched back and forth based on subtle reasons, emphasis on participation has never wavered. An effective trainer encourages as much involvement and participation by the learners as is practically feasible.

Sometimes, obstacles exist that prevent trainers from providing as much par-ticipation as they would prefer, for example, time limitations, facility availabil-ity, organizational culture, group size. If those are not a consideration and you're still interested in increasing the amount of participation, examine your competency based on various aspects of delivering training.

Perhaps you have designed the perfect experiential learning activity. Yet par-ticipants are not getting involved the way you thought they might. The fol-lowing areas may give you some ideas of what may inhibit participation and what you need to do to increase participation in your sessions.

Communication

Good communication skills encourage participation naturally.

- **Listen well.** This skill is at the top of almost any good-skills-to-possess list. If you expect participation, this is one you'd better master. You know all the right things to do: Listen to understand, avoid hasty judgment, don't interrupt, ask clarifying questions, and focus on content and intent.

- **Accept input.** When you receive suggestions, comments, or responses that are not quite right, you need to accept them — at least initially. You of course do not want anyone to leave the session with incorrect information, but you can thank the person, and then ask the group, "What do the rest of you think?"

- **Project assertiveness.** A trainer needs to be assertive with individuals at times — for example, disruptive participants, argumentative individuals — to ensure participants have the correct information.

- **Ask questions.** This is probably the most used way to encourage participation. You may ask closed or open-ended questions or rhetorical questions. You may ask for volunteers or call on someone specifically. Allow participants to develop their own answers and accept them.

  If you ask participants a question, give them enough time to answer it. If you answer your own question because you're uncomfortable with the silence or because you think participants don't know the answer, then eventually, they will let you answer *all* the questions.

- **Encourage questions.** If you ask for questions, allow enough time for participants to formulate and ask them. If you find yourself asking people to hold their questions too often, it means the participants are ahead of you. Perhaps there is something wrong with the design. Asking participants to hold questions is one of the biggest deterrents to participation. Use the parking-lot tip found earlier in the "Use facilitative skills when you present" section in this chapter, but don't overuse it.

- **Practice silence.** Silence is a way to communicate also. Pause regularly to allow participants to think and process information. They can't talk if you are.

Interpretive skills

The ability to read participants' nonverbal messages and to understand the *intent* of verbal messages, as well as the *content,* takes communication skills to another level. Learners need to know that you "get it" to increase their participation level.

- **Relate to situations.** The ability for a trainer to empathize and visualize from the participant's view increases participation. Participants gain trust and believe that you really do understand.

✔ **Appreciate hot buttons.** Know your participants' hot buttons. If you can ignore them, do so. If you cannot ignore them, prepare your response so that you both save face.

✔ **Be sensitive to nonverbal meanings.** Watch participants and try to interpret the messages their nonverbals are really saying. If you don't understand, don't be afraid to ask. Sometimes, this is better done during a break and away from the rest of the group.

✔ **Translate correctly.** Interpreting what participants say and transferring their thoughts and ideas correctly to the rest of the group verbally or writing them on a flipchart page encourages others to speak up.

Personal traits

Several basic characteristics will encourage participation if they are evident. If they are absent, these may discourage participation faster than any others.

✔ **Sense of humor:** Use humor to lighten the experience. Laugh at incidents. Laugh at yourself. Do not laugh at participants.

✔ **Patience:** Give participants the time they need to learn or practice skills that will make them successful.

✔ **Trustworthiness:** Do what you say you're going to do.

✔ **Openness to ideas:** Be open; at least acknowledge even wild ideas.

✔ **Sincerity:** Sincerity may be one of the most important to encourage participation. People know if you truly want them to participate.

Interpersonal style

The style you exhibit allows participants to trust you and adds to their willingness to contribute to the training session. You display a set of characteristics that are natural to your unique style, yet the most successful trainers are also flexible enough to adapt all the style characteristics required to ensure participation.

✔ **People-oriented and approachable:** Encourage participants to ask you questions. It's a good sign if they are asking you questions at break that have nothing to do with the session. It means they are comfortable asking for your thoughts and find you easy to talk to. Smile.

✔ **Willing to share yourself:** Let people in on who you are. Share something about you. Share your experiences, your successes, and your failures. Be real. They will feel more comfortable about sharing something about themselves.

✔ **Organized:** Participants will trust that you can help them if you're prepared and organized. Being organized also ensures that you have the maximum amount of time to give to your participants.

> ✔ **Respectful of all opinions:** Trainers can't play favorites if they want to encourage participation. You don't need to agree with all opinions, just respect them and try to understand what it means.

Learning techniques

Effective teaching skills do come into play. Think back to teaching your children or younger siblings. You probably used techniques that continue to work with adults who are learning new skills. An effective trainer will have adapted some of these learning techniques to adult learners.

> ✔ **Provide clear directions.** Anything that needs to be done correctly needs to begin with clear directions. Don't set your participants up for failure by giving poor directions.
>
> ✔ **Catch 'em being good.** Reinforce participants as they achieve success. In addition, provide feedback for the behaviors that contribute to a participative environment, such as volunteering and contributing. Say, for example, "Thanks for doing. . . ."
>
> ✔ **Allow the learning process to occur** even if participants experience some struggles. Survival and learning is often dependent on the process.
>
> ✔ **Provide feedback.** Give participants honest feedback about their progress.
>
> ✔ **Coach.** Coach participants about both the skills they are learning as well as appropriate participation behaviors.

Think through all the techniques you use to encourage learning. Ensure that you remember to use adult-learning principles as the basis for your techniques. Don't destroy the environment for the sake of "the right answer." For example, if you ask participants to identify a list of anything in small groups, don't follow up with a handout of your list of the same thing. Adults may resent it, thinking that you could have just given it to them in the first place or, even worse, that somehow their list was defective in some way and your list is "the right answer."

Attending skills

Sometimes tossed in with good communication skills, attending skills in a training session do much more than open communication. Attending skills help to show that you care about your participants and that you want them to succeed. That's a powerful message when trying to increase participation.

> ✔ **Provide consistent eye contact.** Face the participants; ensure that you make real eye contact so that you can read them. (Don't look at the tops of their heads.) Learn to talk and walk backward. Truly the skill of a gifted trainer!

✔ **Balance eye contact.** Scan the group regularly. This will help you know whether anyone is confused, distracted, or focused. This is a critical one for good participation.

Trainers tend to extend the majority of their eye contact to 75 percent of the room to their non-dominant side. To encourage participation of everyone, remember to look at those participants sitting near the front of the room to your dominant side.

✔ **Demonstrate attentive moves.** Move around the room as you encourage discussion. Move toward individuals to encourage them to get involved in the discussion or to signal you're about to call on them.

✔ **Provide affirmative non-verbals.** This means body language like nods and smiles.

✔ **Stay engaged.** Even while participants are working on activities or small groups, stay engaged. This is not a time to call your office or take a break. Move among the groups, offering assistance, listening for understanding, and answering questions.

Process factors

The process you use to encourage and balance participation is the final area to consider. Participants may interpret a lack of somewhat equal participation by learners as your playing favorites or ignoring quieter participants.

✔ **Balance participation.** Encouraging the quiet, yet not shutting down the vocal participants. Reinforcing the correct response, yet not negating the incorrect. Allowing participants to bring up issues, yet staying on track. Balance is the job of an effective trainer.

✔ **Maintain flow of interaction.** Observe who speaks to whom and how often. Encourage participants to speak with each other rather than to direct all comments your way.

✔ **Build participation.** Consider how you methodically increase expectations. You may start by asking for a simple show of hands, requesting volunteers, using a round robin, calling on specific people, asking individuals to participate in small groups, and eventually encouraging an individual to act as the spokesperson for a group.

✔ **Create an inclusive environment.** When participants feel psychologically safe in your session, they will want to be a part of it. Encouraging everyone to participate, including quiet learners, demonstrates to everyone (not just those who are quiet) that you value everyone's opinions.

REACTing

There are so many things you may think about to facilitate and encourage participation. Don't worry about learning and perfecting all of them. Many of them will become as natural as good communication skills. That's because many are natural. In effect, it comes down to your reaction to the learners and the learning situation. How do you REACT to ensure an environment that encourages the best opportunities for participation? How do you REACT to create the best learning experience? This *mnemonic,* a tool for remembering, will help you remember the basics for encouraging participation.

- ✔ Relaxed and informal atmosphere
- ✔ Encourage participation
- ✔ Accept them where they are
- ✔ Communication is open, friendly, and honest
- ✔ Take control of their own learning

I wish I knew to whom to attribute this quote. I do not. It speaks volumes about why some facilitators are successful and others are not. Attributed to anonymous: "Adults want to know how much you care before they care how much you know."

Chapter 9

It's Showtime: Delivering Success

*S*howtime! You've conducted a thorough needs assessment, written clear objectives, designed an interactive training program, and developed materials. You're on!

Stage Four, Implementing the Design, displayed in Figure 9-1 is most likely the part of The Training Cycle that most people think about when they hear any terminology about training. It is certainly the part that everyone sees; now you can see that it is actually the culmination of a huge effort that focuses on the learner and what needs to be accomplished to ensure a successful training.

Now that you've made it to this point, how do you ensure that you deliver successfully? This chapter addresses opening the session with a bang and creating a supportive learning environment. It will share ideas to help you get to know the participants better and how to continue to address their needs by training like a pro, using questions and answers that lead to learning, and bringing closure to the session.

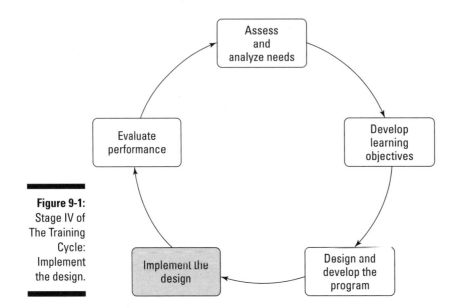

Figure 9-1:
Stage IV of
The Training
Cycle:
Implement
the design.

Opening Your Training Session with a BANG

You completed all the preparation steps to ensure that the room, the equipment, and you are as ready as you're ever going to be. You have arrived an hour early, and you have been welcoming participants as they arrived. It's time to start the session. Many things happen when you deliver a training session, but few are as important as the opening.

You will want your opening to be informative, yet creative. It should be practical, yet promote excitement. And it should be helpful, as well as enthusiastic. Start your session with a BANG!

Build interest in the session.

Ask what participants know and what they want to know.

Note the ground rules and what to expect.

Get them involved.

In the following sections, I examine each of these.

Build interest in the session

Start the session on time and grab their attention right from the start. Save the ground rules and the housekeeping details for later. Be creative with your opening. You may use props, tell a story, state an unusual fact, ask a provocative question, or make a promise. Participants will want to know what's in it for them: how what they will learn will be useful to them personally or how it will make their jobs easier.

Ask what participants know and what they want to know

Understanding your participants' needs is critical for you, so conduct a mini needs assessment by asking for a show of hands about their experience, expertise, or knowledge. This also demonstrates that you want to know about them. Ask participants about their expectations. Listen well. You may wish to capture these on a flipchart and then post them on a wall so they can be seen throughout the session.

You may wish to have the "expectations" flipchart page prepped with a title. Although it is a little thing, it sends a message to the participants that you spent time to prepare for them.

Be honest about expectations that are unrealistic for the session or for you. For example, if one of the participants wants to learn about a topic that is too complex or lengthy or will not fit into the agenda, you could say, "We probably won't have time to add that to the agenda, but I would be happy to chat with you off-line or follow up with a reference next week."

Note the ground rules and what to expect

Save time by stating any given ground rules up front, such as start and end time (if they are not flexible). Ask participants to add others. Again, you may wish to capture and post the ground rules for ready reference. What are the most common ground rules?

No sidebars	Cellphones and pagers on silent mode
No dumb questions	Respect others' opinions
Timely break	Stop and start on time
Allow for interaction	Participate willingly
Keep an open mind	What's said in here stays in here
One person speaks at a time	Okay to move around as needed

Briefly note any administrative details and share what participants can expect beyond the ground rules. Pay particular attention to the word "briefly." Don't dwell on the mundane.

If you must provide a telephone number regarding an administrative detail, post it on the flipchart. If you don't, you will repeat it a dozen times during the day.

Go over the session objectives and the agenda so that participants know what they will learn. Put participants at ease by explaining their role as learners and how you intend to conduct the session.

I do not put specific times on the participants' agenda. Participants become nervous if they see that you're behind by 30 minutes. They don't understand that you may be currently covering something that was planned for later or that you know that what they are addressing now is much more important than something later and that you can decrease time on another activity.

I print my personal agenda on brightly colored paper. I use bright paper so that I can see it if it gets lost under handouts or whatever. I include the timing of activities so that I stay on track. I like to allow flexibility to meet participants' needs, but I also need to take full responsibility for achieving the learning objectives.

Get them involved

Start with a show of hands, and next help everyone get to know each other. Participants learn as much from each other as the program, so start quickly with introductions that are tied to an icebreaker. Knowing something about the other individuals in the session will make it easier for them to listen, to contribute, and to get involved. Several tried-and-true icebreakers are listed in Chapter 23.

If you want a list of the best icebreaker books, check my Web site at www. ebbweb.com. I provide a complete resource list to support this book.

The classic four questions answered by participants in a training session include:

- ✔ Who are you?
- ✔ Where do you work?
- ✔ What do you hope to learn?
- ✔ What's something interesting about you?

These four questions are usually embedded in the introductions in some way. Remember that your participants will want to know the same things about you.

Always start on time. Anything else teaches participants that it is okay to be late. You're training them to be late. Waiting for a few stragglers punishes those who made the effort to be on time. If you anticipate a tardiness problem, you can always be prepared to start with something that is interesting but not critical for everyone to know.

Identify all that you want to accomplish in your opening. These things may include:

- ✔ Establish a participative climate.
- ✔ Introduce participants.
- ✔ Introduce the agenda.
- ✔ Clarify the participants' expectations.
- ✔ List objectives of the training.
- ✔ Build interest and excitement.
- ✔ Learn something about the participants.
- ✔ Determine some minimum rules of engagement (ground rules).
- ✔ Establish your credibility.

Plan how you will accomplish what you need to lay the foundation for the rest of the training session. First impressions are critical. A good trainer will catch and hold participants' attention right from the start. That's why it is important to start with a BANG!

Looking at Six Disastrous Debuts

Trainers need to be prepared with an opening — what to say and what to do. If you're unprepared, you may find yourself saying things you didn't mean to say, getting ahead of yourself, forgetting what you were supposed to say, and just generally confusing your audience.

Be prepared so you don't fall into one of these disastrous debuts:

- ✔ Asking obvious, contrived questions
- ✔ Talking too much, wandering from point to point with no direction
- ✔ Telling individuals they are wrong

> ✔ Making a participant the brunt of a joke
>
> ✔ Forcing your beliefs on the participants, telling them what to do or how to think
>
> ✔ Trying to be funny

Not one of these works. Trust me. I've seen them all. Don't do them.

Creating a Supportive Learning Environment

To successfully create a supportive learning environment you need to get to know your participants, and that means remembering and using their names. It also means that you will want to let them know something about you.

Get to know your participants

If you have opened with a BANG and gotten early participation, learners will expect to be involved in their learning. Don't change the expectation now! Continue to implement activities that encourage discussion and involvement. Begin to call participants by their names immediately to create a supportive learning environment.

I like to use name tents (cardstock folded in half lengthwise) for their names. I usually have my name tent completed as a model when they walk in the door. I also place broad-tipped markers around the tables so that their names can be written to be seen from a distance. If everyone has not completed the name tents by the time introductions have been completed, I ask them to do so.

Have participants put their names on both sides so that you and other participants can see the name from all sides of the room.

You started to get to know your participants through introductions and by conducting a mini needs assessment during your opening. Select questions that help you better understand the group's skill level, knowledge, experience, and expertise. In the case of a train-the-trainer, for example, I may want to know how long they had been trainers, whether they had ever attended a train-the-trainer, whether they had designed training, and finally whether they thought that training was their destined profession. How do you do this? You may simply ask for a show of hands. If more complex, you may wish to have them complete a few brief questions. (Note, however, that this process doesn't encourage participation, nor does it inform the rest of the participants). If you want to add movement, you may ask participants to stand if their response is yes or to move to a certain spot in the room based on their response.

Getting to know your participants early in the session is one of the best investments you can make in the session. After you have created a learning environment in which participants feel comfortable to participate, to ask questions, and to learn, the session has the best chance of success.

What's in a name: Five secrets to remembering names

To establish an environment that is conducive to learning, trainers need to build trust and let their participants know that they care about them. Because most people are flattered when someone takes the time to learn and use their names, this is one obvious way to build a positive environment. Oh no! Can't even do that at a party when you meet only one person? Now I'm suggesting that you learn 10, 20, or more participants' names all at once?

Obtain a copy of the roster prior to your training session. I read it over and try to get a big-picture vision of how many people, men, women, and names. I also look for names that may be difficult to pronounce so that I can take extra care to listen when they introduce themselves.

These five techniques will help you as the facilitator to learn participants' names.

Use name tents

I highly recommend that you use name tents on which participants can write their names. Name tents are 8½"-x-11" sheets of cardstock that are folded in half lengthwise and sit on the table like a tent. (Which is why they are also called *table tents*.) Most organizations have their logos printed on them. Provide fat, dark markers so that you can read everyone's, even those who sit way in the back of the room. I usually say something like, "Use the marker to write your name or whatever you wish to be called for the next couple of days (hours) on the name tent. I have completed mine, and it is sitting up front as a model." Sometimes, this is all participants need. They see the model and imitate it before I even say anything.

Ask them to print their names on both sides of the name tent so that everyone can see it no matter where they are in the room. This is actually as much help to you as anyone. When you see hands go up to make a comment, a quick glance at the name tent and you can easily say, "Tedman, how would you answer that?"

Be sure you don't have anything in your line of sight between you and the name tent — no glasses, no water pitchers, no props. Otherwise, you will constantly be craning your neck to read names.

Some organizations insist on preprinting the name tents with participants' names. I oppose this for several reasons. First, there is a chance that a name is misspelled, or, worse yet, the person's name is missed completely. Second, it adds a sense of formality that I do not want as a part of my sessions. Third, it adds to the logistic nightmare. Participants need to find their name tents in a stack or someone needs to be available to pass them out. Or a worse solution, they are placed around the tables and participants are not able to select where they want to sit. Fourth, and worst of all, usually the typeface is too small for anyone to read across the length of the room, so it is all for naught! The only reason you would want preprinted name tents is if the trainer required assigned seating.

Work the introductions

You may think that you can relax a bit while everyone is going around and introducing themselves. Perhaps use the time to get organized for the first information sharing? Not a good idea. Remember these first few minutes are a critical time to build rapport. As people are introducing themselves, listen to what they are saying, look at their names on their name tents, and begin to connect their names and faces. Also, use their names at least twice during the introductions. You can say, "Welcome [name]," or "[Name], thank you for telling us. . . ." Start planting those names in your brain.

Use small-group time

I usually have participants remain in their seats for the first small-group activity. They may either turn to the person next to them or form a group of three or four sitting next to each other. My rationale is that while they are completing the task in the small group, I spend a portion of the time matching faces and names again. If I forget anyone's, the name tent is nearby and provides the cue for me. I set a goal to know everyone's names by the first break. Set a goal for yourself.

Play a game

Several name games work well. If you have time for an icebreaker that focuses on people learning each other's names, you may try these. They are fun, and they teach everyone, not just the trainer, the names of the participants.

- ✔ **How Many Can You Name?** If your icebreaker includes individuals meeting as many other people as possible, you can let them know that you will "quiz" them on how many people they actually "meet," meaning they remember their names. Before you debrief the icebreaker, ask how many names each participant remembers.

✔ **Chain Name:** As you go around the room with introductions, each person reiterates all the people before. For example, person number one only introduces himself or herself. Person number two introduces person number one plus himself or herself. Person number three introduces number one, number two, and himself or herself. It becomes more and more difficult, but the rest of the participants begin to help those at the end. The activity establishes a good environment, and everyone learns names.

✔ **Doodles:** Have participants add a doodle to their name tent. The doodle must start with the same letter as their first name. For example, Opal may add oatmeal and Dominick may add a dog. The alliteration will help you, and the other participants, remember names.

✔ **Name It:** When participants introduce themselves, ask them to add something about their names: the history or meaning of their names, who they were named after, what they like (or dislike) about their names, or any other unique fact about their names. The added discussion about the name itself helps everyone to remember more names.

Cheat

Finally, when all else fails, do what I do — cheat. Before the session starts I draw a sketch of the room and the table arrangement. As participants introduce themselves, I jot the person's name at the corresponding place in the sketch. I can use that later as I practice everyone's name.

Participants feel good when you use their names. Work at remembering them.

Let them know about you

Let participants in on who you are — both professionally and personally — to create a supportive learning environment. I tend to be low keyed about my expertise and experience. I may drop subtle hints related to the discussion or the content about who I am. I would probably not say, "I have written 16 books." But I would say, "In my last book, I interviewed 45 training managers who said. . . ." You do not need to be subtle at all. You do want to establish credibility with the participants.

How about personally? How much you let them in on who you are personally is entirely up to you. I like to get to know participants, so I spend breaks with them as much as possible. I find things out about them that we have in common and then use that information to continue our discussion. Sometimes, as an energizer, I ask participants what they want to know of each other. I get into the fray, and they can ask questions of me as well.

You will want to build professional credibility with your participants. You will want them to know you as a human being as well. Don't keep yourself on a pedestal that prevents you from building rapport with your participants.

Training Like a Pro

As you discovered in the last chapter, trainers have two key skill sets they master when they are conducting training. First, they facilitate small-group activities, large-group discussions, and learning in general. Second, they present new information, data, and knowledge. Both of these skill sets are requirements for the job. I examine the facilitator role in Chapter 8. Now, I examine how trainers can be effective presenters.

Presentation skills

Trainers need to present information. It would be nice to never have to deliver a lecturette, but that just isn't going to happen.

Mel Silberman, author and consultant, is well known for his concept of active training. Yet he knows that as a trainer you will need to present information at times. Even, so, Mel believes that participants can be actively involved in the learning. See his "Ten suggestions to turn a lecture into active learning" sidebar.

When you present, whether it is a lecturette, simply describing a concept during a discussion, or responding to a question, the participants will not only hear your content, but they will also "hear" and "see" your presentation style.

It is easier for your participants to learn when your presentation is interesting, and even better when it is exciting. How interesting, competent, and exciting do you sound? What do participants infer about you based on your presentation techniques and style?

What do they hear? The six Ps

Vocal expression adds vitality and energy to your ideas. Several characteristics make up the audio part of your presentation. Think of these as the six Ps of your presentation: projection, pitch, pace, pauses, pronunciation, and phillers.

- **Projection** refers to how loudly the message is heard. Do you project enough volume? Loudness results when air is expelled from the lungs with maximum force and intensity. The appropriateness of a loud or soft voice depends on the room size and the need for vocal variety. Variations in volume can be used to indicate urgency, exasperation, and importance.

- **Pitch** in a conversation flows up and down the scale naturally. But when some trainers stand in front of a group, their voices become dull and flat. I learned to picture pitch from Kevin Daley, founder of Communispond.

He says to picture pitch, think of the states of Kansas and Colorado. Kansas is flat; even when you say the state's name, it comes out quite flat. Now picture Colorado with its rolling hills, mountains, valleys, streams, lots of variety. Even when you say "Colorado," your voice can't help but roll up and down the scale. Pitch variety adds interest to your voice, but it also helps you to emphasize important ideas or to signal transitions. Both are important to keep your learner tuned in to what you're saying.

✔ **Pace** is the rate of delivery and is determined by the duration of sound and the number of pauses between sounds. Words can be spoken fast or drawn out. Like projection and pitch, the pace can also signal importance. Try saying $50,000 quickly, as if it is just a small amount of money. Now, say it again, this time slowing your pace and adding emphasis on every other syllable. It can really make a difference.

Select a pace that is comfortable for you. Don't try to speed up or slow down. Your brain is accustomed to working with your mouth in a certain cadence. However, if you're told you speak too rapidly, try punctuating your presentation with more pauses. Right. Just snap your jaw closed. If, on the other hand, you're told you speak too slowly, check on a couple of things. First, make sure you're using no fillers. Second, be certain you're not repeating the same information. And third, know your material cold. Practice your content aloud a couple of extra times.

✔ **Pauses** can actually add more emphasis than anything mentioned so far. A judiciously placed pause before and/or after an idea can focus attention right where you want it. Pauses allow you time to think. Pauses also allow you to observe the participants for feedback. Pauses are the sign of a seasoned presenter, because most inexperienced presenters are uncomfortable with silence. Practice your pauses.

✔ **Pronunciation** is critical to make it easy for your participants to understand and learn easily. Speaking articulately, clearly, and distinctly is a sign of a pro. Learn to enunciate clearly. Take care that you do not run words together or let the ends of your sentences trail off so your learners have difficulty hearing.

✔ **Phillers** are those nasty little nonsounds that sneak in when you aren't listening to yourself: um, ah, and ah, er, okay, ya know, like. All are fillers that can hypnotize your participants into a trance or can grate on their innermost nerves. No matter which occurs, you can be sure that they will not hear your content but may instead be counting fillers. The sad thing is that most people do not hear their own fillers.

The only way I know to eliminate fillers is to hire yourself an Um Counter, someone who will listen to your presentation and provide you with feedback about how many fillers you use per minute and which ones. The shock seems to awaken something so that you can finally hear yourself.

What do they see?

The other half of your presentation is what your learners see. What they see should convey the same interesting, competent, and exciting message.

✔ **Body stance** is one of the first things participants notice. Good posture and poise convey confidence in your message, and your participants will want to know the content. When standing in front of the room, plant your feet and avoid shifting your weight. Moving around and among the participants is good. It uses up some of your nervous energy and helps to create a natural and comfortable environment. However, repetitive moves, such as pacing back and forth in the same spot, are distracting.

Try to never have your back to the group. Learn to talk and walk backwards! How about sitting? Sitting certainly changes the tone. It would be rare, but you may sit or even lean against a table. Your stance then says "informal." The tenor of the presentation has changed. In the past I have purposefully pulled a chair in the middle of the room and, while sitting, had a heart-to-heart discussion with a group that was disagreeable. So the question is, what is your purpose for sitting? What atmosphere do you want to convey?

✔ **Gestures** help to convey enthusiasm and help your participants follow your presentation. Keep them natural. If you start with your hands at your sides, they will come up naturally. Think about speaking and gesturing to those seated farthest from you. This enhances your gestures, as well as your projection. Avoid crossing your arms, playing with your marker, or touching your head.

How about putting your hands in your pockets? It depends. Are you putting your hands in your pockets because you're nervous or they feel awkward and you don't know what to do with them? Or are you putting your hands in your pockets because you're relaxed and you want to send a message of relaxation to your audience? If you're putting your hands in your pockets for the first reason, then the answer is no, don't do it. Your hands will just get into trouble jangling change. On the other hand, if your reason is to send a message of relaxation, then fine, go ahead.

✔ **Facial expression** should be congruent with your words. In fact, your face can express more than your words! Facial mobility is an indication of a relaxed speaker. Use it to add emphasis to your message and to display energy. Be aware of your expressions and what they may convey.

Early in my career, I was surprised when a participant said to me, "You don't want us to ask questions." This was of course exactly the opposite of what I wanted. I did want them to ask all the questions necessary to understand the skills they were learning. When I asked why she made the statement, she said, "Whenever we ask questions you frown." Wow! I was unaware of frowning. I realized that I was concentrating on their questions, and when I concentrate my face appears to be frowning. It was a great lesson. What are your facial expressions saying about you?

✔ **Eye contact** is important in all conversations. In the United States it represents caring, understanding, and trust. Good eye contact builds rapport with your participants. Avoid looking at the ceiling. Don't just sweep the participants or try to get by with looking at the tops of their heads. People know whether you're making eye contact. Good eye contact means that you see their facial expressions and can tell if they are following and/or agreeing with you.

Be sure to look at all of your participants. I find that most trainers ignore the 25 percent of the people closest to the front on their dominant side. Are you aware of where you're looking? One other thing — I have noticed that good eye contact decreases the number of fillers. Somehow, it's tougher to look someone in the eye and say "um!"

Eye contact is a cultural preference. It is not viewed the same in all cultures. If you're training in another country or training other cultures in

Ten suggestions to turn a lecture into active learning

by Mel Silberman

Lecturing is one of the most time-honored yet ineffective ways to teach. By itself, it will never lead to active learning. In order for a lecture to be effective, the instructor should build interest first, maximize understanding and retention, involve participants during the lecture, and reinforce what's been presented. There are several options to do just that.

Building Interest

- Lead off with a story or interesting visual. Provide a relevant anecdote, fictional story, cartoon, or graphic that draws the audience's attention to what you're about to teach.

- Present an initial case problem. Present a problem around which the lecture will be structured.

- Use a test question. Ask participants a question (even if they have little prior knowledge) so that they will be motivated to listen to your lecture for the answer.

Maximizing Understanding and Retention

- Reduce to headlines. Reduce the major points in the lecture to key words, which act as verbal subheadings or memory aids.

- Use examples and analogies. Provide real-life illustrations of the ideas in the lecture and, if possible, create a comparison between your material and the knowledge/experience the participants already have.

- Have a visual backup. Use flipcharts, transparencies, brief handouts, and demonstrations that enable participants to see as well as hear what you're saying.

Involving Participants During the Lecture

- Spot challenges. Interrupt the lecture periodically and challenge participants to give examples of the concepts presented thus far or answer spot-quiz questions.

- Illuminate with exercises. Throughout the presentation, intersperse brief activities that illuminate the points you're making.

Reinforcing the Lecture

- Apply a problem. Pose a problem or question for participants to solve based on the information given in the lecture.

- Encourage participant review. Ask participants to review the contents of the lecture with each other or give them a self-scoring review test.

the United States, you will of course respect other values. Other cultures view eye contact differently. Some consider it rude or aggressive. Be familiar with the culture of your participants.

✔ **Nervousness** is displayed in numerous ways: pacing or swaying, fidgeting with a pen, jingling change in your pocket, perspiring, shaking, clearing your throat, grimacing, tenseness, and dozens of other things. However, if you have interesting content, your participants will not even notice. The number one rule regarding nervousness is "Do not say that you're nervous." Nervousness is covered in greater depth in Chapter 12. Check it out for additional information.

How about some feedback?

Feedback is good for learning new skills and improving performance. It is nearly impossible for you to give feedback to yourself. I recommend that you give a copy of the form in Table 9-1 to a colleague. Tell them you want honest feedback about what they heard and saw in your training. Then, when they share their observations with you, be quiet and listen. After you have the observations, you can get started on any performance improvements necessary.

Table 9-1	Training Feedback
I am interested in improving my skills as a trainer. Thank you for agreeing to observe my training session. Please provide feedback to me in the following areas. Thank you for your time.	
What do you hear (the six Ps)?	
Projection:_____	
Pitch:_____	
Pace: _____	
Pauses: _____	
Pronunciation: _____	
Phillers:_____	
What do you see?	
Body stance:_____	
Gestures: _____	
Facial expression:_____	
Eye contact: _____	
Nervousness: _____	
What suggestions do you have for improvements I can make?	

The participants' materials

Encourage the participants to use the materials provided. First, it will help them to understand the content better. Second, they will more easily find any information should they need to after the training session.

- ✔ Always refer to every page, even if you won't use it. Tell the participants why it's there, for example, "the resource page is information you may refer to after you return to the workplace."

- ✔ Decide whether you will have the handouts available as participants arrive, after the session starts, or at the end of the session. Each has advantages and disadvantages.

- ✔ Remind your participants what page they should be on as you move through the content.

- ✔ During presentations or activities, tell participants whether the information is in their manuals or handouts so they can choose whether to take notes.

Notes: To be or note to be

Whenever I conduct a train-the-trainer session, I am asked about notes. Should I use them? Or should I memorize everything? Should I hold them? Should I keep them in the trainer's manual? Should I use an outline? Should I speak from key words? Should I use paper? Should I use note cards? Should I write them in my own words?

My answer is "Yes."

There is no secret about using notes as a trainer. Do what works best for you. My best advice is "Yes, use notes." Your participants are there to see you succeed. They want you to stay on track. They want you to remember everything you're supposed to tell them. They don't want you to memorize a "speech." They want you to converse with them. They want you to be comfortable with the content so that you can interact with them and address their unique needs — even if they aren't on the agenda.

I cannot advise you of the one way that works best. I can, however, provide you with a few techniques and ideas from experience. I hope you will try a couple and find what works best for you.

- ✔ **Use the trainer's manual as your guide.** If a trainer's manual has been developed, it is probably filled with most everything you will need to conduct the training session. You may want to go through it, crossing off parts you will not be using or even removing pages that you will not need. If it is an off-the-shelf training program, you may want to customize it for your organization, adding your own examples, questions, and stories. See Chapter 6 for ideas about how to do this.

✔ **Use the participant manual/materials as your guide.** This is my preferred method. I start with a participant's manual. If it is bound and printed on both sides, I copy it on one side only. I use the information from the trainer's manual (if there is one) and add pertinent notes. I note the time at the top of the page (that it should be when you reach that particular page). I underline key ideas, add notes about media, props, or handouts, and include special information about putting the participants into small groups.

✔ **Develop your own notes.** Some trainers create their own notes. This of course gives you the maximum amount of creative license to develop your notes so that they work best in your format. Some trainers use an outline, some use key words, and some develop an entire manuscript. I caution you about developing a manuscript. It's a great deal of work. Also, trainers who tend to do this are usually good writers, and after they have written their "good stuff," they want to read it as it is. Be careful. Your learners do not want you to read to them.

Another method is used by trainers who rely on their visuals and media to guide them through the session. They may add notes on the frames of their overhead transparencies or in the margins of their flipcharts. Some develop their notes using the note feature of the PowerPoint slide presentation and then use the printed pages to guide them.

Experiment a bit until you find the technique that works best for you.

Things I know for sure about notes

Notes will help keep you on track: both time and topic. They are your support system, so use a format that works best for you

Become intimate with your notes. Practice with them and become familiar with what's on each page and where. You should be able to trust that anything you may need will be found in your notes. Therefore, do not write new notes just before your training session. Yes, you practiced with them. They are a little bent and crinkly. You folded them when you didn't mean to. You even spilled a little latte on module three. But don't redo them now. Better that they are well worn and familiar to you than that they are pretty and aren't familiar at all. If you practiced with them, you know where to find the list of five ways to recognize a good leader and the "don't forget to tell the learner."

Number your pages. Whether you use your own pages/cards or modify the trainer's guide, number them. If you use the trainer's guide as a starting point, you may add pages that are more pertinent or delete pages that will not be a part of the training session. Renumber the pages. If you drop them, you will be able to put them in order again. I once sat in the audience and watched a man shuffle his notes as he delivered his opening lines. The audience did not hear a word he said. We were all aghast at what he was doing. He realized it and recovered by putting us into buzz groups. Fortunately, he had numbered his note cards.

Cue yourself. Whatever technique you use, develop a plan to cue yourself about where to find information. Use highlight markers, underlining, boxes, clouds, arrows, or different colors. You may for example, underline all the places where you need to use a type of media. You may put stars in front of the questions you need to ask. You may draw a miniscreen as a cue to use PowerPoint. You may put red boxes around the times of the session.

If you use the trainer's guide as your notes, it will give the times in some formula that denotes how far into the training you are. For example, 0315 means that three hours and fifteen minutes have passed since you started training. If you actually started at 8:00 o'clock and you have built an additional 15-minute break into the session, you would replace it with 11:30 a.m.

Don't fold or staple your notes. Folding them makes them weak, and stapling prevents you from being flexible with them. I usually keep my notes in a three-ring binder and remove only the page or pages I intend to use during a specific amount of time. When I am finished, I return the pages and pick up the next one or two. I keep the binder at the upper-left-hand corner of the table. I always know where my notes are.

If you create your own note pages, use a heavier stock of paper. It will hold up better. If your hand tends to shake, it won't rattle either! If you use note cards, use larger cards than the 3 x 5 cards. The larger cards will provide you with much more flexibility — and of course room.

One last note: Make your notes work for you; don't be a slave to them.

Asking and Answering Questions

The art of asking and answering questions and encouraging participants to ask questions is a valued skill of trainers. Don't take it lightly. Beyond simply eliciting answers or facts, questions can stimulate interaction and discussion. Questions enable you to assess what your participants know and what they still need to learn. Questions can be used to emphasize and reinforce significant points. Questions encourage participants to evaluate their own knowledge gaps and think about how to address them. Questions encourage thinking.

Encouraging participants to ask questions ensures understanding, enhances interest, increases learning, and prompts interaction.

Encouraging participants to ask questions

Participants may ask questions for different reasons. They may be positive reasons to acquire information. On the other hand, they may ask questions to irritate the trainer or to impress other participants. Fortunately, most often participants ask for positive reasons. So how can you encourage more questions?

- ✔ At the beginning of the session, encourage participants to ask questions at any time.

- ✔ Go through your training program. Try to anticipate questions that may come up. During your presentation, pose these questions to the participants if they don't pose them to you.

- ✔ Stop at natural points in the training and ask for questions.

Have participants work in trios to create a question about the information that you're presenting. Have them write the question on an index card. Collect the questions and redistribute so that each trio has a different question to answer.

- ✔ If a participant looks puzzled, stop and ask whether there is a question.

- ✔ If two or more participants are talking among themselves, ask them whether there is something they would like clarified.

- ✔ Allow time for participants to ask their questions privately. They may be too shy to ask in front of the entire group.

Make it okay to ask questions. Assume that there will be questions. At the same time, convey a message to your participants that you expect questions. You can do this by how you ask for questions. Instead of saying, "Are there any questions?" say, "What questions do you have?" It may be subtle, but it works.

Guidelines for answering questions

These guidelines provide suggestions as you master the art of answering questions.

- ✔ Anticipate your participants' questions. Being prepared is always good. If you get the same questions often, you may wish to add the content to the training. Practice answers out loud.

- ✔ Inform participants of your expectations for asking questions early in the session.

- ✔ Listen carefully to each question for both content (what is asked) and intent (what is meant). Listen for the emotion that may not match the words of the question. If it seems that the individual's intent doesn't match the content, you may be heading for a let's-see-whether-we-can-irritate-the-trainer situation. If you do receive a hostile question, avoid showing your feelings. Remember, the group is usually on your side.

✔ Treat a "why?" question like a "how?" question. "Why" questions may put you on the defensive because it seems as if you must justify your rationale. However, if you think about it from a "how" perspective, you will respond from a fact basis rather than an opinion basis. For example, if someone asks you, "Why do you think your process is better?" respond by stating *how* your process is better. Do you see the small nuance that will help you maintain your composure?

✔ Paraphrase the question to ensure that everyone heard and that you understood the question. This prevents you from answering the wrong question. You may also choose to paraphrase all lengthy questions to ensure clarity.

Another reason to paraphrase a question is that it gives you time to organize your response before plunging in with an answer.

✔ Take care with how you paraphrase. You do want to clarify what the question was, but you don't want to come across as condescending. Saying, "What you mean is. . ." or "What you're trying to say is. . ." may come across as insulting.

✔ Keep your answer short and on target. Choose your words carefully. Don't build a watch if the individual has only asked for the time. Avoid using the word "obviously," because this implies that the participant should already know the answer. I also try to avoid "you should," "you must," and other terms that appear to be controlling or moralizing. These words may discourage others from asking questions.

✔ Direct your response to the entire group, not just the person who asked the question. You may start by responding to the person who asked the question, but then look at the other participants during your response. This ensures that the rest of the participants feel a part of the discussion. In addition, it discourages the person from tagging on a second question, which may lead to a conversation between the two of you.

✔ Watch the person's body language. If you're uncertain about whether you hit the mark, verify your response with, "Is that what you were looking for?" or "Would you like more detail?"

✔ If you don't know an answer, redirect it to the participants, to another source, or state your follow-up plan for getting the information. In addition, "I don't know" is an acceptable answer. Just be sure to tell the participant what you will do (and by when) to find the information. "I don't know the answer to that, but I can call the office on break to obtain the information." Don't make up an answer. Don't fake it.

✔ If the question refers to something you will cover at a later time, ask the participant to write the question on a sticky note and place it in the parking lot. Address it specifically at the time that the topic is introduced.

✔ I avoid saying, "That's a good question" or "Gee, I'm glad you asked that question." If you provide a compliment after every question, it may come across as insincere. On the other hand, if you say it sometimes, some participants will wonder if their questions were not "good questions" or if you're not "glad they asked a question." It may seem minor, but if you just avoid the situation, it will be one less concern for you.

Asking questions

Questions are wonderful tools to get participation, to personalize a presentation, or to provoke participants to think about your message. To be effective, you will want to think about these.

✔ Plan your questions in advance. When should they appear in your presentation?

✔ Consider your reason for including them. Are you looking for a correct answer? Are you trying to initiate controversy? Or are you asking a rhetorical question?

✔ Early on, ask the question that will yield involvement by the most participants. For example, if you're asking for a show of hands, ask the question that will cause the most people to raise their hands in response.

✔ Keep questions short and clear.

✔ Ensure that they are relevant to your presentation.

✔ Know whether you want information or opinions.

✔ Go from general to specific when asking a series of questions.

✔ Get participation by asking questions early. Further, be sure to balance to whom you direct the questions.

✔ Be sure that you're asking open-ended questions.

✔ Say the participant's name first, and then ask the question. There is no need to "catch them" in a mini-vacation.

✔ Pause after asking. Too often, trainers are uncomfortable with silence. So they will ask a question. When they do not get an immediate response, they will ask it again. If still no response, they will answer it themselves. This teaches participants that if they wait long enough, the trainer will answer as well as ask all the questions!

✔ Be prepared to take action if you don't get a response.

Asking questions is one of the most useful tools you have to encourage participation. Hone your questioning skills.

Questions in action

Think about how you may be able to apply some of what you just read. Think about the next training session you will conduct. Then complete the appropriate information in Table 9-2.

Table 9-2	What Questions Will They Ask?

Anticipate five questions your participants may have in your next training session. List them, and then add your response.

Question: _____

My response: _____

_____

Question: _____

My response: _____

_____

Question: _____

My response: _____

_____

Question: _____

My response: _____

_____

Question: _____

My response: _____

_____

If you anticipate these questions, should you build something into the training that would address them before they come up?

Now think about your use of questions. How could you make your training more dynamic by adding questions? Where? What kind of questions would they be? What would be the purpose? Identify three questions you could ask your participants in Table 9-3.

Table 9-3	What Questions Will You Ask?
Question I could ask: _____	
Purpose of the question: _____	
_____	
Question I could ask: _____	
Purpose of the question: _____	
_____	
Question I could ask: _____	
Purpose of the question: _____	
_____	

Using Smooth Transitions

Keep your learners in mind as you transition from one topic to the next. Take them with you on a smooth journey as you move through your agenda. Help them see the relevance and the relationships. Help them see the big picture and how things are connected. You will look like the professional that you are. These tips will assist you.

- ✔ **When you're designing the training, make sure it has a logical flow or sequence.** This in itself will enable smooth transitions.

- ✔ **Make sure you properly wrap up the previous topic before going on to the next.** Ask whether there are questions. When there are no more, say, "Now let's move on to _____."

- ✔ **Use mini-summaries to transition out of a section.** You may present these summaries, but you do not need to. Ask for volunteers to do this for the group. Or place participants in small groups and ask each group to identify two or three summary statements.

✔ **Pick a common theme that relates to both the previous and the upcoming topic.** Address that theme while moving from one topic to the next. Tell them how the role play you just completed is related to the next module.

✔ **Use the building-block approach.** In your transition, summarize the concepts from the previous discussion that will be the foundation of the upcoming discussion.

✔ **Use visual cues.** If you're following an agenda or a flowchart, show the change from one point to the next. I've used props at times. For example, I used two-by-four blocks to "build" a structure when discussing the Ten Building Blocks of Teams.

✔ **Although it is difficult to practice an entire training presentation, it is very easy to practice transitions.** Go through every lesson of your training, and write down key points for each. Next, look for relationships with the activity or presentation before and after. Last, develop and write the transitions in your training notes. Finally, rehearse them until they are smooth.

Wrapping Up an Effective Training Session

Remember that the conclusion should provide a sense of closure for the learners. You have created a design to ensure that the following occur. What are your responsibilities to wrap up your training session? You will need to ensure that expectations were met. You may want to conduct a group experience. Most training sessions end with an evaluation and sometimes ask for additional feedback for improvement. A closing activity may get commitment from participants. You will most likely want to have some final words of wisdom planned as a send-off. The closing is a time to wrap up all loose ends and shift the focus from the training session to the workplace.

Ensure that expectations were met

One of the most common ways to address this is to review the expectations that were developed by the participants at the beginning of the session and posted on the wall. You can also conduct a verbal check with participants.

Ensure that you have answered all the questions in the parking lot and that there are no loose ends left undone.

Provide a shared group experience

Many closing activities exist. One of the most creative closing activities I've heard of is to develop a video or a PowerPoint collage. First determine the equipment you will use. Use it to take a video or pictures of the training room before participants arrive. Continue to capture pictures of the group through-out the training session working in small groups, on individual activities, or as a large group. Be sure that everyone is represented in the shots. If you're taking digital shots, put them together in a collage presentation. You may wish to add appropriate music. Then near the end announce that you want to show them all the hard work they have completed during the session. Sit back and enjoy the show. This is a very motivational way to end a session.

Check the resource list on my Web site at www.ebbweb.com for books that feature closing activities.

I have taken 35mm pictures during team-building sessions. Then on the last day I have them developed at a one-hour photo shop. I have doubles made and share one set with the participants. Again, if you do this, ensure that you get everyone in the pictures.

Evaluate the learning experience

All training sessions based on an instructional design model will include an evaluation element. You may evaluate participant reaction, knowledge gained, application of the skills and knowledge, and/or business results. Chapter 13 provides more details about evaluation. You may also consider conducting a feedback session.

You may also wish to request feedback and improvement suggestions for future sessions. One method that works well is to ask participants what went well and what improvements are needed. Use two flipcharts with a "What went well?" heading on one and "What would you change?" on the other. You may alternate making the lists on both flipcharts at the same time.

Summarize the accomplishments and gain commitment to action

You may wish to review the agenda and the objectives. Ask whether every-thing was covered. Commitment to action can be worked into a closing activ-ity in which you may ask:

✔ What was the most valuable part of the training session?

✔ What will you implement back at the workplace?

✔ What will you change as a result of what you've learned?

You may conduct these discussions in small groups that report out to the larger group. To ensure transfer of learning, you may also want participants to pair up with a "buddy." Buddies will support each other after the session has ended. This is a good time for the buddies to exchange contact information and make plans for the first contact.

A favorite activity that I use is to have participants write memos to themselves committing to some actions and/or changes. They put them inside envelopes, self-address, and seal them. I collect the envelopes and mail their commitment memos back to them six to eight weeks later.

Send them off with a final encouraging word — or two

Have your ending designed as tightly as you have your opening planned. Based on this section, you have a number of things to complete. In addition, you will want to have a formal send-off message for the participants. You opened the training with a BANG! End it with the same kind of fanfare.

Help participants remember the experience, give them encouragement, and send them off with something to think about after the session. What could that be? It could be a call to action, a poem, a quote, a moral to a story, an anecdote or illustration, a visual, a reference to the introduction, a rhetorical question, a demonstration, a challenge, a magic trick, or something that makes the point. I will forever remember stabbing a plastic straw all the way through a raw potato, as the facilitator said, "Positive thinking moves mountains. Believe that you will be successful and you will be."

Bob Lucas, author, trainer, and consultant, likes to end day-long training sessions by reading from the Dr. Seuss book *Oh, the Places You Will Go!* The book's message of optimism and reaching goals has high impact. Bob adds his own statement encouraging learners to achieve their goals.

Lastly, stand at the door, shake participants' hands, wish them luck, and say good-bye.

Focusing on the asking-and-answering questions section, a quote by my favorite author, e.e. cummings: "always the beautiful answer who asks a more beautiful question."

Chapter 10

Mastering Media and Other Visuals

* *

In This Chapter

▶ Selecting the best media or visual to do the job

▶ Selecting and using visuals

▶ Using powerful visuals that add to the learning

▶ Looking like a pro using specific media techniques in training

* *

A picture is worth a thousand words. Of course this is a cliché, yet it tells you exactly what this chapter is all about. I touch lightly on visuals in Chapter 5, but in this chapter, I focus solely on visuals: what's available to you, why you should use them, a few more tips for designing them, and most important, techniques for using them with your learners.

Before you begin this chapter, consider the expertise you have now by using the self-evaluation in Table 10-1.

Table 10-1	Evaluate Your Audiovisual Expertise

Use this scale to evaluate your expertise when using visuals in the classroom.

1. No expertise; heck, I'm not even sure I know what you mean!

2. Minimal expertise; pretty darn average.

3. Expert; I have mastered this one.

    ____ I plan the visuals to support the learning objectives.

    ____ I consider the participants' needs when designing visuals.

    ____ I design simple and clear visuals.

    ____ My visuals speak in headlines, phrases, not complete sentences.

    ____ My visuals can be seen from the back row.

    ____ I use sans serif typeface.

    ____ I know exactly when and where to use the visuals for maximum impact.

    ____ I arrive early to check out equipment and organize my visuals.

    ____ I do not block the view to my visuals.

    ____ I maintain eye contact even when using visuals.

    ____ I avoid reading my visuals.

    ____ I keep my visuals organized in the training session.

    ____ I have learned and use tips and tricks that add to my professionalism.

    ____ I ensure that the visuals support the presentation rather than become the presentation.

How'd you do? Ready for a few tips and techniques?

Select the Best Visual to Do the Job

You have a number of choices available with regard to the type of media — everything from computer displays to paper. The media should support your training session and make it easier for the learner to acquire the skills or knowledge intended.

What's available?

PowerPoint presentations have taken the training world by storm. They are easy and fast to create. The tools to design them are sitting on everyone's desktop inside their computers. They can be changed or updated on the spot. They add color automatically and may include animation and sound effects or video clips.

They may also be boring, overused, and less effective than other forms of media and visuals that are available. This list of media and visual support provides an overview of what is available to you.

- ✔ **Computer projection systems:** This includes PowerPoint presentations and SMART Boards. Both use computer technology to project images. PowerPoint presentations are convenient, and most trainers use the technology. SMART Boards are a combination of a giant computer screen and a whiteboard on which you can write. In addition, your hand can act as a giant cursor to move things from one place to another.

- ✔ **Videos and DVDs:** You may show a video clip to demonstrate a skill, illustrate behavior, or to have an expert deliver content in a way that you could not. You may decide to show a video in its entirety or just a segment that makes the point. You may also use videos to tape participants' practice sessions. This allows them to critique themselves. Most people are their own best critics.

- ✔ **Overhead projectors:** Information written on an 8-inch-x-10-inch transparency is placed over a light source. The light is collected in a periscope-like device, and the image is projected on a screen. They are useful for two specific reasons. First, you can write on them while you speak. The trainer can capture the participants' ideas and change the projected image as participants add ideas, respond to questions, or even revise a design. Second, it is easy to use layers to build a complex model or image.

- ✔ **Flipchart easels and chart packs:** Flipcharts are large pads of newsprint mounted so that individual sheets can be torn off and hung on the wall or flipped over the top of the pad. The pad is mounted on a large easel about six feet high. Trainers can write on them with chisel-tip markers. Flipcharts work well for creating on-the-spot lists, capturing ideas generated by the group, and creating real-time plans. There is a sense of immediacy and spontaneity to the information presented. Flipcharts are very valuable when you're called in to do some spur-of-the-moment facilitating.

   Flipchart packs of paper are available in a preglued format that acts like a giant sticky notes pad. Pages stick directly to the wall as opposed to using masking tape.

✔ **Blackboards, whiteboards, magnetic boards, felt boards:** Whiteboards are making a comeback! A new paint covers an entire wall and has magnetic properties so that a trainer can use magnets. In addition, some training rooms still have boards on the walls or on a movable stand.

✔ **Electronic whiteboards:** This whiteboard is combined with a copier mechanism. It translates whatever you write on its 3-foot-x-5-foot surface to an 8-inch-x-11-inch page of paper. Participants can each walk out the door with whatever ideas were captured on the board.

✔ **Props:** Props usually do not plug in, turn on, make sounds, show animation, or have glitches. While props have nothing to do with media, they may be great visuals. Props capture or refocus attention. They may serve as a metaphor for any aspect of the content. Props may include samples, models, demonstrations, or any article that a trainer holds to drive a point home. The best prop I use is a $20 bill that I borrow from the leader in the group. I ask whether participants can provide examples of the cost of waste (due to poor communication, poor quality, or whatever the topic is) and begin to rip it up as I restate the examples and throw the pieces on the floor. It drives the point home that waste costs money. By the way, I always return the leader's $20 off-line. It's a small price to make an important point.

What are the benefits?

The benefits of visuals to you and your participants are clear. Your participants learn through their five senses. Research suggests that the proportion of learning that occurs visually is much higher than the other four senses combined. Learning that takes place through each is approximately:

✔ **Taste:** 1 percent

✔ **Touch:** 1.5 percent

✔ **Scent:** 3.5 percent

✔ **Aural:** 11 percent

✔ **Visual:** 83 percent

About 70 percent of Western culture is a visual-learning culture. Adding visual support to your aural message is a major benefit to your participants. Participants will grasp the information faster, understand it better, and retain it longer if visuals are added to your training session.

As you discuss the content with participants, visuals will help you be clearer and more concise.

Ensure That the Visual Adds to the Learning

I list several types of visuals you may wish to add to your training session. Under what circumstances may you use each? The following lists a number of situations in which each media or visual performs best. You will also determine others depending upon the learning objectives and the curriculum of your training session.

Computer projection systems

PowerPoint presentations are useful for guiding your participants through the training session. They will probably be the foundation of your media presentation with others added as appropriate. You will use PowerPoint for these at a minimum:

- Provide the outline to the session
- Cue that you're switching to another module or topic
- Provide introductions to topics
- Present new information in any format
- Present processes in sequential order
- Show relationships, for example, pros and cons, advantages and disadvantages, parts to a whole
- Display charts and graphs, for example, bar graphs for change over time or as a comparison, pie charts to display the division of a whole
- Pictures of new products
- Sketches and diagrams
- Organizational relationships
- Directions to complete an activity during the session
- Mini quizzes or challenges
- Cartoons (with appropriate copyright approval) or mindbenders
- Video clips of a message from top management or subject matter experts (SMEs)
- Close the session with a statement, call to action, quote, reference to the introduction, or a rhetorical question

SMART Boards have a more unique use. They would not be appropriate for a large group because most are smaller than the required screen size. Still, they may be useful for some of the same things. Due to your ability to interact with them, SMART Boards may also be used to

✔ Create or revise a document as a small group

✔ Brainstorm

✔ Problem solve

✔ Change a process

Videos and DVDs

Videos and DVD presentations work well when it is difficult to recreate a scenario in the training session. You may show a clip to do any of the following:

✔ Demonstrate a skill

✔ Illustrate behavior

✔ Deliver content by an expert

✔ Set up a scenario

✔ Show the wrong way

You may tape participants' practice sessions to allow the following:

✔ Participants review and critique their own skills

✔ Obtain feedback from other participants and the facilitator

✔ Facilitate a comparison to later, more improved skills

Overhead projectors

Use overhead projectors when you do not have PowerPoint available. They also provide a spontaneous and efficient way to introduce new information that has not been included in the session. To use overhead projectors to obtain large-group participation, the facilitator takes notes or lists ideas on transparencies as participants provide input. Useful at times like these.

✔ Create a list of ideas as a large group

✔ Track list of brainstormed solutions or ideas

✔ Build a model or concept as a large group

✔ Use in small groups to summarize activity and present to entire group

✔ One of the easiest AV tools and you do not need to worry about a technology meltdown

✔ Easy to leave out some transparencies without participants knowing whether you're running behind or making a conscious decision to eliminate a portion of your presentation

✔ Use for same situations as PowerPoint

Flipcharts

Flipcharts are the reliable, no-computer-glitch, flexible tool trainers find useful. They are the only practical tool that allows the trainer to display information for a period of time. As information is recorded or discussed, the trainer can remove the pages and hang them on the wall. One drawback — flipcharts are best for groups of 40 or fewer participants. Flipcharts are portable and an instant resource. Useful for many other situations as well.

✔ Prerecorded information can be presented like any other media

✔ Use for spur-of-the-moment facilitation requests

✔ Capture on-the-spot lists

✔ Record input and ideas generated by the group

✔ Create real-time plans

✔ Track action items, next steps generated during the session

✔ Brainstorm ideas

✔ Reinforce or supplement a lecturette

✔ Track participants' questions or concerns

✔ Display lists or content throughout the session

✔ Make a decision by voting with sticky-back flags

✔ Prioritize a list of items by having the participants vote with stickers

✔ Used by small groups to organize their results

✔ Emergency backup when any technical equipment fails

Boards of all types (including electronic)

Whiteboards, magnetic boards, and all other boards can be useful when available in these situations:

✔ Use for same situations as a flipchart

✔ Use for building a description step by step

✔ Tack up ideas, questions, or concerns

✔ Hold, display, and/or move sticky notes for discussions

✔ Create an affinity diagram

✔ Prioritize a list

✔ Group ideas into categories

Props

Props include a diverse assortment of three-dimensional items that the participants use for discussion or practice. They may be used as practical hands-on support.

✔ Display samples of product, errors, and so on for participants to examine

✔ Introduce models of actual equipment, locations, buildings

✔ Practice skills using actual tools, equipment, or materials

✔ Demonstrate a correct process or procedure

✔ Use props as a metaphor to make a point visually

✔ Make a closing statement

Look Like a Pro

A trainer is a professional. Using visuals can enhance your image and increase the confidence participants have in you. On the other hand, if you do not have professionally designed visuals, if you have not practiced, and if you don't know the best way to use them, your participants may lose all confidence in you.

Visuals are only effective when

✔ They are relevant to the subject.

✔ They are visible and understandable to the participants.

Use the following tips to ensure you look like the professional you are. First attend to the general tips useful for all visuals and media. Following those tips, you will find guidelines for using each of the types of media discussed.

The Competency Study from the American Society for Training and Development (ASTD) lists presentation tools and media as key knowledge required for delivering training.

Tips for using visuals in general

Experienced trainers have learned a number of tips to ensure that they provide the best learning experience for their participants.

Participants must be able to see the visuals

Some of the best presentations are doomed for failure if the participants are unable to see the visuals. These tips will prevent that from happening.

- ✔ Don't block the view.
- ✔ Sit in the participants' seats to ensure that they can see the visuals.
- ✔ Visuals must be readable. Keep a tight focus on what is shown.
- ✔ Reveal only one point at a time.
- ✔ Limit the number of ideas on one visual to four.
- ✔ Use a pointer to focus attention.

   Cocktail sticks work great as pointers for overhead transparencies. They are pointed, and the light shows through those that are colored and translucent.

- ✔ Turn projection lights off between visuals.

PowerPoint presentations can dissolve to a black slide so that participants are not distracted. You can also force a black screen by touching the "B" key.

Orient the visuals for the learner

Imagine that you are one of the participants and that you are seeing the visuals for the first time.

- ✔ Tell learners what they are looking at: "Here are four criteria for perception checks."
- ✔ A good visual may not need words to describe it.
- ✔ Allow enough time for people to take notes.

Be well-practiced

It should be comfortable and natural to use your visuals. That comes with practice.

✔ Charts roll easily (you may need to practice this).

✔ You know how to operate the equipment.

✔ You have prepositioned your equipment and organized your supplies beforehand.

✔ Turn off the projector at the end of the last frame, transparency, and so on.

✔ After its use, leave the equipment alone until after the training session has finished. Don't bother about rewinding a video or putting equipment or visuals away. You owe your time to your participants.

Visuals should enhance your performance rather than replace it

Your visuals should not take center stage, but they should help to explain or clarify the concepts you are presenting.

✔ Visuals should become an extension of yourself as you use them to explain the content of your presentations.

✔ Visuals are tied together with a common element, for example, a graphic, a color, or a sketch.

You're prepared for an emergency

Emergencies that occur during the presentation don't have to be a complete disaster. These may help to reduce the effect on your participants:

✔ Have an extra bulb, adaptor plug, marking pens.

✔ Know how to change the bulb.

✔ Know how or where to obtain an extension cord.

✔ Have an alternative plan if the electricity fails.

✔ Call a break as you address the emergency.

And finally, in the words of that famous trainer, Anonymous: "Keep it simple, keep it simple, keep it simple."

Guidelines for using specific media and visuals

You have read some general tips to ensure success with using the media and visuals. How about a few guidelines for each specific media type?

LCD projector guidelines

Keep the limited flexibility in mind when using LCD-projected PowerPoint. It may be difficult to get participants involved in the visuals. Use other media to create and display their ideas. To design PowerPoint slides that incorporate effective techniques, return to Chapter 5. In addition, try some of these guidelines:

✔ Plan ahead to know where you will be standing.

✔ E-mail the presentation to yourself as a backup.

✔ Some LCD projectors will identify the lifespan of the bulb.

✔ Focus and set up before the training begins; some LCD machines may not be compatible with all computers.

✔ Mark the projection table placement with masking tape on the floor in case you need to move it.

✔ Use a wireless advance control and try it out ahead; have extra batteries available.

✔ Turn off lights immediately in front of the screen but keep them on in the rest of the room.

✔ If the projector has an automatic keystoning setting, don't increase the projection angle over 30 degrees.

✔ Know the password for the computer you will use.

✔ Ensure that the computer uses an appropriate screen saver.

✔ Turn off instant messenger, Outlook, and other communication tools loaded on the computer.

✔ Ensure that both machines have proper ventilation around them.

✔ Ensure that the LCD has the right number of lumens of light for the size of the room.

✔ Prepare your participants for what they should be learning, seeing.

✔ Allow an average of 10 to 20 seconds of reading time per slide. Viewers' eyes should have time to move over the entire visual but not become "fixed" on it. Interject your comments accordingly; otherwise, hypnosis may set in.

✔ Speak to the participants, NOT to the screen.

Film, DVD, and video guidelines

Use video judiciously. Take care that if you include a film clip that it uses the right amount of time. Also, always preview the tape before showing it in your session.

- ✔ Set up the machine before your presentation.
- ✔ Practice setting the sound and dimming lights.
- ✔ Cue the tape and have it ready to play.
- ✔ Check the sound.
- ✔ Never leave videos, CDs, or DVDs in a hot car.
- ✔ Before playing, provide an introduction that tells why you're showing the tape.

Trainers sometimes encounter participants who claim they cannot relate to a setting or video because it is not the same occupational setting as the one they are in. Defuse this issue in your introduction by stating up front that they will see a setting that is different from theirs, but it should not make a difference because the goal is to learn a technique that is transferable to any setting.

- ✔ Show only the portion that you must to make the point; provide a brief explanation about what happens up to this point.
- ✔ Before you show the tape, tell participants what to do during the viewing, for example, take notes, look for a specific behavior.
- ✔ Don't turn off the lights if people will be taking notes.
- ✔ Follow the viewing with at least one question to get participants quickly involved again.
- ✔ Allow for discussion and highlight key points.
- ✔ Ensure that participants are clear about the objectives of the film and what they should have learned.
- ✔ Rewind the video after the training has been completed; you owe your time to your participants.

If you're actually filming or videotaping, remember these guidelines for a smoother training session:

- ✔ Test the camera beforehand; learn zoom, turning on/off, tripod adjustment, and other techniques.
- ✔ Determine whether you will need an additional person to assist with the taping.
- ✔ Have extra videotapes on hand.
- ✔ Be prepared for cameras that automatically shut off after a time period.
- ✔ Adjust the tripod to the appropriate height.
- ✔ Do a microphone check beforehand.
- ✔ Test the VCR and monitor beforehand.

Overhead transparency guidelines

Overheads may not be the most-cutting edge technology, but they continue to be the most versatile and flexible when you need to address unanticipated participant needs.

✔ Maintain eye contact with audience; there is no need to look at the screen.

✔ Number the transparencies for easy ordering each time.

✔ Turn the projector off between transparencies.

To avoid the constant on/off clicking sound, you may cover the light source with cardstock.

✔ Project large images.

✔ Don't block your visual.

✔ Prevent keystone distortion by tilting the screen forward at the top.

✔ Use a pen or small pointer to draw attention to a specific point or to assist your learners to follow the content.

Use a swizzle stick or plastic cocktail pick to create a unique and colorful pointer. Take care that you don't put your hand over the light source. The image of your large hand will be a *big* distraction.

✔ Use the reveal technique to control how much your participants see at one time.

Use cardstock in a bright color and place it under the transparency. Use a bright color so that you can find it on your table of supplies. Place it under the transparency so that you can see the next point and prepare to discuss it.

✔ Record participants' comments on the transparencies to make your transparencies living documents and to increase participation.

✔ If you have written on the transparency with markers, remove all traces before putting them away. Even water-based markers leave a stain if left too long.

✔ If ceiling lights shine directly on the screen, dim those nearest the screen for a sharper contrast.

✔ Do not three-hole punch your transparencies to place in a binder; the holes will show up on the screen.

✔ Put transparencies in transparency frames after they are designed and for storage; frames keep them flat and protect them until the next training session.

Purchase protectors or frames specifically designed for transparencies. Page protectors do not provide as clear an image.

Flipchart guidelines

Flipcharts may sit patiently waiting in the corner of a training room. When you pull them out, however, be prepared with these guidelines to look like a pro.

- Charts for displaying information should be to your dominant side; charts for writing on should be to your nondominant side (this ensures that your back is to the fewest participants when you're writing on the chart).

- Write on every other page so that participants cannot read through to the next page; this also provides a page to absorb pen marks that may bleed through.

- Select and stage the color of markers you will use before the session.

  Mr. Sketch makes the best markers for flipcharts. They do not bleed through the paper, are washable (even out of your clothes), and as a bonus they smell great!

- Printed letters should be 1 to 3 inches high.

- Use some of the new flipchart stickers and fluorescent tape to highlight words, add borders, or use for emphasis in other ways.

- Pencil small cues in the margin.

- Bend the lower corners (two pages together if you have written on every other page) closest to where you will stand so that you can reach down without looking to turn a page.

- Practice rolling the pages over to the back of the easel.

- Use sticky-back tabs to locate specific information on predesigned charts.

- Don't try to talk, write, and spell at the same time.

- After writing, pause and turn toward your participants before you begin to speak.

- Clear the visual: Tell participants what is on the entire page in one succinct statement before discussion on each individual point. This will help them stay focused and with you as you explain the content.

- Stand beside the chart.

- Talk to your participants, not to the chart, using a *touch, turn, tell* process.

- Lined pads are available for those whose writing strays from horizontal.

- Put the marker down when you're not writing.

- Turn pages out of sight when they are no longer pertinent.

- When appropriate, tear off sheets and hang them on the walls with masking tape.

✔ Place two-inch strips of masking tape on the back side of the easel to use to tape pages to the wall.

Plan where and how you will hang your charts. Hang them so they can be read left to right. Use the same color marker for charts that belong together.

Hang your charts in a straight vertical line — not going uphill, or downhill. To do this, the first one must be precisely vertical and perpendicular to the floor so that you can use its edge as your guide as you hang the rest. You can accomplish this in at least four ways. First prepare by attaching tape to the top of the chart.

   ✔ If wallpaper covers the wall, find the seam and align it.

   ✔ If there is a pattern on the wall, use that as a cue.

   ✔ If you have time, position two pieces of transparent tape, equal distance from the floor, to serve as a guide.

   ✔ When all else fails, grasp the chart with both hands equal distance from the top of the page, stand with your feet flat on the floor and reach the same height with both hands, and attach it.

To complete the task, step back and eyeball the first chart. Make any adjustments. With a little practice you will be able to hang them perpendicular without any guide at all.

Blackboard, whiteboard, electronic whiteboard guidelines

Though you may not use them too often, follow this guidance to improve their effectiveness.

   ✔ Be absolutely certain that you're using the correct marker; permanent markers or inappropriate markers spell disaster.

   ✔ Avoid dark clothing if you know you will use a blackboard; chalk dust will soon find its way to your clothes.

   ✔ Star, box, or circle items for emphasis.

   ✔ Use the darkest marker if you intend to copy from an electronic whiteboard; even red doesn't copy well.

Use this idea if you do not spell very well and you find yourself writing in front of groups. When a participant uses a word that I cannot spell, I print a dozen arbitrary letters in the corner of the board or flipchart, making sure they do NOT spell anything. I then turn to the audience and say, "I am not a very good speller. So if you see that I have forgotten a letter in a word, please just take it from the pile of letters and insert it where it belongs. Thank you."

Prop guidelines

Props are used whenever possible to make a point or to give participants hands-on practice. A few tips will make their use easier.

- ✔ Keep props out of sight until you're ready to have participants interact with them.

- ✔ Stretch, be creative, find the link that allows a prop to be a metaphor for key points in your training.

- ✔ Have them readily available for use and touch during breaks.

Take a trip to your local dollar or hardware store to find props and workshop themes that will help your participants learn faster and retain longer than any other media or tool you can use.

Hot Tips for a Cool Ending

The tips listed here are things I have picked up from the best trainer of all, experience. They will not make or break your session. Some are so logical and practical you will wonder why someone else hasn't published them before.

- ✔ Practice tearing flipchart pages off the pack with razor-sharp precision. Many trainers yank them off hard or pull them up against the cardboard strip. Both techniques result in ragged edges. Instead, start the chart gently at the perforated tear line, and then continue pulling the page straight *down*. It's like the "Ole!" cape motion of a bullfighter! You'll have a perfect rip nearly every time.

- ✔ If you want to get a head start on your perfect flipchart tear, you may rip the perforation about an inch or two before your session starts. That way you will have a "perfect" start to each page.

- ✔ When you're given a flipchart that has lots of ragged edges at the top where trainers did not know how to tear off the charts, simply flip the first page to the back to cover all the rough tears.

- ✔ Masking tape can remove certain kinds of paint from walls. If you're uncertain, test the wall in an inconspicuous place.

- ✔ Blue painters' tape works better than masking tape; it holds the paper in place and is safe for all surfaces.

✔ When conducting a training session at a hotel, be sure to ask whether your room will be used that evening for another group. If it is, recognize that when you return in the morning your visuals and equipment will be moved, perhaps even discarded.

✔ If you have a flipchart at the training site, create a "welcome to the training" page.

✔ If flipchart pages fall off the wall, you often can remedy by putting more tape on the *wall,* not more on the paper chart.

✔ You can pre-position flipcharts on the wall. Fold the bottom of the chart up to the top to cover the information until you want it. Use masking tape to make a tab in the center of the chart. When you're ready, pull the masking tape tab down to reveal the information on the chart.

✔ All markers are not created equal. Bring your own; do not depend on someone else's markers.

✔ Cap your markers as soon as you're finished writing; don't allow them to lay around without caps and dry out.

✔ Purchase only water-based markers. They won't bleed through paper, and if you drop markers on your clothes, the color washes out.

✔ Use a variety of bullets in front of lists. One that I like to use is an empty shadowed box. As the class finishes discussing each item, I fill in the box or add a checkmark.

✔ Wash the glass on your overhead projector and the cover of the light source for all your projectors. You may be surprised at how few trainers clean their equipment.

✔ Personalize visuals by adding the company's logo. Add yours if you're an independent trainer, too. You can even trace one on flipcharts.

✔ Ensure that your visuals are the highest quality possible.

If you must apologize for any of your visuals, get rid of them.

✔ Most important: Have a backup plan. The greatest cause of problems in training sessions is something to do with the media and/or visuals. Have a backup plan.

Use pictures or charts instead of words whenever possible. Will Rogers stated, "People's minds are changed through observation and not through argument."

Flipchart graphics

Adding graphics to your flipchart assists visual learners, maintains focus, and adds color and fun to the session. The icons in this sidebar get you started replacing words with graphics. Practice with these icons, and then add your own special touch to these or create your own.

 ✔ A star person indicates people and can show connections between individuals or groups and ideas.

✔ Arrows show movement and can indicate progress or connections. Two arrows pointing at each other may depict conflict.

✔ Light bulbs are used to highlight good ideas.

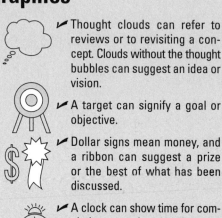 ✔ Thought clouds can refer to reviews or to revisiting a concept. Clouds without the thought bubbles can suggest an idea or vision.

✔ A target can signify a goal or objective.

✔ Dollar signs mean money, and a ribbon can suggest a prize or the best of what has been discussed.

✔ A clock can show time for completing a project or the next steps.

Chapter 11

Training with Style

Chapters 1 through 10 focus on the basics of the training and workplace learning profession: understanding adult-learning theory, understanding the steps of the training cycle, practicing good presentation skills, and selecting and using audiovisuals.

This chapter goes beyond the basics to an intermediate level of training skills and knowledge. It covers several topics to ensure that you're a skilled professional trainer. It presents four training styles so that you can identify your style and use your strengths to the best advantage for each session. This chapter also explores group dynamics and what it takes to create an energizing and exciting environment.

Understanding Your Training Style Strengths

Every trainer brings a unique set of strengths to a training session. The effective trainer recognizes these strengths and builds off of them. To do this, it is helpful to have an understanding of the styles and the behaviors that make up the model.

The more you know about yourself and your training style, the better trainer you will be.

✔ When you know your own style, you recognize your weaknesses and can make an effort to improve them.

✔ Knowing other training styles helps you appreciate aspects of training that are important to all participants, thus getting into everyone's learning comfort zone.

✔ The more you know about training styles, the better role model you are for others.

Even though everyone exhibits characteristics from all style types, everyone has preferences that are ours alone. Ideally, a trainer is balanced among all four styles. However, having a perfect balance is almost nonexistent. Equally as good as a balance is the trainer who is flexible enough to fulfill all roles.

Building the training style model

All trainers have personal preferences that are based on who they are as individuals. It would be a boring world if everyone was the same, whether in food preferences or communication styles. Training style is the same, and some training styles appeal to some learners more than others. Professional trainers adapt their training style to meet the needs of everyone in the classroom.

✔ **The training style foundation:** The trainer style model is based on four dimensions of training: content, process, task, and people. These dimensions can be placed on two scales that, when combined, create a grid displaying four styles.

✔ **Content/process continuum:** Trainers may be either content or process focused, so the horizontal scale is a continuum with content at the left end of the scale and process to the right end of the scale, as presented in Figure 11-1. Each trainer may be anywhere along the continuum, depending on his or her preference.

The *content* is the purpose of the learning experience. A trainer who is more interested in ensuring that the information contained in the course is delivered accurately to the participants is content focused. Trainers work hard at ensuring that content is accurate and that everything has been put before the learner. A trainer who prefers content over process may try to squeeze everything in. A trainer who prefers this end of the continuum may say such things as "information you'll need" and "other resources available include."

Process is the overall flow of a training program and the flow of events within the program. Process includes such activities as facilitating discussion, forming small groups, and moving from one topic to another. A trainer who prefers process over content may forsake content to ensure a great experience for participants. A trainer who prefers this end of the continuum may say such things as "that discussion went well" and "everything is going smoothly."

Which is better? Neither! You need both a content and a process focus in order to have a successful training experience.

✔ **Task/people continuum:** The vertical scale is a continuum with task at the top and people at the bottom, as presented in Figure 11-1. Again, trainers may be anywhere along this continuum depending on their preferences.

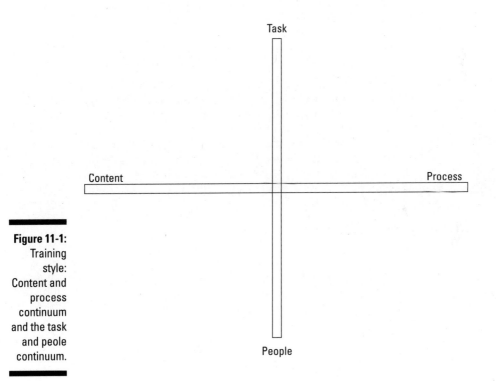

Figure 11-1:
Training style:
Content and process continuum and the task and peole continuum.

The *task* dimension focuses on everything a trainer needs to do to manage a learning environment. The tasks may enable learning such as setting up a simulation, or they may be purely administrative such as record keeping. They may include setup tasks such as rearranging the tables, creating the schedule, and placing materials on the tables. A trainer who prefers tasks over people may forsake discussion or breaks to stay on schedule. Trainers who have a preference for the task end of the continuum may say such things as "I must complete this before" and "we'll need to stop this discussion and move on."

The *people* dimension refers primarily to the participants and may include others related to the training program. Trainers focus on the people when they do such things as modify the program to meet participant needs, encourage introductions and discussions, and schedule timely breaks. A trainer who prefers people over task may not stay on schedule very well and may need to shortchange some topics to "catch up." Trainers who have a preference for the people end of the continuum may say such things as "what do you think about" and "you will probably want to."

Which is better? Neither! You need both a task and a people focus in order to have a successful training experience.

All four dimensions are important for a successful training session. How do you see yourself? Perhaps you relate to one end of the continuum more than the other. Perhaps you believe you are balanced between the two ends. You probably demonstrate characteristics at both ends of the continuum. It simply means that you are able to do all of it.

Think instead about what you "prefer" to do — those things that come naturally to you. This is important because when you're pressed for time or are under stress, you tend to do what comes naturally. It is at these times that trainers need to push themselves to remember to do it all. Most successful trainers can move easily along the continuum depending on the situation. Yet each person does have a preferred spot on the continuum when no one is asking you to be anything but who you are naturally. Spot yourself and your preferences on each of the two continuums.

Exploring the four training styles

When you superimpose one continuum over the other, you create a grid that displays four different training styles as pictured in Figure 11-2. When you combine the content end of the horizontal scale with the task end of the vertical scale, you have a trainer who enjoys delivering content, is organized, and is in control. I call this training style the *presenting style*.

Training Style Preferences

Presenting

Strengths
Delivers interesting presentations
Enjoys being in front of a group
Is a positive center of influence
Is organized and in control
Is comfortable giving information
Is engaging, thinks on his or her feet

Cautions
May not enable or allow participants'
  self-discovery
May have to deal with own ego
May be manipulative or dominating
May be too structured

Guiding

Strengths
States clear expectations and boundaries
Respects participants' active role in learning
May be most appropriate for hard skills
Preempts difficult participants by creating
  ground rules to hold them accountable
Delivers a systematic presentation with a
  logical approach

Cautions
May not be appropriate for soft skills
May be less flexible during the presentation
May not be aware of lagging interest or other
  dynamics
Less ability to "wing it" when mechanicals
  malfunction

Coaching

Strengths
Supports the individual in the process
Motivates and encourages
Heads participants in the right direction
Offers sincere enthusiasm and positive
  attitude
Easily encourages participation
Provides reinforcement naturally

Cautions
May not bring closure to topics or sections
What is taught may not become the
  resource; the coach becomes the
  resource
May not be strong on content details
May lack respect or credibility

Facilitating

Strengths
Encourages active participation
Is a good listener
Tries to be on an equal level with participants
Encourages interaction
Embodies Malcolm Knowles' principles
Draws on and validates experiences

Cautions
May be less focused on content and too
  focused on discussion
May have a short attention span
May not be good with logistics
May lose control and/or lose track of time

Figure 11-2:
Four training
styles.

When you combine the process end of the horizontal scale with the task end of the vertical scale, you have a trainer who states clear expectations, is systematic in presentations, and uses a logical approach. I call this training style the *guiding style*.

When you combine the process end of the horizontal scale with the people end of the vertical scale, you have a trainer who is generally a great listener, encourages discussion among participants, and confirms and reinforces participants. I call this training style the *facilitating style*.

When you combine the content end of the horizontal scale with the people end of the vertical scale, you have a trainer who is motivating, directs participants to the answers, but does not tell them straight out, and who cheers participants on to bigger and greater things. I call this training style the *coaching style*.

Now, before you start reading your personal definitions into the labels for each of these training styles, I am going to caution you to relax. None, let me repeat, *none* of the training styles is any better than any of the others. This information is *only* to help you understand your personal preferences so that you know which areas are your strengths and which areas you need to improve.

In the following bullets, you can explore some of the additional strengths of each of the styles. Also consider cautions for each of the four styles. The cautions are areas that each style needs to be aware of, especially during times of stress.

Presenting style strengths:

- ✔ Delivers interesting presentations
- ✔ Enjoys being in front of a group
- ✔ Is a positive center of influence
- ✔ Is organized and in control
- ✔ Is comfortable delivering information
- ✔ Is engaging, quick-thinking

Presenting style cautions:

- ✔ May not enable or allow participants' self-discovery
- ✔ May have to deal with own ego
- ✔ May be manipulative or dominating
- ✔ May be too structured

Guiding style strengths:

- ✔ States clear expectations and boundaries
- ✔ Respects participants' active role in learning
- ✔ May be more appropriate for hard skills
- ✔ Preempts difficult participants by creating ground rules to hold them accountable
- ✔ Delivers a systematic presentation; takes a logical approach

Guiding style cautions:

✔ May not be appropriate for soft skills

✔ May be less flexible during the presentation

✔ May not be aware of lagging interest or other dynamics

✔ May be less able to "wing it" when mechanicals malfunction

Coaching style strengths:

✔ Supports the individual in the process

✔ Motivates and encourages

✔ Heads participants in the right direction

✔ Offers sincere enthusiasm and a positive attitude

✔ Easily encourages participation

✔ Provides reinforcement naturally

Coaching style cautions:

✔ May not bring closure to topics or sections

✔ What was taught may not become the resource; the coach becomes the resource

✔ May not be strong on content details

✔ May lack respect or credibility

Facilitating style strengths:

✔ Encourages active participation

✔ Is a good listener

✔ Tries to be on an equal level with participants

✔ Encourages interaction

✔ Embodies Malcolm Knowles' principles (see Chapter 2)

✔ Draws on and validates experiences

Facilitating style cautions:

✔ May be less focused on content; too focused on discussion

✔ May have a short attention span

✔ May not be good with logistics

✔ May lose control; may lose track of time

Does one size fit all in training?

by Jean Barbazette

One of the difficult issues trainers and course designers face is to match a lesson to the needs of the learners. Homogeneous audiences make a trainer's task of design and facilitation an easier one. When learners have the same level of experience, interest, and past training, one lesson fits the needs of all the learners. So, what's the best way to design a training session for a diverse audience?

The answer: Design all training using an experiential learning model. Several models with differing numbers of steps have been offered to trainers over many years to teach through simulations. These models include

1. Setting up the learning activity

2. Conducting the learning activity

3. Asking learners to share and interpret their reactions to the activity

4. Identifying what was learned through the activity

5. Planning how to use what was learned

An experiential learning model helps all learners begin from where they are and grow from a shared experience. Because experiential learning actively involves the learner, it is possible to use the same activity with a diverse audience. Granted, some learners will get more out of an activity than others.

Trainers need a range of skills to facilitate each step of the experiential learning model. In Step 1, setting up the learning activity, adult learners become motivated when they understand the benefits or importance of the activity to themselves and their work. To be successful, set up the activity so learners understand what they are going to do and why they are going to do it. A trainer needs to be directive by giving instructions and ground rules for how the learning activity is to be conducted. Setups may also include elements such as the following:

✔ Tell participants about the purpose of the learning activity.

✔ Divide participants into groups and assign roles.

✔ Provide ground rules.

✔ Explain what the participants are going to do.

✔ Tell participants why they are doing the activity without giving away what they will "discover" as a result of engaging in the activity.

In Step 2, a learning activity will be successful when adult learners are involved as much as possible. It is also appropriate to consider how the activity will appeal to the senses of sight, hearing, and touch. This step includes any learning activity, including lecture, discussion, case study, role play, simulation or game, inventory, and independent study and/or reading.

Depending on the activity selected for Step 2, the trainer's style can be anywhere on a continuum from presenting to facilitating.

In Step 3, learners share their reactions to the activity by identifying what happened to them and to others as well as how their own behavior affected others. Often, questions such as these are asked:

✔ "What was your partner's reaction when you did . . . ?"

✔ "What helped or hindered your progress?"

✔ "Summarize the key points from the lecture, role-playing activity, or case study."

Learners in diverse groups learn different things from the same activity. The trainer's role in this step is to facilitate a discussion and ask the learners what happened to them (not what was learned) during the activity.

During Step 4, the trainer again uses a facilitative role and helps learners discover the concept or idea underlying the activity. This is the "So, what did I learn?" step. Questions that develop concepts may include "What did you learn about how to conduct an interview? Discipline a subordinate? Teach a new job?" and so on."

If this step is left out, learning will be incomplete. Certainly, participants will have been entertained by the training activity, but they may not be able to apply new learning to similar situations outside the classroom. Indeed, it is only when concepts are inferred from an activity that adult learners are ready and able to apply them to future situations. Diverse learners can learn different things from the same activity. The trainer's role as a facilitator is to be sure each learner takes away something of value from the activity.

During Step 5, the trainer continues in a facilitative style. This is the "So, what now?" step.

During this process, learners are asked to use and apply new information learned from the activity to their own situations. This step often involves an action question such as "How will you use this questioning technique the next time a subordinate asks you for a favor?" or "In what situations would you be more effective if you used this technique?" Like the preceding four steps, if this step is left out, then learners may not be able to discern the relationship between the learning activity and their job (or situation) and may not be able to see how what was learned can be useful to them in the future. Diverse learners definitely take something different from the lesson because different jobs require different applications. The trainer's role is to be sure enough questions are discussed so application of the concept is possible for all learners.

So does one size fit all in training? A trainer can use the same activity for diverse learners. A skillful trainer uses a variety of styles — presenting, guiding, coaching, and facilitating — to be sure all learners find value in the same activity.

No one style is any better than another, so there is no reason to think that you would want to change your style. It is just who you are, with your strengths and areas that you need to attend to more than others.

Using your training style

Even though you have preferences, that is not an excuse for not improving the areas that need to be improved. All of the dimensions are defined by skills — skills that you can master and abilities that you can acquire.

Take time right now to think about your training style. What are your preferences? Are you balanced in your use of all four dimensions? Or do you have strong preferences? What are your strengths? What areas need improving? What insights have you gained by thinking through this content? What can you do differently as a result of the knowledge you have learned?

Jean Barbazette is one of the few people who addresses training styles in an orderly way. She developed one of the first trainer style inventories in 1996. Although her model is different from the one presented in this book, her philosophy is similar, as presented by her in the "Does one size fit all in training?" sidebar. Jean is president of The Training Clinic, a train-the-trainer company in Seal Beach, California. She has designed and presented train-the-trainer workshops since 1977. The focus of her work in training and development has been to make training programs practical, useful, and concrete. She is also the author of *The Trainer's Support Handbook: A Guide to Managing the Administrative Details of Training* and *Instant Case Studies: How to Design, Adapt, and Use Case Studies in Training*. See the "Does one size fit all in training?" sidebar for more information from Jean.

Gauging Group Dynamics

Group dynamics develop when people interact with one another. The study of group dynamics is a more complex undertaking than space allows me to discuss here. Yet understanding group dynamics is important so that you are aware of why your participants are acting the way they are and how it may affect other participants and ultimately your training session. Therefore, I present here a general overview of the kinds of things that can affect group dynamics. This section barely scratches the surface of what many know about the topic.

Numerous elements can affect group dynamics, such as the composition of the group, the atmosphere, the norms under which the individuals operate, the values of the individuals and the group, the communication and participation among the group, the roles that participants play, and the power and influence that exists and is exuded within the group. The following sections examine some of these.

Composition

Composition refers to a number of things. The size of the group may have more effect on team dynamics than anything else. If the group is too large, you may have difficulty in keeping everyone's attention and balancing participation.

Consider the reasons participants are attending the training. Very different dynamics occur when participants believe that they have a choice about attending the training than if they believe they were sent against their will.

The feelings participants have about each other is another composition aspect that can affect the group dynamics. Do they like the other people in the training session? Do all the departments respect each other? Previous as well as current work relationships with each other can affect the dynamics as well.

The formation of subgroups affects group dynamics, too. Consider this as you prepare for your session. And you may prepare for the exact opposite, depending upon the situation. For example, if you are teaching team skills, you may want subgroups to form. In that case, you can create opportunities to strengthen these teams. At other times, you may need to find ways to break up cliques and get the already formed subgroups to split up and work with other participants.

Atmosphere

Begin to examine the dynamics caused by the atmosphere by looking toward the physical setting. Is the room spacious? too spacious? crowded? Is the lighting bright? dim? natural? Are the tables spacious? crowded? Are the chairs comfortable? hard? Is the temperature comfortable? too hot? too cold? Can you control it? It doesn't matter how great your training session is. If the participants are not comfortable, I guarantee it will affect group dynamics negatively.

How formal is the training session? Is the timeline flexible enough to accommodate participants' needs and requests? If it isn't, you may influence group dynamics in a positive way by determining how you can build in time for unique participant needs.

The level of interest participants have in the subject affect group dynamics. The amount of laughter you hear is an indicator of how much fun participants are having. Paired with how interested participants are in the content, both affect the dynamics.

How congenial people are to each other, how participants express themselves, and how well they accept others and the session are other aspects of the atmosphere that may have either a negative or positive effect on group dynamics.

Norms

When people think about group dynamics, they often think first of norms. *Norms* are what people have grown to expect of each other and the rest of the group. Included in norms are attendance and punctuality expectations. Is it common to show up five or ten minutes late and still be counted as timely? Is that true for some of the group or all members of the group? Is everyone expected to attend fully? How about phone calls? Can participants leave to return messages? Each of these affects group dynamics — especially if everyone in the session operates under a different set of norms.

The amount and type of participation that is acceptable is a part of the organizational norms. Trainers sometimes stretch individuals, encouraging them to be more participative than they normally would be. That is generally seen as good. Take care that you do not stretch them too much. For example, don't expect engineers to enjoy role plays. This is one of the reasons to find out all you can about participants before the training session.

The topics of the training session may affect the group dynamics, but interestingly, the topics that are *avoided* may also affect the group dynamics. If participants are listening to content that they believe is good but not displayed within the organization, they may feel the training is a sham. Having an opportunity to express what they are thinking may help the group dynamics.

The norms that individuals operate under when working with the rest of the group are also important. For example, do they treat each other with respect? Do they cooperate during tasks? Are some more competitive than others? Is information shared willingly or withheld? Each of these affects the small-group exercises in the training session.

Values

The values that individuals bring to the session affect the group dynamics. Ideally, individual, group, and organizational values are the same. When this is not true, however, it can affect the interaction negatively. You may see some people stop interacting if certain beliefs are brought up. The direction the group wants to take as a result of differences in values can be a positive experience. In most cases, it is wise to allow a discussion of the differences to take place. Unfortunately, it is sometimes difficult to bring closure to these discussions.

Another way values can affect the dynamics of a group is if hidden agendas exist in the group. It may take a while, but, generally, hidden agendas are uncovered by the behaviors that are observed or the comments that are made. By the way, hidden agendas do not always need to represent a "bad" objective. However, a lack of openness may lead to distrust among the group.

Communication and participation

As a trainer, you have a role in displaying good communication and encouraging participation. Participants bring their skills and beliefs into the training session, and this affects the group dynamics. The degree to which some participants want to be involved may be different from others. This may affect large-group discussions as well as small-group activities. The communication and participation aspect of group dynamics is one area over which the trainer has the most control.

Group dynamics are affected by many things that you do as a trainer. For example, how you handle disagreements and conflicts is observed by participants. The factors that contribute to the misunderstanding also affect group dynamics. How you address challenges and how you deal with interruptions affect the level of trust and respect participants have for you.

Participants observe how silent members are treated. Are they brought into the discussion slowly, respecting their personal needs? Or are they forced to participate before they are comfortable? Or are they ignored?

Listening skills of both the trainer and the participants affect the group dynamics. Participants may have a hard time respecting a trainer who is not a good listener.

Roles

The roles participants play affect the team dynamics. Roles are frequently divided into task and maintenance behaviors. Individuals play these roles naturally.

✔ *Task roles* are those things that individuals do to get the job completed. Task roles supply the information, ideas, and energy necessary for the group to accomplish its objectives. These roles get things started and may include asking for information or opinions, clarifying comments, sharing facts or ideas, or suggesting solutions or methods. Task roles may also help to organize by coordinating or clarifying relationships, comparing concepts, defining positions, or summarizing what has happened. Task roles may also focus on action-type events by offering suggestions, prodding the group to take action, or simply keeping the group on task.

✔ *Maintenance roles* are behaviors that are completed that ensure a positive atmosphere. Maintenance roles establish and maintain interpersonal relationships and a pleasant atmosphere. They are generally focused on people and the atmosphere. Individuals may play roles to mediate differences or referee disagreements. These roles include searching for common elements in conflicts or offering a compromise. Maintenance roles also include motivators who offer praise of and support to others. Maintenance roles include finding the humor in a situation and bringing in participants who otherwise may not speak. Maintenance roles encourage participation, build trust, and relieve tension in a group.

Power and influence

Power and influence are potentially one of the most problematic areas of group dynamics to a trainer. Power is often described as coming from three sources:

positional power, informational power, or charismatic power. Each of these three has the potential to affect group dynamics — either positively or negatively. Individuals do not like to feel powerless. Therefore, how individuals use power determines how it affects the dynamics of the group. Using power to lead positively or to contribute appropriately will enhance group dynamics. On the other hand, flaunting power or using it negatively can be destructive.

Individuals who have reporting relationships are often a dilemma for trainers. It may be uncomfortable for a participant to be in a session with the boss present. The subordinate may not feel comfortable contributing during the session.

Rivalry between departments or individuals may also cause group dynamics problems for a trainer. If individuals do not get along outside a training session, the situation can be exacerbated by forcing them to sit in the same room and interact during a training session.

Many things can affect group dynamics during a training session. A good trainer learns as much as possible about the participants and prepares for anything that may cause a disruption. On the positive side, a trainer's knowledge of the participants may also be used to enhance the training session.

Trainers need to be proactive about managing groups and the group dynamics. Should subgroups remain the same for key projects? Or is it better if they change? How do you determine whether the large group is mixing and mingling enough? What do you do to include everyone but not impose on those who prefer to participate by listening? What do you do when you sense tension? How do you deal with someone who may be using power inappropriately? Each of these affects group dynamics and how you address each affects it also.

This section alerts you to some of the most common aspects of group dynamics. Awareness is the first step: Observe your participants. When you address various aspects, be sure to note what happens. Later, determine why. You may even want to discuss what occurred with another trainer. People being who they are, it is impossible to identify every situation you may encounter. However, your experiences and what you learn from them will equip you to handle future group-dynamics situations.

Creating an Energizing, Exciting, Encouraging Environment

You always want to establish an environment that's conducive to learning. However, there are times (most times) when you want to go beyond the basics to create an energizing or exciting and encouraging environment. How do you do that? You can add energy and excitement to a training session with a little extra planning. Here are some suggestions.

Coloring outside the lines

Remember that old joke "What's black and white and red all over?" As I recall there were a couple of right answers: a newspaper and an embarrassed zebra. As a trainer, you need to ensure that you're looking outside the lines — the black-and-white lines — of training and encouraging the colorful, creative world of training.

This book touches on the topic of color a couple of times when I explore media and visuals. One of the advantages of using visuals is that you can add color. However, you can add color in other ways as well.

TIP

If you experiment with various colors on visuals, check them out from the back of the room to ensure readability.

Color affects everyone, and each color is associated with specific emotions. Marketing folks have depended on color for years to encourage you to purchase one product over another. Trainers can use color to

✔ Excite and stimulate participants' senses

✔ Encourage participants to get involved in activities

✔ Energize participants to learn and apply the knowledge and skills they learn

Consider some of the emotions associated with specific colors, as shown in Table 11-1.

Table 11-1	Color Associations
Color	*Using Color to Evoke Emotions and Energize*
Red	Red says, "Pay attention!" It evokes power, anger, achievement, excitement, and intensity. It tells us to stop. It may send a negative message due to financial shortages. Red should be reserved for highlighting, circling hot spots, or trouble. It can indicate tension or stressful areas also.
Yellow	Evokes happiness, cheerfulness, and warmth. While it can be mellow and indicate optimism, it can also suggest caution. Although it stimulates thinking, it is impossible to see on its own, so use it to fill within the lines. Use it to find ideas and to support creativity.

(continued)

Table 11-1 *(continued)*

Color	Using Color to Evoke Emotions and Energize
Blue	Blue creates a feeling of reliability, trust, maturity, authority, peace, and tranquility. Dark blue projects a masculine image, while light blue projects youth. Use blue early in a session to establish trust.
Green	Indicates productivity, growth, youth, and health. Instills a positive image and forward motion, "go." Suggests money or prosperity. Use green branches on a tree to suggest strength or growth. Light green is energizing, but dark green is easier to read. Use it when reaching consensus or finding compromises.
Orange	Stimulates energy, enthusiasm, and positive thinking. This lively color works best for highlighting, but it may be difficult to read in rooms with fluorescent lighting. Use to highlight a subject or create connections.
Purple	Projects assertiveness, boldness, passion, and power. May be used to signify royalty, richness, or spirituality. Works well with other colors and stimulates ideas during brainstorming.
White	Usually indicates cleanliness, honesty, innocence, or goodness. White space provides visual rest. Use white space to assist with clarity and order.
Black	Creates feelings of independence and solidarity. As opposed to red, suggests financial solvency. Has a serious side by representing death, somberness, or gravity of a situation. Easiest of all colors to read by everyone. Usually highlight with a bright color. Because it means finality, it is not the best color to use when brainstorming.
Brown	Indicates strength, support, solidly earthy, and a lack of superiority. It may affect some folks negatively. This is an easy-to-read color but may be depressing or drab on its own.
Pink	Light pink indicates femininity and fun. It is upbeat and youthful. Bright pink creates excitement and passion. Combines well with other colors and may be a good wake-up color after lunch.
Gold/silver	These prestigious hues project elegance and an image of status. May also suggest riches.

So how can you use color in your training? Here are a few ways I add color:

✔ Place brightly colored sticky notes in front of participants, so that the notes are available for them to jot a note or to mark something in their participant materials.

✔ Use colored paper for specific activities. For example, I have a page of creativity techniques that has a light bulb in the background that I copy on bright yellow paper. In another training session, I conduct a killer-phrases exercise, where the participants list killer phrases on red paper and end up wadding up their pages and throwing them.

✔ Place a variety of brightly colored sheets of paper in the center of tables for use with small-group activities that require blank paper.

✔ Place crayons or colored pencils on the tables and ask participants to complete certain activities using them. A favorite is to use them to decorate their name tents.

✔ Hang posters that are related to your training session around the room. They may also be posters that encourage thinking positively, that deliver a message, or provide a quote.

✔ When voting on positive and/or negative issues, you can use sticky flags on a wall poster. For example, use a green flag to vote for the characteristic that our team is best at and a red flag to vote for the characteristic that our team needs to improve the most.

✔ Instead of dark on light, surprise your participants and have them write light on dark. Use white, silver, or gold marking pens and dark paper in red, green, and even navy blue. These items are easy to find in your local office supply store.

Don't use colors willy-nilly. Think through how you will use them. For example, colors can be a great way to transition from one module to another. Use highlighting to assist learners to note the key areas. Think about which color combinations work best. Use brighter colors to infuse energy after lunch.

Energizing the group

Many of the ideas discussed in this book energize participants:

✔ Obtaining participation

✔ Conducting learner-centered activities

✔ Varying activities

✔ Creating an active learning environment

✔ Celebrating success

✔ Being enthusiastic yourself

All of these are important, but sometimes you need just a bit more. If you see energy waning or enthusiasm wavering, it may be time to move people around the room in the form of an energizer.

How to determine whether you need an energizer

How do you know whether you need an energizer? There are lots of ways to tell. Try these for starters.

✔ Participants agree with everything you say.

✔ Participants are sharing the scented markers.

✔ The most interested contributors are reading ahead.

✔ The doodlers are creating works of art.

✔ Someone's head thumps on the table, and he or she does not awaken.

✔ Twenty-five percent of the group has left the room and the rest are wiggling.

✔ Seventy-five percent of the group is watching the fly circling the doughnuts.

✔ Magazines have been pulled out of backpacks.

✔ Participants are entertained by their watches' second hand.

Yes, this is a tongue-in-cheek list. Don't wait until these things are happening. Attend to both participants and the time so that you will sense a break or an energizer is needed.

Purpose of energizers

Energizers are used to change the mental and/or physical state of participants. They may be used to change the pace of a program; for example, if the session is bogged down in heavy discussion, you can use an energizer to speed up the pace. Or the opposite, you may be able to use an energizer to provide quiet personal reflection after an energetic group activity. Energizers are great to use if participants have been sitting for a while and need to get up and move about.

Energizers are useful in many ways:

✔ Change the pace of the session

✔ Revive the energy of a group when it is lagging

✔ Create a transition from one topic to another

✔ Provide movement for kinesthetic learners

✔ Subtly break up subgroups that may have formed

✔ Give everyone a break from listening or sitting for a long period of time

Selecting energizers

Use the same common sense for selecting an energizer that you would when selecting an icebreaker. Numerous books have been written about energizers, and sometimes you can adjust an icebreaker to be an appropriate energizer.

✔ Consider the participants' expectations.

✔ Consider the size of the group.

✔ Place the energizer at the appropriate time.

✔ Have a clear purpose for selecting and scheduling the energizer.

✔ Initiate appropriate risk, ensuring that it is comfortable for everyone.

Energizer examples

So what does an energizer look like? This list displays the wide range.

✔ Participants find "their mate" based on anything from clothing to birthday to someone they don't know. Once there, a task is assigned.

✔ Teams race to complete a puzzle, word game, or "test" related to the content.

✔ Participants write one thing they have learned on a sheet of paper and then turn it into a paper airplane. Fly the planes, and whomever it goes to reads the item on the plane.

✔ Hold a relay race or ball toss to review content.

✔ Participants select toys, tools, office supplies, or anything as a metaphor related to the content or to their opinions about the session.

✔ Led by you, participants stretch, relax, deep breathe, or do "shake out" exercises.

✔ Use music: Sing rounds, make up songs, hand out kazoos, or hum.

For variation, hum using the sounds of various vowels: a, e, i, o, u.

✔ Sometimes, just a regular break serves as a great energizer.

Any of the preceding can be used to energize your group. Experiment with various energizers. You will soon have your own repertoire of energizers.

The Internet opens a whole world of energizers. Search for books from publishers such as American Society for Training and Development (ASTD), Bowperson Publishing, Gulf Publishing, HRD Press, Lakewood Publications, McGraw-Hill, and Pfeiffer/Jossey-Bass.

Let me entertrain you!

Humor can be the best thing for a training session — or the worst. Especially if it falls flat. A few guidelines will help you to successfully interject humor into your training session. My friend Jeanne builds humor into her presentations in a very natural way. She even calls herself an *entertrainer* and believes that humor adds a great deal to training. What are some of the advantages of adding humor to a training session?

✔ Can be used to get participants' attention

✔ Keeps participants interested in content

✔ Clarifies a point

✔ Ensures that key points are memorable

✔ Creates a relaxed atmosphere

✔ Builds a positive relationship between you and your participants

✔ Can ease the way through difficult content

Laughing while they learn

Notice that I have not mentioned telling jokes. Some people are good at telling jokes; some are not. If you are in the second category, don't bother. Keep your humor natural and relevant to the content. Know your participants and what will be funny to them.

Being natural is best: Humor should fit naturally into the content. Relevance is more important than humor. Do not tell a story or joke that is not related to the content.

Keep a funny file. Build your own list of humorous stories. Keep a file with stories you may use, examples of things that happened to you, jokes, cartoons, and funny quotes. Look for visuals as well. Your file will fill with experiences.

Keep it clean. I shouldn't have to address this, but I will just to be certain. Humor should not use offensive language. Race, religion, sex, stereotypes, and politics are off limits.

What if you don't get a laugh? You have two choices. You can ignore it and move quickly into content, or you can try again with a quip such as "That's the last time I try out my material on a group of trainers" or "That's the last time I ask (name of one of the participants) for new material." Sometimes, you can pick up these one-liners watching stand-up comedians on television.

You may wish to check out Chapter 22 for ten ways to add humor to your training. Many of the ideas are based on things that happen naturally in a training session.

You ought to be in show business

Participants want to have fun. Now how can trainers create their own material? Write your story in a conversational tone. Keep it short. Practice it out loud. Try it out on someone or two. Rewrite it to clarify or simplify. Make sure the words and timing are right. Be sure your punch line is clear, concise, and of course — funny!

Customize your joke for your audience. It is guaranteed to get a laugh! You can customize it using names of the people in the organization, competitors of the organization, or the location of your training. For example, the age-old joke "I'm afraid to fly. It's not the plane, it's the drive to the airport," can be customized for the location. If you are in Washington, D.C., you could say, "I'm afraid to fly. It's not the plane, it's the drive to Reagan National!"

Celebrating success

Remember when you were a kid and your family celebrated all those little accomplishments, like the first time you rode a bike or taking a blue ribbon at the science fair? Well, adults like to celebrate success, too. Another way to create an energizing, exciting, enthusiastic environment is to celebrate participants' success.

Use rewards and reinforcement to celebrate success. Trainers use intrinsic rewards such as thank yous, feedback on performance, and other verbal recognition. Trainers also use tangible rewards, such as candy, gum, small team prizes, and individual doodads. Or break out a special prize for everyone (a big bag of candy-coated chocolate).

Check out sources for inexpensive (some as low as a dime each) doodads. Oriental Trading, at www.orientaltrading.com, is a favorite for toys, holiday items, puzzles, key chains, hats, and more things than you ever thought existed. While it is fun to check its Web site, it's even more fun to get on its mailing list and have its monthly catalog delivered to your door!

Reinforce what participants learn throughout the training. You could try some of these or make up your own.

- ✔ Participants write on flipchart pages posted on the wall.
- ✔ Participants complete a crossword puzzle format or word search.
- ✔ Participants stand in a circle, toss a ball, and state one thing each learned.
- ✔ Participants write a memo to their supervisors.
- ✔ Participants write a memo to themselves that the trainer mails later.
- ✔ Review key concepts using a game-show format such as *Jeopardy!*

All of these work to enhance and celebrate learning.

Celebrate success at the end of the session as well. Certificates are an inexpensive reward, as is reenacting a graduation ceremony playing "Pomp and Circumstance" or playing any engaging or celebratory tune that brings closure such as "Happy Trails" or "Goodbye, So Long, Farewell." Bob Lucas, trainer extraordinaire, likes to read from Dr. Seuss's book, *Oh, the Places You'll Go!* The book's message is about achievement and reaching goals.

If you use music in your training session, be sure to get copyright permission from BMI or ASCAP.

Putting It All Together

Many concepts have been presented in this chapter. Can you really do it all? Should you try? Well, that's a trick question. You shouldn't "try" to do anything. You absorb this information and use it when appropriate. Everything presented in this chapter sets a stage for you to add energy, excitement, and encouragement to your sessions. Knowing your training style is the first step to understanding what you will feel comfortable doing.

Training with style means not only ensuring that you get the job done but that you get the job done right — and ensure that you and the participants enjoy everything along the way. You will learn more. Your participants will learn more.

Or, as Plato stated, "You can discover more about a person in an hour of play than in a year of conversation."

Chapter 12

Addressing Problems: What's a Trainer to Do?

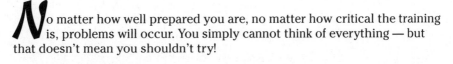

In This Chapter

▶ Preventing training problems

▶ Dealing with unexpected training problems

▶ Managing disruptive participants

▶ Mastering your presentation anxiety

*N*o matter how well prepared you are, no matter how critical the training is, problems will occur. You simply cannot think of everything — but that doesn't mean you shouldn't try!

It's not the disaster that matters; it's how you manage the disaster that counts. Your participants will be watching you as a role model, because they may someday be in the same situation.

In this chapter, I introduce you to the COOL technique to manage any disasters that may come your way. Staying COOL makes you appear to be the pro that you are. Most trainers have experienced these problems at one time or another — that's how you know what works best! Your main problems are likely to involve inadequate training facilities, disruptive participants, and your own attack of nerves. What follows is a primer of problems, with the tools you need to cut them off early without losing a beat.

Problems in the Classroom

A host of problems may occur during training. Just when you think you have encountered almost anything that could happen, a new problem will be tossed in your path.

Problems with logistics

Logistics can create big headaches for trainers. Chapter 7 provides guidance for how to prepare and prevent many logistical nightmares from occurring. Here are a few others.

Rooms not conducive to training

You may find yourself conducting training in a room that was never intended to be used for that purpose. You may be in a boardroom with a large table and no room to divide into small groups. You may find a large pillar in the center of the room. You may be in a room that is so filled with furniture there is little space for your participants. You may even find that you have no room at all. I once found myself relegated to the end of a hallway to conduct a training because the carpeting in the training room was being torn out as I arrived!

In any of these cases, if you do not find out until 60 minutes before the session starts, it is most likely too late to do anything about it. You should at least ask whether there is a different room available or that could be available at the next break or lunch. If nothing is available, you need to do a quick shuffle in the design and make the most of it. Check for space outside the room for breakout groups.

Furniture not conducive to training

It may not seem like your job, but ensuring that participants have comfortable chairs and tables that don't fall down is your responsibility. You can tell the second you walk into the room whether the chairs will be comfortable or not. You may even find that the participants will need to squeeze into one-piece desks like those you used in high school.

You probably want to look for other space for breakout sessions. On these occasions I've even taken participants outside to sit on picnic tables for small-group activities. Participants appreciate even the smallest things you do to provide additional comfort.

Logistics problems

Preparation is key to preventing logistics problems. You certainly will never be able to think of everything, but the more you plan ahead, the fewer problems you will have. Learn from each experience. Begin to create a generic preparation checklist of items to help you remember what questions to ask, whom to ask, and when.

Equipment problems

Nothing can be as frustrating as equipment problems. If something critical is going to go wrong, equipment is the area that will take you down.

What can go wrong?

What can possibly go wrong? Try this for a comedy of errors. The address given the trainer was for 1423 East Oak, but the church was on West Oak. It didn't matter anyway because when she finally arrived, the door was locked and she couldn't get in. She had the director's name and cellphone number, but the director was an hour away and participants started to arrive before anyone could get into the building. Just before the director arrived another trainer showed up who had a key. Unfortunately, this trainer believed that he was assigned the same training room. In fact, they were double booked.

Another room in the basement of the old church was available. Although the trainer was just over five feet tall, she had to duck to miss some of the overhead pipes. Participants jumped in to help her set up and carry her boxes of supplies. When she tried to plug the overhead projector into an outlet, she found that the three-pronged plug would not fit in the archaic, two-holed electrical receptacle. She broke the third prong off to accommodate the electrical requirement.

When the training session started, the overhead pipes began to perspire and drip on the participants' materials, the overhead projector transparencies, and the trainer. The trainer learned that the participants were unaware of why they were attending the training and thought that it was some sort of punishment. The air conditioning kicked in as soon as it was turned on but quickly blew a fuse, and no one knew how to replace it. The receptionist who was supposed to have opened the church never arrived. Therefore, the phone in the room next to the training room rang every few minutes with no one to answer it.

By the way, the good news was that the trainer's suitcase, which was temporarily "lost" by the airline, was delivered just before she left to go to her hotel for the evening.

Yes, this happened to me when I first started training. The funniest thing about the situation is that the participants said it was the best training they had ever attended.

What could occur?

Almost anything can go wrong with equipment, starting with it simply not showing up: Someone forgot, it was delivered to the wrong room, or perhaps it is simply not available.

With overhead projectors, the worst thing that can happen is that the bulb may burn out. The flipchart pad may be filled with used paper. You may not have enough copies of the handouts for participants. Perhaps someone did not count correctly. Perhaps more participants showed up than you anticipated.

Prevent these problems

Some problems with equipment can be prevented. Others cannot. But that doesn't mean that you shouldn't try to prevent them from occurring.

Always double-check on your equipment needs. Order it at least a month in advance, follow up one week before your session, and, finally, call the day before to confirm date, time, location, and type of equipment.

I obtain the name and office and cellphone or pager number of the person who is responsible for setting up the equipment. This has come in handy more often than I can count.

When you arrive at your room, check the equipment first. Make sure it all works, turns on, and has a spare bulb and that the cords are taped down. Check to make sure that the flipchart pad is filled with unused paper. If at all possible, have the equipment delivered to your room and set it up the day or night before your session.

And when you can't prevent equipment problems . . .

When problems occur anyway (and they will), you can do two things. First, have a backup plan, and second, keep your cool and follow a specific process.

✔ **Have a backup plan.** It is almost certain that your equipment will fail at just the moment your presentation is dependent on your visuals. If you're prepared to deliver your presentation without the visuals, all will not be lost. If using slides, have a hard copy so that participants can see on paper what they would have seen on a screen. I always have a flipchart in the room. It is available for sketching diagrams, creating lists, highlighting key points, or getting your participants involved in the presentation.

Remember, you will now be the focal point of your presentation, and all eyes will be on you, so you need to attend to your presentation skills: good eye contact, animated gestures, planned body movement, and confident stance. You may also need to use more descriptive language, add more examples, and paint a verbal picture for your participants that they would have otherwise observed visually.

✔ **Follow a specific process.** Know what to try and in what order to try it. Almost everyone uses an LCD projector and laptop computer. If this equipment malfunctions, ask these questions:

- Is everything plugged in and turned on? Be sure to check extension cords, too.

- Are all the cables firmly connected to the correct input or output ports?

- Are the projector and your laptop set up properly? Be sure that your laptop is selected as the source and that the projector is not in the standby mode.

- Has your laptop been set to display through the external video port? Every laptop computer has multiple display modes and a utility that allows you to toggle among these modes. When toggling between modes, allow at least 15 seconds for the setting to change before trying another mode.

- Have you tried to reset the equipment? Sometimes, simply shutting everything down and turning it back on works.

> • Have you used your laptop with this type of projector in the past? Some computers are not compatible with some projectors. Although it is rare, it has happened to me.
>
> ✔ **Be positive.** If your equipment failure occurs in front of participants, don't complain about the equipment or the situation. Offer a brief apology, take no more than four minutes to fix it, and move on. You may wish to call a short break, but don't allow your participants to sit and watch you pull, poke, and prod your equipment.
>
> Yes, equipment can be one of the most frustrating problems a trainer may face. But if you're prepared, it doesn't have to throw you off center. Always learn something from the experience. If you were unable to fix the problem, try to fix it after your participants leave. You may wish to consult with the audiovisual technician. Know how to fix the problem. If it happened once, it is likely that it will happen again.

Difficult personal situations

Sometimes, things happen to you that create problems. In many cases, it won't seem like a big deal the next day, but that doesn't help when you're in the middle of it. What may happen and what could you do?

You forget what you were going to say

Many trainers are afraid of going brain dead in front of the participants. It happens to everyone during daily conversations with others. However, when it occurs in front of participants, it may be more uncomfortable. You may wish to adapt some of these techniques to your style.

> ✔ **Admit that you forgot, just as you would in a typical daily conversation.** Continue on and return to the point when you remember it.
>
> ✔ **Take a sip of water that you have at your table.** Often, the 30-second pause will be enough time to recall your train of thought.
>
> ✔ **Try to fill in by repeating the last point in a different way or giving an example.** Like the sip of water, it will give you a couple of seconds of thinking time.
>
> ✔ **Refer to your notes.** Ensure that your notes work for you: You have the information on them that you need, and you have it displayed in a way that you can find what you need.
>
> ✔ **If it is not obvious, shift the attention back to the participants.** Ask them what questions they have at this point. Because no one knows exactly what you were going to do or say, it is highly unlikely that anyone will notice the shift.
>
> ✔ **Have a standard phrase that you will use,** such as, "I lost my train of thought. Perhaps one of you can find it" or "I just went brain dead. Do any of you remember what I was going to say?"

You do not feel well

Unfortunately, there is not much you can do about feeling under the weather. The show must go on, and as a trainer, you rarely have someone to back you up. Certainly, if you have something contagious or if you're so ill that you will be unable to facilitate the session, you may need to cancel. It is difficult to cancel a training session because so many other people are counting on you. At times, others may have traveled hundreds of miles for the training event.

If you do not feel well and you're going to continue to conduct the training, consider these suggestions.

- ✔ Don't tell the participants you're not feeling well, or if you do, don't make a big deal out of it. You may get sympathy, but is that what you want?

- ✔ Shift the session to put more emphasis on participant involvement and activities. You will most likely have participants who have experience and expertise related to the topic. Ask them to assist with delivering information, or leading a discussion.

It is never any fun to work when you do not feel well. Being a trainer is one of those professions, however, that allows little flexibility when illness occurs.

You get off track

It is so easy to get off track. Thousands of detours cross your path. Sometimes, participants may take you off track with a question. At other times, you may take yourself off track because you tell a story or you add information that is nice to know.

As soon as you recognize that you're off track, steer the group back. Try these techniques to help you.

- ✔ Try to connect what you're saying to where you should be.

- ✔ Humor may work. Wrap up the topic quickly and say something like, "My, that was a distracting little detour!"

- ✔ If it is difficult to get back on track, take a break.

You're new to the job

Everyone has to start somewhere. Being new to training is not something, however, that you need to announce to the group. Imagine that you were getting on a flight from San Francisco to Frankfurt. You probably do not want the pilot to announce that this is her first flight. Likewise, you do not need to announce that this is your first training session.

In fact, you should never need to make excuses. Using the phrase "bear with me" makes participants feel as if they are putting up with something that is uncalled for. Don't use it. "Bear with me, this is my first training!" may establish a hesitancy from participants right from the start.

Difficult group situation

Sometimes, it may seem that the entire group is creating a problem — and it could be true.

Why might this occur?

Participants' style may not be a match for the training design. For example, if the design calls for a great deal of participation and the audience is made up of analytical styles, you may not get the level of discussion and involvement that is required.

The group may also be preoccupied by other thoughts. For example, if you're training them to learn how to improve processes or make change of any kind, and they know that the company needs to become more efficient, they may be concerned about whether downsizing may occur and how it may affect them. They may also be preoccupied with less threatening thoughts; for example, when training is held to support a change, everyone may feel overwhelmed with the additional work required after the change is implemented. At other times, they may simply be concerned with the work that is piling up on their desks while they are attending the training.

Participants may have never been told why they are attending training. They may think that it is punishment because they are not doing their jobs well enough. Participants need to understand how the training affects performance and the vision and mission of the organization, as well as what's in it for them.

It is impossible to identify all the reasons an entire group may be causing difficulty. Techniques exist that help to prevent these problems and to address them when they do occur.

Preventing these problems

You may be able to prevent some of these problems.

- ✔ Focus on participants' needs during the design.
- ✔ Know as much as possible about the participants who will attend the training session, including such things as their communication style, their attitude toward training, what changes may be going on in their workplace, whether they are all at the same level, and why they think they are attending the training session. You may want to ask what expectations participants are bringing with them to the session or what professional issues participants may be dealing with.
- ✔ Refer to the needs assessment to give you insight about why the training is being held.
- ✔ Interview participants prior to the training session to identify concerns and how you will approach them.

> ✔ Be certain that the problem isn't one that you created. For example, you may not have clearly stated how the training is related to the participants — what's in it for them. You may not have established your credibility. Or you may not be providing enough breaks.

If you encounter a difficult group, unexpectedly, it is almost always best to address the issue as soon as you're sure. How can you do this?

You may wish to probe a few participants during the first break with "The group seems reluctant to speak up" or "Everyone seems preoccupied, is something happening that I should know?"

You may also just stop the training session and admit that something seems amiss and address it with the group. When I do this, I usually make some dramatic shift that says "We have changed focus." I may pull up a chair in the middle of the room and sit down and begin a discussion. After a hostile or negative statement, I may take a very long pause, cap my pen, and close my facilitator's guide, and say, "Okay, we need to talk." How do I open the discussion? I state the behaviors I have observed and then say something like "It seems to me that we need to address the cause of these behaviors before we can be successful with this training." I then pause and wait for someone to speak up. At some point I may list the issues on a flipchart page to prevent people from repeating what has already been stated.

If you have a group that is not responding to you or the content of the training, it is best to address it as soon as possible. If you do not, you will probably just be wasting time — yours and the participants.

Note: Sometimes, it may seem as if you have a problem group on your hands when in reality only a few individuals may be causing the problem. Managing individual participants who may make the training difficult is addressed in the "Managing disruptive types" section later in this chapter.

If training is not the solution

Even though you have conducted a needs assessment and the organization has determined that training is required, you may find that training really is not the solution. There is probably little you can do on the spot except to ensure that you create a meaningful experience for the participants. In many cases, you may not change the agenda much, but you may refocus the discussion to topics that provide more usable information.

I was hired many years ago to conduct a Communications Training. I found a group of 20 men who would not speak up, were angry, and obviously did not want to be there. After the introduction module, I quickly called a break and discovered that all of these people had been slated for a downsizing and the training in communication skills was a part of development for outplacement.

No one had told me. After the break, we identified some of the issues they were facing, and I adjusted the communication training material, making it as meaningful and useful as I could.

Using a process similar to the one in the "A ten-step solution when training is not" sidebar, I uncovered what communication skills they thought they would need given the situation. I adjusted the program accordingly and salvaged what was going to be a worthless day for the participants.

A ten-step solution when training is not

If you're facing a situation where training isn't the solution or perhaps the training isn't focused on the right topic, you can follow these steps to make the best of the situation.

- ✔ Call a timeout. Put the program agenda on hold because the participants are probably not ready to hear or use the information anyway.

- ✔ Summarize your understanding of the range of viewpoints you've heard expressed.

- ✔ Use a flipchart and ask participants to help you list all the reasons the program is meaningless (or whatever else their key issue is). Allow enough time for them to list all the reasons they can think of. Post all the responses on a wall.

- ✔ Explain that if they take a look at their list, they may notice that some of their issues are controllable and some are not. Ask for a few examples about any of the items they believe are out of their control. Allow sufficient "ventilation" time.

- ✔ Acknowledge that when situations are out of someone's control, there's nothing that can be done to change those situations — for the moment. Explain that the best opportunity for change starts by focusing on what's controllable. Give an example based on one of the items posted on the wall and ask for agreement.

- ✔ Say something like "So here's the challenge: Look over your list, and let's try to come up with a new list — a list of what you have control over." The group may be slow to start. Don't panic; hang in there and restate the question. When they catch on that you're serious and will stay with the question until it's been answered, you will get responses.

- ✔ Record their ideas on flipchart paper and encourage input with "Good. How about another one?" As their energy starts to ebb, congratulate them for putting together a great list. Explain that you will give them a break now, and when they come back you'd like them to think about how to apply the balance of the program information they'll be receiving in terms of what's controllable. Check for agreement.

- ✔ Tell them that you're going to remove the obstacles currently posted on the wall and replace them with the flipchart listing what the group believes is controllable. Do so. Use the break to rethink what you will cover and how you will cover it during the rest of the time allocated for the program.

- ✔ When participants return from break, explain that it was important to make time to discuss their concerns. Describe your plan for how to proceed and get agreement. Check in with participants toward the end of the session or during another appropriate time to learn their current thinking.

- ✔ Privately congratulate yourself.

Taking a COOL approach

You may have done everything that has been suggested so far in this chapter, and something may still go wrong. If something happens when you least expect it, you need to be prepared to think on your feet. I suggest you use a COOL approach.

Calm down immediately

Although it is difficult to do, the first step is to remain calm. Take a deep breath, focus on the situation, and determine the root cause. After the oxygen hits your brain, you're better able to determine what to do next.

Open yourself to all the options

When something goes wrong, a can-do attitude may get you into trouble because you want to charge right in and "fix it." There is no one right answer to any problem, so be open to all possibilities. If others are with you (participants or another trainer), ask for their ideas. Do a quick pros and cons assessment of all the alternatives in your mind and select one option.

Optimistically implement your options

After you have selected the solution, move forward optimistically knowing that you have chosen the best alternative considering all the factors. I don't mean be dogmatic about your choice no matter what. I do mean be positive and move forward. Don't second-guess yourself with "should haves."

Look at it from another perspective

A friend of mine taught me to always look at problems from a "What's good about it?" perspective. You could look at any problem from other perspectives as well, such as "What's funny about it?" or "What lesson did I learn from this?" Whether you try to find what's good about the problem or some other perspective, this technique will maintain your professionalism. It will also ensure that you learn from the experience and transfer that learning to future situations.

Using humor to deal with problems

In some cases, humor may be your only option. For example, if you're using a microphone that isn't working, you can ask, "How many in the back can read lips?"

Humor is not for everyone. If it isn't natural, or if you feel as if you're forcing it, don't use it. You don't need to be funny to get through problems. Efficiency, grace, kindness, and a positive attitude work, too.

---

ebb's ten laws of training trip-ups

I work diligently at preparing for and preventing problems that plague trainers. It seems that something new always comes along. I have found a sense of humor to be invaluable. Over the years the staff at my company, ebb associates inc, have created this list of things that can trip up training. Although it is written tongue-in-cheek, at times it is oh so true!

✔ If you're expecting 15 participants, 30 will show up.

✔ If you're expecting 30 participants, 15 will show up.

✔ The electricity will go out exactly when you're ready to show a video.

✔ The only typo in your entire program will show up on the handout about quality.

✔ The day you order fruit in the morning, the group will want jelly doughnuts with real butter.

✔ The day you order jelly doughnuts, the group will want fruit with yogurt.

✔ The room reservation you made will cancel itself only on days when there are no other rooms available.

✔ The contact person at your training site will be sick on the day of your training.

✔ If you arrive at the training site early to do some last-minute preparation, the most talkative participant will arrive early as well.

✔ A perfectly open room will sprout a pillar right in the middle of your U-shaped table arrangement.

Maintaining a sense of humor as well as a sense of flexibility is critical to your success as a trainer. Flexibility and humor may also be critical to your sanity, as you can see in the "ebb's ten laws of training trip-ups" sidebar. Although the sidebar humorously suggests that no matter how well you prepare something may go wrong anyway, you still must prepare as well as you can. The key message is to maintain your sense of humor.

Managing Disruptive Behaviors

Sometimes, you can see them walking in the door — the disruptive behaviors. They may be vying for the center of attention, are boisterous, or are negatively outspoken. On the other hand, they may ignore everyone and refuse to make eye contact right from the start. Disruptive behaviors interrupt the flow of the training session and have a negative effect on the positive climate you're trying to create.

In this book, I emphasize the importance of interaction and participative learning in almost every chapter. Of course, most positive things usually have a negative correlation. As you increase interaction and participation among your participants, you give them a high level of flexibility, and you always risk the chance that some participants may get out of hand, easily leading to more active disruptive situations.

Preventing disruptions

The best approach to disruptive behavior is to prevent the disruption from occurring in the first place. Both your attitude and how you manage disruptive individuals sets the stage for the ease with which you manage disruptions.

Create a climate in which participants feel free to give each other feedback on their behaviors: Build trust, reward appropriate behavior, ignore inappropriate behavior, and develop ground rules.

You will facilitate the group to establish ground rules at the beginning of the training session. These ground rules will prevent many problems from occurring — but not all. As you establish the ground rules, ask the participants to help you manage them.

Allowing participants to determine their own ground rules gives them ownership. You can guide them to include rules that address the kind of behavior you want to foster, such as these:

- ✔ How to address punctuality. For example, "We will return from breaks on time." Or "We will start and end on time."

- ✔ How participants will communicate during the training session. For example, "We will take turns speaking during the session." Or "Questions are encouraged."

- ✔ What level of participation is expected. For example, "Participation should be balanced among participants." Or "We will encourage each other to speak up."

- ✔ How everyone will demonstrate respect toward each other. For example, "We will respect each other's ideas." Or "We will not interrupt when someone is speaking." Or "Attack the concept, not the person."

Post your ground rules so that they serve to guide behavior; then, you don't need to be the bad cop in enforcing appropriate classroom behavior. Instead, you can ask, "What did we agree upon in our ground rules?" and allow the participants to police themselves with their answers.

In a multiple-day training session, be sure to review the ground rules each morning and ask whether the group would like to add any others or even to rate itself on how well members are upholding the ground rules. You can use other general strategies throughout your session that will help to manage disruptive participants. For example, you will

- ✔ Reward and model appropriate behavior.

- ✔ Show genuine interest in all individuals.

- ✔ Be open to and invite individuals' comments, ideas, and disagreements.

If someone disagrees with you, be professional and respectful. Acknowledge that there are different ways to think about the topic. Take care that you do not become defensive nor are you drawn into an argument. Thank the person for offering a different viewpoint and respond appropriately. If you expect a long discussion, you may tell the participant that you're interested in the discussion and request that you continue it during the next break.

These kinds of strategies build trust with your participants and help to make the learning environment one that is productive for everyone attending your training session.

Managing disruptive types

Even after you do all you can to prevent disruptions, disruptions will still occur. When they do, I like to give the disruptive participants the benefit of the doubt. In many cases, they are unaware of the disruptions their behavior is causing. Often, all you need to do is let the disrupters know how their behavior is affecting you and the rest of the class.

Remember, some folks bring some very heavy baggage into the training with them. A participant may have recently suffered a bereavement or have a child who is not doing well in school. Another may be unhappy on the job or is anticipating a downsizing. Facilitators need to be sensitive to the fact that something may be causing the behavior and they may never know what it is.

Many disruptive behavior types exist. Movie Stars, Deserters, Comedians, Blockers, Attackers, and Dominators are six of the most common.

Movie Stars

Movie Stars like attention and want to be the center of the action. Sometimes, Movie Stars just have lots of pent-up energy and need to focus it in a positive direction. To address Movie Stars, you can:

- Ask them to help with demonstrations or other tasks, thus using their desire for attention to your advantage.

- Point out to them that you want to get others' ideas first: "Let's see what others have to say."

- Assign a specified amount of time for each response.

Deserters

Deserters come in several models. One deserter may have side conversations that prevent participation; another deserter may simply be reluctant to speak up; still another may have participated earlier in the session but now has pulled out.

Each of these participants has reasons for playing the Deserter role — and some may be positive. For example, the side-conversation deserters may be so excited about the concepts you're delivering that they want to share how they will implement them with their neighbor. They are often not even aware that they are causing a disruption. Some Deserters are reluctant to speak up and may simply be shy. Many have told me that they feel they are participating 100 percent. Others are analyzer types who like to think more than speak.

It is a third type, the Deserter who was a solid participator earlier in the session, but now has pulled out, that concerns me the most. Something has happened that changed the participation level. Perhaps the person received some bad news during a break. Perhaps something happened during the session that upset the participant. It behooves you to find out whether this is the case. To deal with Deserters:

✔ Manage side conversations by casually sauntering behind the two talkers and continuing to present over their conversations. This often works.

✔ Ask a question directly of the Deserter who is reluctant to speak up, starting with easy questions that don't test knowledge. The round robin (going around the group, one person at a time) is a good tool to use with this Deserter. You can also form smaller discussion groups to bring out the shy participant.

✔ The Deserter who was once active but now is not should be a concern to you. Pull the person aside at the first opportunity (perhaps during a break) and ask what has changed. Often, something happened outside the training session. If so, you need not pry. However, sometimes, you may have inadvertently done something that made the participant pull out.

✔ If you desire participation from everyone, ask the class to write their answers on index cards before verbalizing. This technique gives everyone a fair chance. It keeps the vocal participants busy writing while the quiet participants have a chance to think through their responses.

Comedians

Comedians, the class clowns, may also be looking for attention through humorous remarks. I like to give these folks the benefit of the doubt. They may have a very positive attitude and are trying to add levity to the training session. To deal with Comedians:

✔ Ignore the humor as long as it is not disruptive. Unfortunately, most people laugh at the first couple of comments and that keeps the Comedian going.

✔ Ask Comedians to relate their point to the discussion at hand.

✔ Give feedback to the Comedian during the next break if the disruption continues.

> ✔ Ask Comedians serious questions. If they cannot provide serious answers, you know you have a problem on your hands that probably needs to be addressed one on one with the person.
>
> ✔ If the disruption spreads throughout the group or if it gets out of hand, you may wish to call a break.

Blockers

Blockers are the naysayers in the group. They are the ones who are negative and don't believe anything will work. I give these folks a break because often I have found them to have valuable background information, but have not figured out how to get them to appropriately explain their side of the story. To get them to disrupt less, you could

> ✔ Ask what alternative they are willing to propose.
>
> ✔ Be sure that they do not take the class off on a tangential topic, based on some hidden agenda they may have.
>
> ✔ Ask the group for other opinions regarding what a blocker may have said.
>
> ✔ Ask them, "What would need to happen in order for the idea (concept, change, or others) to work?" Expect them to respond with "It won't work." Keep asking what would have to happen and by the third or fourth time a response will roll out of their mouth. In my experience, their thoughts are worth pursuing.

Attackers

Attackers toss out barbs directed toward the trainer, other participants, or the content. They may call people names and give dirty looks. I've often found that Attackers have never learned an appropriate way to disagree. To deal with Attackers:

> ✔ Ask them to confine their comments to the situation, not the people.
>
> ✔ Refer them to the ground rule that addresses respect.
>
> ✔ Some attackers may not be aware of how they come across. In this case, the trainer's feedback may be accepted and even appreciated.
>
> ✔ Ask other participants whether they agree with the statement.
>
> ✔ Sometimes it is appropriate to explore their comments further.
>
> ✔ If not directed at individuals in the room, ignore until a break when you can discuss with the Attacker to identify the root of the problem.

Dominators

Dominators take up much air time by talking, sometimes repeating themselves, and sometimes speaking slowly and in great detail. You can't ignore the dominators; other participants will get frustrated, bored, and lose interest. To address Dominators:

- ✔ Break eye contact with them and call on others by name for answers.

- ✔ Consider holding your hand up as if trying to stop a car if they continue to talk without being recognized.

- ✔ Impose a time limit on all participants' statements.

- ✔ Break into the middle of a long statement when they take a breath and ask for others' opinions.

- ✔ Assign a gatekeeper role to one of the participants.

- ✔ To balance participation with a dominator or two in your training session, pose a situation or question and ask people to raise their hands if they have a response. Then call on someone other than the dominators.

- ✔ Create a bin list or parking lot (a sheet of flipchart paper on which you write questions or ideas). Parking lots are used to post comments that are not appropriate for discussion at the current time but will be addressed later in the session. If you have pads of sticky-back notes on the table, you can have dominators write their comments and post them on the parking lot. This prevents repetition of the same comment.

Although other types of disruptive participants, such as the Rambler, the Clueless, and the Know-it-all, exist, knowing how to address the preceding six will prepare you for most situations you encounter. In all situations, you would be wise to identify the disruptive person's needs. That may help you determine a solution.

Remember, ignoring a disruptive behavior is one way to address it. I usually ignore most things the first time. It is repetitive disruptions that affect the results of your class. You can always call a break if things get out of hand. Never hesitate to pull the person aside at a break to identify the problem and what you may be able to do about it.

On very rare occasions, you may need to ask the participant to leave. If you have pulled the person aside and you can't reach a win-win agreement about how to handle the situation, tell the person what kind of cooperation you need. Ask whether the person would be more comfortable staying — and agreeing to your request — or leaving. Reassure the person that you would prefer him to stay and benefit from the session, but you can't allow others' learning to suffer from continued disruptions.

If you have established a climate of trust and support, often the rest of the participants will take care of the disruptive participant for you.

Remember that most of the problems identified are outside your control. You could not have prevented them nor predicted them. Ask yourself whether you could have done something better. If yes, consider it a lesson learned; if not, chalk it up to experience. Accept the fact that people attend training packing their baggage with them. And sometimes, you do the best that you know how and move on.

Sweaty Palms, Parched Throat: Overcoming Nervousness

Stage fright. Presentation anxiety. Nervousness. Platform panic. Pre-performance jitters. Butterflies. Training fear. Nervous tension. Being keyed up or flustered. Whatever you call it, it is normal to be nervous near the beginning of a training session. Several studies show that more American adults are more fearful of talking to a large group than they are of dying!

If you ask other trainers, most will tell you that they experience a bit of anxiety at the beginning of every training session. And they are in good company, too. History suggests that Abe Lincoln shook the first few minutes of every speech. In an interview, Yul Brynner admitted to stage fright after appearing on stage in *The King and I* more than 600 times. Jack Benny, Jane Fonda, Mark Twain, and Ali McGraw are all people who have admitted to nervous tension prior to a big gig.

Recognize first that nervousness is a normal response. Almost everyone gets butterflies. The key is to master your nervousness and get those butterflies to fly in formation!

Understanding pre-performance jitters

Where do those performance butterflies come from? They are caused by a natural fear response. Your brain perceives a threatening situation and prepares your body for a flight-or-fight situation. This is the same fight-or-flight mechanism that helped early humans battle rampaging saber-toothed tigers and other ferocious beasts. Adrenalin and thyroxin are dumped into your bloodstream, causing your heart to race, your blood pressure to rise, and your pupils to dilate. Your liver gets busy pumping sugar, and your blood increases its ability to clot. Your body is on red alert — ready for the worst!

Here's the good news. You do not want to eliminate all your nervous energy. Just as the flow of adrenalin gives runners the edge to win a race, this same adrenalin can give you the mental edge to be a dynamic trainer. You want to accept your nervousness as a natural phenomenon, and use it to fuel a more enthusiastic and dynamic training session. As you feel the adrenalin flowing, embrace the energy that it brings.

Accepting your nervousness as natural

How can you make nervousness work for you? First and most importantly, don't tell your participants that you're nervous. Remember, they are attending because you're the expert. They expect you to succeed, but if you start the training session by saying "Whew! Am I nervous!" they will begin looking for signs of nervousness. If you never tell them, most will never know. Again, don't admit your nervousness to the participants.

Next, know how your body reacts in this situation and accept it. Perhaps your heart races. Maybe your throat gets dry. Perhaps you fidget with things in your pocket. Whatever it is, know how you react, and then accept it as natural. You may even say to yourself, "Oh, my heart is pounding. I knew that would happen." Accept the reality.

Define how your body reacts. Examine the nervous symptoms in Table 12-1 and place a check in the column that describes when this occurs for you: before or during a training session.

Table 12-1	Identify Your Nervous Symptoms	
Nervous Symptom	**Occurs Before**	**Occurs During**
Voice		
Quivers or crackles		
Speed is too fast/slow		
Monotone		
Change in pitch		
Verbal fluency		
Stammers, halting		
Loss of words, loses place, pauses		
Uses fillers		
Mouth and throat		
Excessive saliva		
Dry mouth/throat		
Clears throat repeatedly		
Repeated swallowing		
Breathing difficulty		
Shallow breathing		

Nervous Symptom	Occurs Before	Occurs During
Facial expression		
Lacks expression, deadpan		
Grimaces, tense facial muscles		
Twitches		
Limited eye contact		
Arms and hands		
Rigid or tense		
Fidgets with _____		
Grips podium		
Lack of gestures		
Waves hands about		
Shakes		
Body movement		
Paces		
Sways		
Shuffles or taps feet		
Crosses legs while standing		
Physiological		
Chest tightness		
Rapid heart beat		
Flushed skin		
Perspires excessively		

Whatever symptoms you experience, these are normal for you. It doesn't matter whether you have checked 2 or 22 items. What is important is that you acknowledge them and that you know how to address them either before or during your presentation.

Mastering nervous symptoms

Okay, so you have three symptoms before the training begins and three different ones that occur during the training. What can you do about them?

Some symptoms you can do little more than camouflage so that your participants won't notice. Others you can actually learn to change. Here are some general things you can do to physically and mentally prepare yourself for your next training event.

Prepare physically: Relax and be ready

You can do many things to prepare yourself and your surroundings before your session. Most of them relate to relaxing and making yourself comfortable.

- **Master relaxation techniques.** Head rolls, shoulder rolls, or dangling your arms at your sides all work well. Practice these techniques as you prepare for your session. Then use those that work best for you just before you begin your session. Even deep yawning helps you relax. A yawn sends a message to your brain that you're ready to relax.

- **Use isometric exercises prior to training.** Tightening various muscles, curling your toes or squeezing on a rubber ball before starting the training session works for many trainers.

- **Practice deep breathing.** Several deep breaths, in through your nose and out through your mouth, add oxygen to and clear your brain. This is especially useful just minutes before you start.

I take a couple of deep breaths while the host is introducing me. No one can see what I am doing. I get oxygen flowing and it helps to focus me on the task at hand.

- **Arrive early to ground yourself with the room and make it yours.** When participants arrive, greet them. Mingle with as many as you can and learn something about those you meet. Getting to know individuals reduces some of the barriers you may have imagined and decreases some of the fear you may have felt. During the training session, find one or two of the friendly faces you met before the training session started. Return to those friendly faces, but be sure that you do not speak solely to them.

- **Don't try anything new.** No new suit, haircut, or shoes. Wear something that you have felt comfortable in before. This is one less thing to worry about. I once saw a trainer who appeared in a new suit — complete with price tags!

A 15-second relaxer

Try this relaxation technique. It takes only 15 seconds and works in almost any situation when you need to reduce anxiety.

1. **Lower your head so that you're looking straight down.**

2. **Squeeze your thumb and index fingertips together on both hands.**

3. **While squeezing your thumb and finger, inhale deeply while silently affirming, "I am calm and relaxed."**

4. **Exhale slowly, relax your fingers, and tell yourself, "I am prepared and confident."**

5. **Repeat four times as you visualize a successful training session.**

6. **Lift your head and smile to whoever is in your eyesight.**

✔ **If you have a crutch, use it.** For some, their crutch is to use audiovisuals early to divert the participants' gazes. For others, it may be to have their notes outlined or highlighted in a particular way. For me, it means having a glass of water nearby. At any time, whether my throat is dry or I forget what I am supposed to do or say, I can reach for the water, take a swallow, and compose myself.

✔ **Organize ahead.** Check out Chapter 7 for specific ways to prepare yourself and the environment. Just knowing that everything is ready to go is relaxing in itself.

✔ **Do something physical.** Take a walk just before the session starts. Do some stretches or wall pushups. One trainer told me that he goes into the men's restroom and does a couple of jumping jacks to release pent-up energy.

✔ **During the session, use up excess energy with gestures and your vocal presentation**. Speak and gesture to the person who is the farthest away from you. Moving about, as long as it is not distracting or in a repeated pattern, for example, two steps to the left, then two steps to the right, will also use up some of your extra energy.

Prepare mentally: Psyching up, not out

You can also prepare yourself mentally. Your brain perceives only what you tell it. If you tell yourself that you're going to be nervous, trip over the cord, and forget what you're supposed to say, you will most likely be nervous, trip over the cord, and forget what you're supposed to say. Get the picture? It takes the same amount of time to paint a good mental picture as a bad one. These ideas will help you psych up for the next training session.

- ✔ **Realize that you will be somewhat nervous.** Accept it as a fact.

- ✔ **Know what to expect when you get nervous and accept it.** When the symptoms occur, say to yourself, "Oh, yes. There it is. I knew my heart would start racing right about now!"

- ✔ **Recognize that the participants want you to succeed.** Forget yourself and put your group first. Focus on the needs of your participants. Think about how important what you have to say is to them.

- ✔ **Think of your presentation as extended conversation.** Imagine that you're talking to your good friend, Dan Greene — except that there are lots of Dan Greenes in the group. Look into their eyes and connect with them on an individual level.

- ✔ **Visualize yourself being successful.** Don't spend energy imagining the worst. Instead, imagine the best. Tell yourself that this is going to be the best darned training these participants have ever attended.

- ✔ **Plan to get your participants involved in the training early.** Ask a question, begin introductions, or start the icebreaker as quickly as you can. After your participants are involved, you will feel more like you're conducting a two-way conversation than a presentation. Going into the training session knowing that within three minutes participants will be actively involved and not staring at you gives you a real mental boost.

- ✔ **Try appropriate humor early to help you mentally hear approval from your participants.** Humor should not be translated as "jokes." Humor can be many things other than jokes. And jokes are not always humorous.

    Humor can make you feel comfortable in front of a group. Telling a bad joke will not. Although you may see speakers who begin with a joke, don't do it unless you know you can pull it off successfully. To be more successful, the joke must tie to content. The joke must be politically appropriate. You must have practiced it at least three dozen times with success almost 100 percent of the time. If you have any doubts about the joke, don't use it.

- ✔ **Keep your presentation in perspective.** What if you do something wrong? Can you correct it? Will the participants even know that something was incorrect? And is it the end of the world if you aren't perfect?

And finally: Practice, practice, practice

In Chapter 7, I discuss practicing the mechanics of your presentation and learning the content. Now you want to think about how practice can assist you with nervousness.

As I mention throughout this book and specifically in Chapter 7, nothing is more important to a successful training session than being well prepared. And nothing is more helpful in overcoming nervousness than knowing your material and knowing that you know your material. That takes practice. Use these suggestions to practice your training material.

- ✔ **Memorize the first couple of paragraphs you will say.** Nervousness goes away for most trainers after 5 to 15 minutes. If you know what you will say for the first few minutes, you can get to the other side of your nervousness.

- ✔ **Practice in front of a mirror.** Many trainers swear by this method. Look yourself in the eye and train away. I must admit that although it works well for many trainers, it doesn't work for me. I prefer several of the next few methods.

- ✔ **Use a tape recorder.** If you record yourself, you can listen to the tape while you're driving or doing other things. An added benefit of listening to the tape is that you can critique your pace, pauses, clarity, articulation, and other vocal characteristics.

- ✔ **Practice activities with your colleagues.** Try the training activities with other people in your department. Practice giving the same directions. Do they understand what you want them to do and the purpose of the activity? I like to ask for a critique as well. What went well? What do they think I could do better?

- ✔ **Practice using the visuals.** Practice several times with whatever audiovisual equipment you will use. Practice turning the equipment on and off. Practice with the actual visuals. Being comfortable with the media you will use will reduce your anxiety level. Your visuals should feel natural — almost an extension of yourself.

- ✔ **Practice out loud.** Practice pronouncing difficult words — or find a way to eliminate them. Practicing aloud allows you the opportunity to time your presentation. You may be surprised at how much time it actually takes to deliver some of the training material. Nervousness decreases the more often you hear yourself state the content.

- ✔ **Present some of the training material to your spouse, significant other, or your dog.** Really! Dogs make great practice participants. They make great eye contact, and some will listen forever, giving you only positive nonverbal feedback.

- ✔ **Get practice in front of groups in other situations as well.** You could try out for a play. You could join Toastmasters, National Speakers Association, or other speaking groups. You can then accept a club office or volunteer to give toasts for special occasions.

The more often you practice your material, the better you'll be prepared for your session. In addition, the more opportunities you have to speak in other situations, the better you will understand, appreciate, and improve your training skills. The better trainer you become, the more confidence you will have, which will reduce your nervousness even more.

Tips for specific anxiety problems

Return to the checklist of nervous symptoms in Table 12-1. The ideas in this section refer to specific symptoms you may have checked. In some cases, your only solution is to camouflage the symptom; in others, you can actually do something about the symptom.

As you read through these tips, remember that the symptoms occur because your body is readying itself for a fight-or-flight situation. Therefore, you must trick it back into thinking that everything is okay again — which it is!

- ✔ **Voice:** Few participants will notice any voice symptoms. A crackling voice usually indicates tense neck muscles or inadequate air supply. Stretch you neck or clear your throat. Deep breathing and a swallow of water may also help. Speaking too rapidly may be the most annoying to the listener. Plan pauses at specific points and write a reminder to yourself in the margin of your notes to "slow down."

  Grandma's warm tea with honey and lemon is a home remedy that really does work. The honey coats your throat, and the warm tea relaxes your throat muscles. Iced beverages tend to constrict your vocal cords even more. Try to avoid them during the initial portion of your training session.

- ✔ **Verbal fluency:** Ensure that you know your material completely. Should you lose your place, simply state that the idea will come to you momentarily and move to another idea. Also, consider some of the ideas in the "Difficult personal situations" section presented earlier in this chapter.

  Um, ahh, you know! If fillers are a problem, you will not eliminate them until you hear yourself say them. Appoint an Um Counter during your training session. This is typically a colleague, not one of your participants. Making eye contact with the Um Counter will remind you to attend to your fillers.

  Write UM in large red capital letters on each page of your notes. Seeing the UM has the same effect as making eye contact with the um-counter. It will remind you to listen to yourself.

- ✔ **Mouth and throat:** Eliminate dry throat by biting on a lemon wedge or spraying with Binaca, a breath freshener. Have a glass of water available, and avoid taking antihistamines before speaking. Also avoid dairy products for four hours prior to a session to prevent the mucus build-up that requires clearing your throat. You can prevent most breathing difficulties by completing deep-breathing exercises.

✔ **Facial expression:** Make eye contact with people you met before the training session started. Think of them as your friends and smile. If a nervous twitch is something you cannot control, camouflage it until it stops by turning that side of your face away from the participants. Experiment with ways to stop the twitch between training sessions. Sometimes, rubbing a twitch or pressing on it will make it stop. Besides, most participants will not likely notice it anyway.

✔ **Arms and hands:** The more you try to control trembling hands or wobbly knees, the more they seem to shake. Instead, isolate one muscle group and shake out the stress just before you present, much like you see athletes do while waiting for their race. You can also use this technique inconspicuously while participants are working in small groups or while they meet other participants during their warm-up exercise. Until the shaking stops, avoid having your hand in front of audiovisual lights or holding flimsy paper. Use note cards instead. They won't rattle and quiver.

If you're a fidgeter, remove everything from your pockets. Also, place all pens in one place and out of your reach. Participants will be distracted if you're clicking a pen. Get in the habit of using a marker, replacing the cap, and then placing it back in its intended location.

✔ **Body movement:** Start by standing near enough to a table so that you can use it like a touchstone to orient yourself to one place. Plant yourself in front of the group with feet slightly farther apart than normal and with your hands at your sides. In extreme cases you may want to focus on keeping your weight on the balls of your feet. Be sure you have not locked your knees. In addition to making you appear rigid, it also adds tension to your system.

✔ **Physiological symptoms:** Sweaty palms? Try talc or antiperspirant, but experiment a couple days before to determine whether it is comfortable and doesn't rub off on your clothing. Have tissues available nearby. Taking long, slow breaths may slow your heart beat. In extreme cases, you may need to breathe deeply and hold your breath just before you begin your session. Camouflage your flushed skin by wearing darker-colored clothing next to your skin. White makes red, flushed skin stand out.

Remember three things about nervousness:

✔ Even if you're very nervous, you will almost always look much better than you feel.

✔ To make those butterflies fly in formation, you must first recognize that you're experiencing a natural feeling.

✔ Focusing on your participants and their needs is a helpful way to overcome nervousness.

It should be somewhat comforting to know that even the most experienced trainers feel some apprehension when stepping in front of a group for the first time. And further, most of the nervousness settles down for most trainers within minutes. Addressing nervousness is not about how to get rid of it but rather, how to manage it. Know how your body reacts to training jitters and be prepared to do what it takes to make those butterflies fly in formation.

Problems Can Be Prevented or Resolved

I hope you're feeling that even though problems are a way of life for a trainer, all is not lost. You can do many things to prevent problems from occurring. And when problems do crop up, you can do many things to resolve them.

I can give you but one guarantee in training. You're going to have problems. When it is happening it's not very funny. A lesson that I have learned, however, is that all those problems eventually become lessons learned. I learn something from them. Even better, I can sometimes turn these not-so-funny experiences into humorous stories for some later training session. Remember, Will Rogers said, "Everything is funny as long as it is happening to somebody else."

Part IV
It's Not Over Yet: The Follow-Up

The 5th Wave
By Rich Tennant

"First of all, let me commend everyone on the teamwork displayed on this icebreaker. Secondly, let me apologize for some of the motivational language I used during this session..."

In this part . . .

You discover the value of follow up. Just because the training session has ended, that doesn't mean your work has ended. This answers questions like, Why is evaluation critical to the training process? How can you use what you glean from the evaluation process to make improvements? What kind of follow-up activities are most beneficial?

Chapter 13

Evaluation: It's Not Over Yet!

· ·

· ·

*E*valuate performance — that's the fifth and last stage of the ADDIE model discussed in Chapter 3. When you reach this stage, you have made it through the entire Training Cycle, and it is now that you can see the beauty of the complete cycle. You will find yourself returning to the earlier stages during the evaluation stage. For example, you will return to the assessment stage to ensure that you're evaluating what you designed the training for in the first place. You may use the objectives you wrote in the second stage to create specific evaluation criteria. You want the training objectives you write to be specific, measurable, and easily converted to items on an evaluation instrument or performance rating.

The evaluation stage of The Training Cycle, highlighted in Figure 13-1, is important to you as a trainer. It is here that you can prove your value as a business partner to your organization. You will be able to answer questions such as, How has training changed employee performance? How has training increased sales or reduced expenses? How has training reduced rework and defects? How has training affected turnover and employee satisfaction? And ultimately, how is training affecting the bottom line?

In this chapter, I expand on the reason for conducting evaluations, describe Kirkpatrick's four levels of evaluation, and provide guidance for how to design your own evaluation plan.

An exciting aspect of this chapter is "The training evaluation guru" sidebar, written by Dr. Don Kirkpatrick. His practical and logical thinking process for how he developed the four levels proves that everything doesn't need to be complicated. Sometimes, less is better. This chapter also presents an interview with Jack Phillips (see the "An interview with Jack Phillips" sidebar), another leader in the training evaluation arena. I feel fortunate to have both of these gentlemen explain their perspective of the development of evaluation.

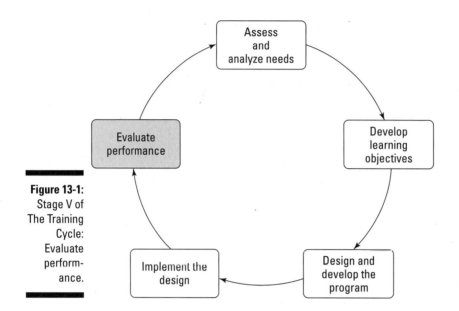

Figure 13-1:
Stage V of
The Training
Cycle:
Evaluate
perform-
ance.

Understanding the Purpose of Evaluations

The purpose of training is to change employees: their behavior, opinions, knowledge, or level of skill. The purpose of evaluation is to determine whether the objective was met and whether these changes have taken place. One way to consider the importance of evaluations is to recognize the feedback it provides. Feedback can be obtained through self-reporting or by observing the learner.

Various kinds of evaluations provide feedback to different people.

- Employees regarding their success in mastering new knowledge, attitudes, and skills

- Employees concerning their work-related strengths and weaknesses. Evaluation results can be a source of positive reinforcement and an incentive for motivation

- Trainers for developing future interventions and program needs or creating modifications in the current training efforts

- Supervisors as to whether there is observable change in employees' effectiveness or performance as a result of participating in the training program

- The organization regarding return on investment in training

The very location of evaluation at the end of The Training Cycle or near the end of this book doesn't mean that you don't think about it until the end. Quite the contrary. You begin thinking about how you will measure the results of the training very early in the design stage — soon after you determine objectives. Decide how you can measure whether the objectives have been achieved.

Reviewing Kirkpatrick's Four Levels of Evaluation

The concept of different levels of evaluation helps you understand the measurement and evaluation process. Don Kirkpatrick originally developed his four levels of training evaluation — reaction, learning, behavior, and results — almost one-half century ago. Although some organizations now add a fifth level for return on investment (ROI), Kirkpatrick's original four levels are as applicable today as they were in the 1950s.

As I discuss each of the four levels, note the elegant but simple sequence from Level I through Level IV. At each level the data become more objective and more meaningful to management and the bottom line. In addition, progressing through each level requires more work and more sophisticated data-gathering techniques.

It is interesting to note that, although the number is increasing, many organizations still only evaluate training at the first level. It is easiest but doesn't really give organizations what they need to measure the value of training.

Before you decide to conduct any type of evaluation, decide how you will use the data. If you aren't going to use it, don't evaluate.

Level I: Reaction

Level I, or participant reaction data, measures participant satisfaction with the training. The reaction to a training that is conducted externally by a consultant or if the employee paid for the experience may be the deciding point as to whether it will be repeated. If the training was presented internally, the Level I evaluation provides guidance about what to change. This is true for externally funded training as well, but sometimes, the provider doesn't have a chance to demonstrate improvements to the company. The employee's company will just not attend another training session. Most training efforts are evaluated at this level.

Sometimes called *smile sheets,* Level I evaluation usually consists of a question-naire that participants use to rate their level of satisfaction with the training program and the trainer, among other things.

If you're conducting a multiple-day training session, it is beneficial to evaluate at the end of each day. If you're conducting a one-day session, you may decide to evaluate it halfway through. It benefits the trainer because it provides feed-back to the trainer to allow adjustments to the design to better meet the par-ticipants' needs. It also benefits participants because it allows them to think about what they learned and how they will apply it to their jobs.

Want to measure reaction at the end of day one and you do not have an eval-uation form? Try one of these two ways.

✔ First, use two flipchart pages. At the top of one write "positives" and at the top of the other write "changes." Then ask participants to provide suggestions about what went well that day, the positives, and what needs to change. Capture ideas as they are suggested.

✔ A second one that I use regularly is to pass out an index card to each participant. Ask them to anonymously rate the day on a 1 to 7 scale, with 1 being low and 7 being high, and then to add one comment about why they rated it at the level they did.

No attempt is made to measure behavioral change or performance improve-ment. Nevertheless, Level I data does provide valuable information.

✔ It provides information about the trainer's performance.

✔ It is an easy and economical process.

✔ If the tool is constructed well, the data can identify what needs to be improved.

✔ The satisfaction level provides guidance to management about whether to continue to invest in the training.

✔ If conducted immediately following the training session, the return rate is generally close to 100 percent, providing a complete database.

Level II: Learning

Level II measures the extent to which learning has occurred. The measure-ment of knowledge, skills, or attitude (KSAs) change indicates what partici-pants have absorbed and whether they know how to implement what they learned. Probably all training designs have at least one objective to increase participant knowledge. Most training sessions also include objectives that improve specific skills. And some training sessions such as diversity or team building attempt to change attitudes.

The training design's objectives provide an initial basis for what to evaluate in Level II. This is the point at which trainers can find out not only how satisfied the participants are, but what they can do differently as a result of the training. Tests, skill practices, simulations, group evaluations, role-plays, and other assessment tools focus on what participants learned during the program. Although testing is a natural part of learning, the word *test* often conjures up stress and fears left over from bad experiences in school. Therefore, substitute other words for tests or exams — even if testing is what you're doing. Measuring learning provides excellent data about what participants mastered as a result of the training experience. This data can be used in several ways.

- A self-assessment for participants to compare what they gained as a result of the training.
- An assessment of an employee's knowledge and skills related to the job requirements.
- If an attitude survey is conducted, it provides an indication of an employee's attitude about the content.
- An assessment of whether participants possess knowledge to safely perform their duties; this is especially critical in a manufacturing setting.

Level III: Behavior

Level III evaluation measures whether the skills and knowledge are being implemented. Are participants applying what they learned and transferring what they learned to the job?

Because this measurement focuses on changes in behavior on the job, it becomes more difficult to measure for several reasons. First, participants can't implement the new behavior until they have an opportunity. In addition, it is difficult to predict when the new behavior will be implemented. Even if there is an opportunity, the learner may not implement the behavior at the first opportunity. Therefore, timing becomes an issue for when to measure.

To complicate things even more, the participant may have learned the behavior and applied it on the job, but the participant's supervisor would not allow the behavior to continue. As a trainer, you hope that's not happening, but unfortunately it occurs more often than you want. This is when the training department must ask itself whether the problem requires something other than a training solution. Due to the nature of Level III evaluation, the measures may include the frequency and use of skills, with input on barriers and enablers.

Measuring Levels I and II should occur immediately following the training, but you can see why this would not be true for Level III. To conduct a Level III evaluation correctly, you must find time to observe the participants on the job, create questionnaires, speak to supervisors, and correlate data. You can also see that even though measuring at Level III may be difficult, the benefits of measuring behaviors are very clear.

- ✔ The measure may encourage a behavioral change on the job.
- ✔ When possible, Level III can be quantified and tied to other outcomes on the job.
- ✔ When a lack of transfer of skills is clearly defined, it can clearly point to a required training design change.
- ✔ A before and after measurement provides data that can be used to understand other events.
- ✔ Sometimes, Level III evaluations help to determine the reasons change has not occurred that are not related to training.

Level IV: Results

Level IV measures the business impact. Sometimes called *cost-benefit analysis* (incorrectly) or *return on investment,* it determines whether the benefits from the training were worth the cost of the training. At this level, the evaluation is not accomplished through methods like those suggested in the previous three levels.

Results could be determined by factors such as reduced turnover, improved quality, increased quantity or output, reduction of costs, increase in profits, increased sales, improved customer service, reduction in waste or errors, less absenteeism, or fewer grievances. You also need to determine the other side of the equation, that is, how much the training costs to design and conduct as compared to the results. Identifying and capturing this data are relatively easy. You would account for the cost of the trainer, materials and equipment, travel for participants and the trainers, training space, and the cost of having participants in a training session instead of producing the organization's services and products.

A cost-benefit analysis is usually completed before a training program is created to decide whether it is worth the investment of resources required to develop the program. Return on investment (ROI) is conducted after the training has been completed to determine whether it was worth the investment.

Measurements focus on the actual results on the business as participants successfully apply the program material. Typical measures may include output, quality, time, costs, and customer satisfaction.

The training evaluation guru

by Dr. Donald Kirkpatrick

Yes, I am the one who originated and published *Evaluating Training Programs: The Four Levels*. And here is how it came about.

I was teaching at the University of Wisconsin Management Institute, and I decided to obtain a Ph.D. in the School of Education. My advisor approved my dissertation, which was called "Evaluating a Human Relations Training Program For Supervisors." I thought that as long as I was teaching in the program, I may as well try to evaluate the effectiveness. These were my thoughts:

If I am going to evaluate, the first thing I am interested in is "How do the participants feel about the program?" After all, they are our customers! I decided to call it REACTION.

My next thought was to try to measure to what extent participants learned the three things we were trying to teach: knowledge of management principles and techniques; skill in knowing such things as how to motivate and how to train employees; whether or not they had changed their attitudes about their company, their job, or the challenges they face in applying what we were teaching. So I decided to call that LEARNING.

My third thought was to see to what extent they applied what they had learned back on the job. So I called it BEHAVIOR. And finally, I decided to try to measure any results that came because they attended this training program. I called it RESULTS.

The editor of *Training & Development* magazine from the American Society for Training and Development (ASTD) asked me to write what I had done. I decided to write a series of four articles in 1959, with each article devoted to one of the four "levels," which they were beginning to be called. Professional trainers read the articles, began to try them out, and passed the word on to others in the training profession. Many trainers wrote to me asking for a copy of the articles.

It wasn't until 1993 that a professional friend, Jane Holcomb, told me to write a book because no one could find the articles any longer but many were talking about the "four levels." The first edition of *Evaluating Training Programs: The Four Levels* was published in 1994. A paper edition was published several years later, and the second edition was published in 1998 with some new case studies. I decided to put some case studies in Part 2 of the book so readers could see how other organizations were applying the four levels. My first contact was with Dave Basarab, an evaluation expert at Motorola. When I told him who I was, he replied, "Don Kirkpatrick! We use your four levels all over the world!" My response was an unbelieving, "You do?" He has not only written a case study but also wrote the introduction to my book.

Since then, the book has been published in Spanish, Polish, and Turkish. And I was invited to those countries to introduce the concepts, principles, and techniques and autograph the books. I have been asked to be a keynote speaker for numerous national conferences and many in-house programs.

People call me a "guru" or "legend," but all I did was come up with four practical and simple ways to evaluate training programs.

Author's note: Dr. Kirkpatrick is currently working on another training evaluation book with his son, Jim.

Guidelines for measuring the four levels

Now that I have given an overview of the four levels, I examine how you can measure each of them. Methods for each level are presented along with guidelines to consider as you develop your evaluation plan.

Measuring Level 1

Level I, or reaction, can be easily measured during the training event or immediately following it, preferably before participants leave the classroom. A questionnaire, composed of both questions with a rating scale and open-ended questions, is usually used. Most recently trainers have started to use Webonnaires. The drawback is a lower return rate.

How do you begin?

1. **Determine what you want to learn about the training.**

   You will most likely want to know something about the content including its relevance to the participants' jobs and the degree of difficulty. You will also want to gather data about the trainer including effectiveness, communication skills, the ability to answer questions, and approachability.

2. **Design a format that will be both easy for participants to complete and presents a way for you to quantify participants' responses.**

   Many formats exist, and the design will be a factor of the first question — What do you want to learn? You may choose to have statements rated on a one- to seven-point scale representing strongly disagree to strongly agree (or poor to excellent). You may also wish to ask open-ended questions, or you may choose to do a combination of both types of questions. Even if you develop a format that has questions that are rated on a scale, it is a good idea to add space at the end for comments.

3. **Plan to obtain 100 percent response ratings that are complete.**

   How do you accomplish all that? Most of it is in the timing. Ensure that you plan time into the training design to complete the questionnaire. Twenty minutes prior to the end of the training session, pass out the evaluations and ask participants to complete them before you wrap up for the day. Allowing time and letting them know there is more to come encourages them to add comments.

Trainers desire honest responses to their evaluations. To ensure honesty, allow for anonymity. Don't require participants to sign their evaluations. In addition, ask them to drop the evaluations off on a table on their way out versus leaving them at their places. If you have a valid reason for wanting to know who made specific comments, for example, to provide feedback, you may wish to make signing the evaluation optional.

Your training department will most likely have determined an acceptable standard against which you will measure results. For example, 5.5 on a 7.0 scale may be considered acceptable by your training department.

If you follow these guidelines, you will be well on your way to finalizing an effective Level I evaluation. A comprehensive training-competency checklist can be found at the end of this chapter. You may want to use some aspects of it to create your Level I evaluation. You and your colleagues may want to use the evaluation to provide feedback to each other on your training skills.

There is a growing tendency for some training practitioners to snub Level I evaluation as too insignificant or perfunctory. Perhaps this is because trainers can conduct more sophisticated evaluations or because it's prudent to tie training to the bottom line. The "smile sheet," as Level I is known, has become a pejorative term to some. Don't fall into that way of thinking. Dr. Kirkpatrick's four levels are built upon each other. Level I is a prerequisite when other levels are used. Even though you're "only" measuring reactions, these are the first-hand reactions of the customers of the training. There are very few more-effective and efficient ways for trainers to obtain feedback about performance. You may have the best training design, but if it is delivered poorly, it does affect participants' ability to learn. Level I evaluation also serves as a way to focus questions on the content. The key here is to design an instrument that measures the essential foundation elements of the training content and how well it was delivered.

Hold on to your evaluations. Use the ideas and suggestions they contain to improve your future performance and program designs. The evaluations can also serve as input to your efforts to continually develop your skills and competencies.

Measuring Level II

Level II, or learning, can be measured using self-assessments, facilitator assessments, tests, simulations, case studies, and other exercises. This type of evaluation should be conducted at the end of the training before participants leave to measure the degree to which the content was learned. Use pre- and post-test results to compare improvement.

Measuring before and after the training session gives you the best data because you will be able to compare the knowledge level prior to the session and after the training has been completed. This is the best way to determine whether participants gained knowledge or skills during the session. How do you evaluate? Remember KSAs from the "Level II: Learning" section? That's what you will measure: the knowledge, skills, and attitudes that the training session was designed to improve. Use tests to measure knowledge and attitude surveys to measure changing attitudes. To measure skill acquisition, use performance tests, where the participant is actually modeling the skill. Like Level I, attempt to obtain a 100 percent response rate.

Some trainers use a control group for comparison. And Dr. Kirkpatrick recommends that you do so if it is practical. While this may be the most scientific way to gather data, it may be wasted time. For example, if participants have another way to learn between pre- and post-tests, then don't send them to training. On the other hand, if training is the only way that participants can gain the knowledge, skills, and attitudes, then why bother with a control group? You'll need to be your own judge about whether a control group is beneficial.

Many types of testing formats exist from which to choose, and each brings with it advantages and disadvantages. True/false tests are easy to develop and cover many questions in a short amount of time. The drawback is that if the test is too easy, having superficial knowledge may lead to an inflated score. Be sure to use a subject matter expert (SME) to assist with the design.

Other options that exist include oral tests, essay tests, multiple-choice tests, and measured simulations such as in-basket exercises, business games, case studies, or role-plays. Assessments may also include self-assessments, team assessments, or instructor assessments. A Web-based evaluation may also be created. Although Web-based assessments are cost and time efficient, they bring a couple problems including guaranteeing that participants are who they say they are when signing in and the ability to protect the questions in the exam banks. Most organizations using Web-based assessments have addressed both of these issues. Whatever testing option you use, be sure that the results are quantifiable.

Create straightforward tests. You're not trying to trip up the participants. You're trying to measure the learning that occurred to ensure improved job performance.

Finally, ensure that testing conditions are optimized by limiting noise, having adequate lighting and comfortable temperature, and eliminating interruptions. Be certain that the test is only as long as it needs to be. Be sure that participants know the rules, such as whether it is acceptable to ask questions during the test.

Pilot any test prior to using it with participants. Also, return measurement results to employees as quickly as possible. The significance of measurement feedback decreases with time.

Measuring Level III

Level III, or behavior, is used to determine the successful transfer of learning to the workplace. Unlike Levels I and II, you need to allow time for the changed behavior to occur. How much time? The experts differ, and with good reason. The amount of time required for the change to manifest itself will be dependent on the type of training, how soon the participant has an opportunity to practice the skill, how long it takes participants to develop a new behavioral pattern, and other aspects of the job. So, how long? Anywhere from 2 to 12 months. You will probably need to work with the subject matter expert (SME) to determine the length of the delay required to allow participants an opportunity to transfer the learning (behavior) to the job.

By the way, like Level II, a pre- and post-testing method is recommended. And again, the question of whether you want to incorporate a control group for comparison needs to be decided.

What do you measure? Each item in an evaluation instrument should be related to an objective taught as part of the training program. Based on the training objectives, you will create a list of skills that describe the desired on-the-job performance. Use an SME to assist you with the design of the evaluation. The SME will understand the nuances of being able to complete a task. For example, a skill may be "uses the four-step coaching model with employees." An SME will know that even though the four steps are essential, what truly makes the model successful is the supervisor's "willingness to be available to respond to questions at any time." Knowing this, your checklist of skills will be expanded to include availability.

After you have identified the skills to measure, select an evaluation method. Evaluation tools may include interviews, focus groups, on-site observations, follow-up questionnaires, customer surveys, and colleague or supervisory input.

Level III evaluation should not be taken lightly. It takes a major resource investment. Know what you will measure; know how you will measure; and most important, know how you will use the data.

All trainers should be skilled in Level III evaluation methods. The most common reason for conducting training is to improve performance due to knowledge and skills transfer, as well as attitude changes. Results cannot be expected unless a positive change in behavior occurs. Therefore, use Level III evaluation to measure the extent to which a change in behavior occurs.

What do you do if the results show that performance has not been changed or skills mastered? You need to go back to the training design. Certainly the first step is to determine whether the skill is required. If yes, you want to examine the training material to ensure that appropriate learning techniques have been used and that enough emphasis has been placed on the skill. Perhaps a job aid is required to improve performance. Sometimes, you may discover something that did not show up in the needs assessment. For example, you may discover that participants are not using the skill because it is no longer important or is not frequently used on the job. In that case, you may want to remove it from the training session. This is a perfect example of how the fifth stage of The Training Cycle feeds back into the first stage.

Getting results that show that performance has not improved is not what a trainer wants to hear. However, it is good to have the knowledge to make an intelligent decision about whether to maintain the training program, overhaul it, or scrap it entirely. Without a Level III evaluation, you would not likely be able to make a wise decision.

Measuring Level IV

Level IV, or results, may be the most difficult to measure. Dr. Kirkpatrick states that the most frequently asked question he gets is "How do you evaluate Level IV?" Even though Level IV is the most challenging, training professionals need to be able to demonstrate that training is valuable and can positively affect the bottom line.

One of the issues of evaluating at this level is that you can never be sure whether external factors affected the business. There is always a possibility that something other than the on-the-job application contaminated the results. Can you really isolate the effects training has on business results? This is one time that using a control group can be helpful to the evaluation results. Yet even with a control group there may be other factors that impact the business, such as the loss of a good customer, the introduction of a new competitor, a new hiring practice, or the economy. Several statistical methods are available to you to consider other evidence. I don't cover them in this book.

So what do you do when management asks you to provide tangible evidence that training is having positive results? A before-and-after measurement is relatively easy because records for the kinds of things you measure (turnover, sales, expenses, errors, grievances) are generally available. The trick is to determine which figures are meaningful.

The second difficultly is predicting the amount of time that should be allowed for the change to take effect. It may be anywhere between 9 and 18 months. Gather the data that you believe provides evidence of the impact of the training. This measurement usually extends beyond the training department and utilizes tools that measure business performance, such as sales, expenses, or rework. Remember, a key issue is to try to isolate training's impact on results. You may not be able to prove beyond a doubt that training has had a positive business impact, but you will be able to produce enough evidence so that management can make the final decision.

You've read in this book and other places that training should align with the business's requirements. How do you do that? Dr. Kirkpatrick suggests that his evaluation levels can be used. Start with Level IV. Determine, with the business managers, what needs to occur (results). Next decided what performance (behaviors, or Level III) are required to achieve the desired results.

Then identify the knowledge, skills, and attitudes (KSAs, or Level II) employees require to achieve performance expectations. Finally, create a plan to offer the correct training, ensuring employees will be receptive to the changes.

Which evaluation level to use?

You may choose to evaluate training at one or all levels. How do you decide? Base your decision on answers to the following questions.

- ✔ What is the purpose of the training?
- ✔ How will you use the results of the evaluation?
- ✔ What changes or improvements may be made as a result of the evaluations?
- ✔ Who are the stakeholders and what do they want you to measure?
- ✔ Is the training expected to impact business goals?
- ✔ What resources will be required for the evaluation?

Just because there are four evaluation levels doesn't mean that you should use all four. After answering the preceding questions, decide which levels will be the most beneficial for each training. Evaluation experts agree that Level III and especially Level IV should be used sparingly due to the time and cost involved. A rule of thumb seems to be use Level IV in those situations where the results are a top organizational priority or for training that is expensive.

Evaluation methods

I have presented a number of evaluation methods in this chapter. In this section, I examine some of these and discuss the advantages and disadvantages to help you choose the one that will work best.

Objective test formats

This method measures how well trainees learn program content. An instructor administers paper-and-pencil or computer tests in class to measure participants' progress. The test should measure the learning specified in the objective. Tests should be valid and reliable. Valid means that an item measures what it is supposed to measure; reliable means that the test gives consistent results from one application to another.

- ✔ Multiple-choice questions take time and consideration to prepare. However, they maximize test-item discrimination yet minimize the accuracy of guessing. They provide an easy format for the participants and an easy method for scoring.
- ✔ True-false tests are more difficult to write than you may imagine. They are easy to score.

✔ Matching tests are easy to write and to score. They require a minimum amount of writing but still offer a challenge.

✔ Fill-in-the-blank or short-answer questions require knowledge without any memory aids. A disadvantage is that scoring may not be as objective as you may think. If the questions do not have one specific answer, the scorer may need to be more flexible than originally planned. Guessing is reduced because there are no choices available.

✔ Essays are the most difficult to score, although they do measure achievement at a higher level than any of the other paper-and-pencil tests. Scoring is the most subjective.

Attitude surveys

These question-and-answer surveys determine what changes in attitude have occurred as a result of training. Practitioners use these surveys to gather information about employees' perceptions, work habits, motivation, values, beliefs, and working relations. Attitude surveys are more difficult to construct because they measure less tangible items. There is also the potential for participants to respond with what they perceive is the "right" answer.

Simulation and on-site observation

Instructors' or managers' observations of performance on the job or in a job simulation indicate whether a learner is demonstrating the desired skills as a result of the training. Facilitate this process by developing a checklist of the desired behaviors. This is sometimes the only way to determine whether skills have transferred to the workplace. Some people panic or behave differently if they think they are being observed. Observations of actual performance or simulated performance can be time-consuming. It also requires a skilled observer to decrease subjectivity.

Criteria checklists

Also called *performance checklists* or *performance evaluation instruments, criteria checklists* are surveys using a list of performance objectives required to evaluate observable performance. The checklists may be used in conjunction with observations.

Productivity or performance reports

Hard production data such as sales reports and manufacturing totals can help managers and instructors determine actual performance improvement on the job. An advantage of using productivity reports is that no new evaluation tool must be developed. The data is quantifiable. Disadvantages include a lack of contact with the participant and records that may be incomplete.

Post-training surveys

Progress and proficiency assessments by both managers and participants indicate perceived performance improvement on the job. Surveys may not be as objective as necessary.

Needs/objectives/content comparison

Training managers, participants, and supervisors compare needs analysis results with course objectives and content to determine whether the program was relevant to participants' needs. Relevancy ratings at the end of the program also contribute to the comparison.

Evaluation forms

Sometimes called a *response sheet,* participants respond on end-of-program *evaluation forms* to indicate what they liked and disliked about the training delivery, content, logistics, location, and other aspects of the training experience. The form lets participants know that their input is desired. Both quantitative and qualitative data can be gathered.

Interviews

Interviews can be used to determine the extent to which skills and knowledge are being used on the job. They may also uncover constraints to implementation. Like no other method, interviews convey interest, concern, and empathy in addition to collecting data. They are useful when it isn't possible to observe behaviors directly. The interviewer becomes the evaluation tool, and this can be both an advantage and a disadvantage. Interviews are more costly than other methods, but they give instant feedback, and the interviewer has the ability to probe for more information.

Instructor evaluation

Professional trainers administer assessment sheets and evaluation forms to measure the instructor's competence, effectiveness, and instructional skills. See an example at the end of this chapter.

All of these evaluation methods work. All give you the information you need. Some work better than others for each of the four levels. The final decision about which method to use will be yours.

It is easy to grow accustomed to your favorite evaluation method. It is much better to incorporate variety in the evaluation methods used. Gaining expertise with several makes you more skilled in knowing which method will be best for each situation, and is an important aspect for achieving certification.

Discussions with employees on an individual basis can give insight into the effectiveness of the training session. Are there things you're doing differently as a result of participating in the training program? Have you noticed changes in your attitudes or relationships that may be related to the training program?

ROI: What's All the Hype?

In recent years a fifth level has been added to Kirkpatrick's Four Levels of Evaluation: return on investment (ROI). Trainers face a persistent trend to be more accountable and to prove their worth — the return on the dollars invested in training. Dr. Jack Phillips has been credited with the development of this fifth level of training evaluation.

As you read more about evaluation, you may see the term ROI used in conjunction with Level IV evaluation. The main difference at the fifth level is how the data is presented. ROI, by definition, is expressed as a percent in Level V.

Level V: Return on investment

This ROI measurement compares the monetary benefits of the training program with the cost of the program. Few organizations conduct evaluations at this level. The current estimates appear to be somewhere between 10 and 20 percent. Even if organizations do evaluate training at Level V, many limit its use only to those training programs that:

- ✔ Are expensive
- ✔ Are high visibility and/or important to top management
- ✔ Involve a large population
- ✔ Are linked to strategic goals and operational objectives

Although many organizations claim to want to know more about training's ROI, few seem to be willing to make the investment required to gather and analyze the data.

What's the ROI process?

ROI presents a process that produces the value-added contribution of training in a corporate-friendly format. The ROI process consists of five steps. Note that Levels I through IV are essential for gathering the initial data.

1. **Collect post-program data.**

   A variety of methods, similar to those identified in the last section, are used to collect Level I through Level IV data.

2. **Isolate the effects of training.**

   Many factors may influence performance data; therefore, steps must be taken to pinpoint the amount of improvement that can be attributed directly to the training program. A comprehensive set of tools is used that may include a control group, trend line analysis, forecasting models, and impact estimates from various groups.

3. **Convert data to a monetary value.**

   Assess the Level IV data and assign a monetary value. Techniques may include using historical costs, using salaries and benefits as value for time, converting output to profit contributions, or using external databases.

4. **Tabulate program costs.**

   Identifying the program costs include at least the cost to design and develop the program, materials, facilitator salary, facilities, travel, administrative costs and overhead, and the cost of participants who attend the program.

5. **Calculate the ROI.**

   The ROI is calculated by dividing the net program benefits (program benefits less program costs) by the program costs times 100. In this step, you also identify intangible benefits, such as increased job satisfaction, improved customer service, and reduced complaints.

Although it feels like a great deal of work, it will be worth it if you need to provide evidence to management regarding the value of training.

Benefits of adding a Level V

Given the extra effort, it's worth examining the benefits of adding a fifth level of evaluation.

Probably the most important one is to respond to management's question of whether training adds value to the organization. The ROI calculations convince management that training is an investment, not an expense. The ROI analysis also provides information about specific training programs: Which ones contributed the most to the bottom line; which ones need to be improved; and which ones are an expense to the organization. When the training practitioner acts on this data, the process has the added benefit of improving the effectiveness of all training programs.

Level V evaluations, ROI, provide an essential aspect of the entire evaluation process.

An interview with Jack Phillips

Q: Jack, it is exciting to be interviewing you. Can you provide readers with some background on ROI?

JP: We developed a systematic and practical way to show value for learning and development. Building on Kirkpatrick's four levels, we added a fifth level for ROI. In addition, we made adjustments in the definition to be more applicable across all types of programs. We added a process model to show how data are collected and converted to monetary value and costs are captured to generate the actual return on investment. One of the most important contributions is the variety of methods to isolate the effects of learning on actual business impact data. This is the most critical step to ensure credibility in an impact study.

Finally, we developed standards for the process and focused on how organizations can implement the methodology based on the assumption that the best model in the world is not going to be used routinely if it's not feasible, practical, rational, and logical. Much of our work is focused on helping others with implementation — the basis for our certification in the ROI methodology.

Q: How was ROI was developed? What's the real story?

JP: My interest in ROI stems initially from my interest and background in quantitative methods. With undergraduate degrees in electrical engineering, math, and physics and a master's in statistics, my personality and interest lie in bottom-line accountability (my Myers Briggs is ISTJ). In 1973, I conducted my first impact study as part of my master's thesis, where I calculated the return on investment for a co-op program at Lockheed Martin (I was the co-op Director).

My next ROI study (1976) was conducted on supervisor training. As training manager, I conducted this study in my organization at the suggestion of a senior executive who wanted to

know more about the impact of training. While we continued to improve, expand, and speak about ROI, I continued to use it internally as an HR executive and ultimately in a banking organization where I served as President and Chief Operating Officer.

Initially, I developed the ROI process using concepts from finance and accounting as well as some of the processes from re-engineering and the total quality movement. The process was built on the foundation of Kirkpatrick's four levels with an added fifth level. I thought the fifth level was necessary to show the ultimate accountability of comparing the monetary value of learning to the actual costs. More important, we developed a process model, created standards, and focused on implementation.

Q: What inspired you to develop a process for measuring ROI?

JP: The initial executive reaction from the second ROI study not only inspired me to continue working with the process on my own work but to also spread the word to others. I began by speaking occasionally, writing articles, and publishing. In 1982, I published my first book, *Handbook of Training and Evaluation and Measurement Methods,* which advocated ROI. Incidentally, this was the first major evaluation book in the United States and is now in its third edition with Butterworth-Heinemann. I continued to see positive reaction and began publishing additional materials. The reaction was overwhelming. My Ph.D. dissertation in the 1980s focused on this issue as well, digging into the issue from a research perspective.

By the early '90s, it was clear to me that there was a need for public workshops and consulting on this methodology. To our knowledge, there were no one- or two-day workshops on training evaluation. At the end of 1992, I launched the process globally, conducting our first two-day workshop in Johannesburg, South Africa. Since then, over 500 two-day workshops have been conducted with 15,000 participants; and over 130 one-week certification workshops have been conducted, involving over 2,000 participants. Its use and adoption throughout the world (in 40 countries) and the continuing feedback we get on this methodology keep inspiring me and our team to continue our work.

Q: Trainers seem to shy away from ROI. Why does that happen?

JP: There is both good and bad news here. First, as indicated above, there is a widespread adoption of ROI. We think that some 15 to 20 percent of training organizations in the USA are using this methodology in some way. Still, that leaves a lot of organizations that do not use ROI. We think some of the primary reasons are as follows:

✔ Many of the trainers have a fear of mathematics and statistics and equate the ROI methodology with mathematics. (This is often a myth and not necessarily the case.)

✔ There's a fear of ROI because it may expose a program or project that is not working well. If a program is ineffective, the last thing a trainer would want to do is publish a report indicating that it's not delivering the value.

✔ This process is very client driven. The trainer must work closely with management groups. Some trainers do not want to do that and will even avoid interaction with the management group.

✔ Trainers do not use ROI because they are concerned about the resources required — both time and money — to make it a reality. (This is often based on a myth and not reality.)

✔ Trainers don't know what ROI is all about and they lack the skills, insight, and knowledge to implement it. The unknown breeds uncertainty, which breeds resistance.

Q: Under what conditions should trainers and training departments be concerned about using ROI?

JP: Trainers should be concerned about ROI from three different viewpoints.

✔ **A defensive posture:** You have to be concerned about ROI when there's a need to justify the budget (or avoid budget cuts) or justify a program (or avoid having a program cut). The ROI methodology provides data about value, and it's the best way that we know to show the value of learning programs.

✔ **A responsive posture:** Trainers should be concerned about ROI if they want to be responsible for making a contribution to an organization. Every professional employee should be held accountable for his or her work.

✔ **A proactive posture:** More trainers these days are concerned about ROI because they want to be proactive, take the lead, and show the value with data that managers appreciate and respect. It's very self-satisfying to see the contribution you've made to the organization, and particularly satisfying for all the stakeholders involved.

Q: Any last words of advice, Jack?

JP: It's important to note that ROI should be used only on programs that are very expensive, strategic, involve a large number of employees, have high visibility, or attract management interest. Collectively, these criteria tell us when to use this process.

Evaluation: The Last Training Cycle Stage but the First Step to Improvement

Bringing a chapter that could be as big as a book to a close can be difficult. I am delighted that, if you chose to read the entire chapter, you were able to read comments directly from the two evaluation experts, Drs. Kirkpatrick and Phillips. Both recognize the value that evaluation holds for making improvements.

You may now be ready to put your evaluation plan together. If so, don't be shy about asking for outside assistance. Statisticians and researchers and other consultants will be able to expedite a process that will meet your stakeholders' needs.

As a trainer, the Level I evaluations are important to you. Don't ignore the feedback. Another practice you should consider is to ask a training colleague to conduct a peer review. Do you have a colleague whose opinion you value? Ask the individual to observe one of your programs — even a portion is helpful. Another trainer will observe things and give you feedback on techniques that participants may overlook.

I am delighted to share with you one of the most comprehensive trainer-competency checklists I've seen in Table 13-1. Copy it and ask a colleague for input on your next training session.

Table 13-1	Training/Facilitating Competency Checklist
Skill	*Comments*
Prepare:	
Appropriately arrange the setting?	
Prepare participants for the session?	
Prepare notes for the session?	
Demonstrate organization?	
Facilitate Learning:	
Provide an effective introduction?	
Use appropriate group facilitation techniques?	
Use a variety of visuals?	
Use visuals skillfully?	
Use a variety of learning activities?	

Skill	*Comments*
Use an appropriate pace?	
Use small groups for learning activities?	
Debrief activities?	
Stay focused on the topic?	
Create a Positive Learning Environment:	
Add creativity to the training?	
Make the learning interesting?	
Share ideas and offer suggestions?	
Use relevant examples?	
Provide honest feedback?	
Handle incorrect answers appropriately?	
Provide time to socialize?	
Reinforce success?	
Encourage Participation:	
Facilitate an appropriate icebreaker?	
Use a variety of methods for learning?	
Establish rapport?	
Make eye contact with all participants?	
Appear relaxed and pleasant?	
Use encouraging body language?	
Provide reinforcement for participation?	
Ask directly for participation?	
Reward risk?	
Share personal examples?	
Exhibit nonjudgmental behaviors?	
Communicate Content and Process:	
Provide an organized delivery?	
Summarize clearly?	

(continued)

Table 13-1 *(continued)*

Skill	Comments
Ask thought-provoking questions?	
Encourage questions?	
Answer questions appropriately?	
Create large-group discussions?	
Listen well?	
Check for understanding?	
Make smooth transitions?	
Use appropriate nonverbal skills?	
Speak and enunciate clearly?	
Project voice effectively?	
Display a thorough knowledge of the topic?	
Use appropriate humor?	
Deliver constructive feedback?	
Deal with the Unexpected:	
Handle unexpected events?	
Manage difficult situations or participants?	
Coach those who were reluctant to change?	
Display flexibility?	
Manage time and topics?	
Ensure Learning Outcomes:	
Assess individual learning?	
Provide time for Q&A?	
Encourage on-the-job application?	
Use relevant examples?	
Establish Credibility:	
Demonstrate understanding of the content?	
Display confidence?	
Maintain composure?	

Skill	*Comments*
Describe personal experiences?	
Answer questions?	
Evaluate the Training Solution:	
Monitor impact throughout program?	
Ask for feedback?	
Note recommendations for improvement?	
Additional Comments?	

Evaluation is the final stage in The Training Cycle, but it is certainly only the beginning of improving training. It will be up to you to take your training efforts to the next level relying on evaluation to help you decide what to improve. In Dr. Kirkpatrick's words, "Evaluation is a science and an art. It is a blend of concepts, theory, principles, and techniques. It is up to you to do the application."

Chapter 14

Transfer of Learning

· ·

In This Chapter

▶ Discovering how to follow-up with your participants

▶ Overcoming barriers to transfer learning to the workplace

▶ Recognizing the importance of planning for transfer

▶ Learning what great trainers do after training

· ·

"*W*ell, that was a great training session; now back to work!" Ever heard a colleague say something like this upon returning from a training session? I have left training with a big binder filled with good ideas. Because work piled up while I was gone, I place the training binder on the side of my desk, promising myself that I would look at it later and implement what I learned. Later came and went, and soon I moved the binder to a shelf next to lots of other binders filled with good ideas. Why does this happen? And when you are the one in the training role, is that what you want to occur? Of course not! But it takes a team effort to ensure that learning transfers to the workplace.

The supervisors, learners, and trainers form a team right from the start to ensure that learning and skills transfer from the training session to the workplace. You know that the pre-training activities are often more critical than the post-training activities in ensuring success. That means planning to ensure transfer should occur as soon as possible. Follow-up actions are useful, to be certain. Just remember that even though transfer of learning occurs after the training session, it is by then too late to plan for it.

This chapter addresses the barriers to transfer of learning and the importance of planning for the transfer. It will also provide suggestions and tips for what trainers can do following a training session.

Making Your Training Memorable: Following-Up

An issue cited by trainers since the beginning of time is that the concepts learned in the classroom may not transfer to the job. The training experience becomes a void — an isolated experience that has no practical application in the real world.

Dana and Jim Robinson have been expressing concern regarding the lack of training transfer to the workplace for years. Trainers need to examine the entire system from an organizational perspective. The reason that learning does not transfer could be organizational (policies, negative consequences), lack of management support, or that the learner lacks the required equipment, supplies, or support system. Therefore, it may not have been a training problem in the first place.

However, assume you conducted a great needs assessment and were correct in identifying a training problem. Yet the training did not transfer. Consider some barriers (see the following section) that may prevent an effective transfer of learning, as well as some steps a trainer can take to overcome these barriers during the design phase.

Note: This section can be placed anywhere in the Training Cycle because transfer of learning starts with the needs assessment to ensure that there really is a training problem and ends with implementation back on the job. I've written a specific chapter to give it the emphasis it needs. However, because you know there is a need for follow-up at the design stage, be sure to build in the strategies you need at that time.

Barriers to transfer of learning

It is unfortunate, but true: Many barriers exist that prevent learning from transferring to the job.

- ✔ It is difficult for participants to change their behavior, so they revert to old habits on the job.
- ✔ Participants may be the only ones practicing the new behavior. Peer pressure may cause them to reject the new learning.
- ✔ The participants' supervisors may not understand the new knowledge, skills, or behaviors; therefore, they do not support or reinforce them.
- ✔ The participants' supervisors may not agree with the new knowledge, skills, or behaviors; therefore, they may undermine them.
- ✔ The participants' supervisors may not be proper role models for the new knowledge, skills, or behaviors.

✔ The informal organizational culture may punish the new behavior. For example, I once worked with an organization that made coded locking systems. They found that their return rate was increasing. They found that the returned systems were defective due to production errors; for example, parts were missing, assembly was incorrect. They thought they needed to retrain all their assembly people. Instead, what they needed to do was to change their compensation system. Employees were paid by the number of systems they shipped on a daily basis, not by the quality of the final product. Of course one would expect employees to work as quickly as they could as opposed to as accurately as they could work.

Strategies for transfer of learning

Even though some barriers may be out of your hands, you can do your part as a trainer to ensure transfer of training. Although the transfer of training occurs after the actual session, remind yourself of what can be done before the training occurs and during the training session.

A comprehensive study about training transfer (Broad, M. & Newstrom, J.,*Transfer of Training*, Addison-Wesley, Reading, MA, 1992) notes that while post-training strategies are important to training transfer, the greater impact is actually in pre-training aspects.

Pre-training strategies

Trainers can implement numerous strategies before the training even begins to ensure that training transfers to the workplace.

✔ **Conduct a needs assessment:** Make sure the training you provide is derived from a well-conducted and -analyzed needs assessment. Be certain the training is aligned with the organization's strategic plan.

✔ **Coach the management team:** If managers have requested specific training for their employees, meet with the managers to gain specific information from them, as well as to let them know exactly what their roles will be in supporting and reinforcing the training. This is a good time to *prequalify managers* to determine how supportive they are of the upcoming training. Encourage them to meet with the learners to prepare them for why attending this training is important.

✔ **Inform managers about the training:** Provide management briefings about the training. Inform them about how the training supports the organizational goals. Let these folks know the objectives, the expected outcomes, and the expected benefits. Alert management to any organizational or top management barriers that may adversely affect the desired outcome. Engage the managers in resolving the barriers and get their commitment to support the group's solution.

✔ **Provide pre-training projects:** Get participants and their managers involved in the training concepts before the training begins. You can do this by having them complete instruments or surveys that will, in turn, be used as resource material or data in the actual training program.

Training strategies — during the session

Trainers can utilize numerous strategies during the session to ensure that training transfers to the workplace.

✔ **Practical application:** Make sure that every topic you cover in the training is job related and has a specific "real world" application.

✔ **Use actual examples:** When conducting role-plays, simulations, and other activities, use actual data and experiences.

✔ **Build in plenty of practice opportunities:** After you know the knowledge and skills required of the learners, design activities that include practice with feedback.

✔ **Poll expectations:** Before conducting the training program, poll the expectations of the participants to assure you are providing them with the skills and information they need. Build in the "what's in it for me?"

✔ **Include transfer to the job in debriefings:** When you debrief on any activity, make sure you include a discussion of how participants can apply the lessons of the activity to their jobs.

✔ **Encourage follow-up actions:** Participants can fortify and augment what they learned by tapping in to additional resources from a list that you provide. They can also schedule an "appointment" with themselves to review their notes. They could plan to discuss with their bosses how they will implement what they learned.

✔ **Create a reminder:** Participants can note their primary goals in their PDAs or other locations where they will see them often. They could also write them on index cards and place them in a conspicuous place at home, work, or in their cars.

✔ **Action plan:** After the training has been conducted, have participants list what they are going to do on the job as a result of training. Discuss participants' ideas with the entire group.

A *self memo* is a unique action planning tool. I've used this tool for many years and participants still love it. Have participants write themselves a memo during the training session and place it in a self-addressed, stamped envelope. Then mail it back to them in four to eight weeks. See Figure 14-1 as an example.

Self Memo

Write yourself a memo, committing to at least three things you'd like to do as a result of this training program. Sign it, insert it in the envelope, address it to yourself, and we will mail it back for your review in six weeks.

1.

2.

3.

Name_____

Date_____

Figure 14-1:
Self memo.

Post-training strategies

To transition learners from "I tried it" to "I'll apply it" requires trainers to design follow-up activities and provide tools to both the learner and the supervisor. In order for learning to transfer, the participant must be committed to the change. In addition, the supervisor must provide the learner with support. The trainer must support both the learner and the supervisor.

These suggestions identify strategies that you can use to ensure that the learners apply what they learn.

- ✔ **Follow-up letters, e-mails, or phone calls from the trainer:** A few weeks after the program is completed, the trainer may write follow-up letters or make phone calls. The communication can remind participants of some of the concepts and ask how they are doing in applying them. The phone call has the advantage of being interactive. It allows participants to share barriers they are experiencing and to get ideas from the trainer to overcome them. The trainer can assist learners with dealing with change. See the sidebar.

- ✔ **Follow-up sharing:** When you follow up with participants, track what you learn. If someone asks a practical question that was not covered in the training, or if the same question comes up several times, take note. Share this information with everyone in the class via an e-mail.

You may wish to credit one of the participants with follow-up: "Dan brought to my attention that we did not _____." This will encourage others to bring these things to your attention.

✔ **Support groups:** The trainer can encourage participants to form support groups. To do this, a small group of people can commit to meeting after a specified period of time. When they meet they can discuss how they have applied the learning, what problems they have encountered, and what they have done to overcome the problems.

✔ **Reunion:** If support groups do not appeal to the participants, you can call for a reunion. Have participants demonstrate how they are implementing what they learned in the workplace.

I've heard of some groups who were so dedicated to reconnecting with the other participants that they met after work.

✔ **Past participants as mentors:** Match participants who have attended the training in the past with participants who have just completed the session. If at all possible bring them into the classroom at some point during the session to meet each other.

✔ **Practice sessions:** The trainer can encourage participants to plan one or two practice sessions. You can even volunteer to facilitate them. The purpose would be to have participants reconvene after having had some time on the job to practice the skills. They could then practice the next higher level of that skill, get feedback, and make a new commitment to continuous learning.

✔ **Other feedback:** Think about other ways to gather data about the success of the session. For example, if you taught a computer class, you can check the help desk calls immediately after the session to determine if there are references to your session. If there are, it means that learning did not occur. Perhaps there is a better method to use next time.

Set up an electronic bulletin board for participants to share successes, ask questions, or just to stay in touch in general.

✔ **Job aids:** Job aids are short, written guides or check sheets that summarize the steps to a task or job procedure. They may also be performance support systems (PSS) or posters that can be taken back to the workplace. They serve as reminders to the participants after the training has been completed. They are especially useful after a skill training program. However, job aids can also be effective in reminding participants of key behavioral concepts.

✔ **Management support and coaching:** The best way to assure post-training application is to have participants' managers provide support and coaching. A trainer may provide a sheet of coaching tips to managers and then follow up to offer assistance to them in the coaching process.

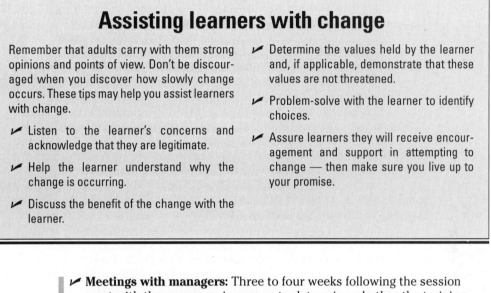

Assisting learners with change

Remember that adults carry with them strong opinions and points of view. Don't be discouraged when you discover how slowly change occurs. These tips may help you assist learners with change.

✔ Listen to the learner's concerns and acknowledge that they are legitimate.

✔ Help the learner understand why the change is occurring.

✔ Discuss the benefit of the change with the learner.

✔ Determine the values held by the learner and, if applicable, demonstrate that these values are not threatened.

✔ Problem-solve with the learner to identify choices.

✔ Assure learners they will receive encouragement and support in attempting to change — then make sure you live up to your promise.

✔ **Meetings with managers:** Three to four weeks following the session meet with the managers in person to determine whether the training addressed the needs and whether the employees are applying the skills and knowledge. You may also use this time to determine what other needs could be addressed in the future.

What Great Trainers Do After Training

Many of the same strategies that you use with participants are things that you can do yourself to ensure continuous improvement. For example, you could write yourself a memo, committing yourself to at least two things you'd like to do better as a result of facilitating your session. Sign it, insert it in an envelope, address it to yourself, and ask someone to mail it back for your review in a month. When it arrives, it will be a reminder of what you were supposed to have accomplished.

Make a habit of reviewing your training notes immediately after the session and make additions or changes while it is all fresh in your mind.

Be sure to study the evaluations. What suggestions do the participants have for you? What can you do differently next time, based on the feedback? Review several sets of evaluations to determine if there are any trends. If so, what are they and do they require any changes on your part or to the materials?

Follow-up with the participants, sending them any materials that you promised you would send. This is a great opportunity to find out how they are doing and how you may be able to help them transfer the skills.

If you do not have a Smile File, start one today. A *Smile File* is a place where you can keep all your kudos. If you did a great job facilitating, you are sure to receive notes, e-mails, and cards complimenting you on something special or thanking you for going out of your way. Your Smile File will be useful when you are having a difficult day. You can pull it out and read the wonderful things participants have said in the past. That will make it all worthwhile.

Connect with the participants' supervisors relatively soon after the training session. Remind them of how they can support their employees. This may be a time to share a "cheat sheet" with them. You could provide a list of the concepts taught, questions that could be asked, or suggestions for how to help learners implement the skills or use the knowledge.

If the training session will be ongoing, consider conducting a focus group with several key supervisors to obtain feedback before conducting the training again. They can tell you what skills seem to be transferring and which are not. They may also be able to provide you with other insight to improve the training session.

There are many other things you could do following training. I think this is enough to get you started. Although short, this chapter is a critical consideration for all trainers. Transfer of learning and transfer of skills beyond the classroom are why you are in business. In this fast-moving world, it would be easier to "call it quits" at the end of the training session. A trainer — a great trainer — makes certain that follow-up activities are completed to ensure transfer of learning has occurred.

As you leave this chapter, remember the words of one of the pioneers in the training profession, Robert Mager, who stated in his book *Making Instruction Work:* "If it's worth teaching, it's worth finding out whether the instruction was successful. If it wasn't entirely successful, it's worth finding out how to improve it."

Part V

The Professional Trainer

The 5th Wave — By Rich Tennant

In this part . . .

You have a chance to explore the professional aspects of being a trainer. How can you constantly upgrade your skills? How do you become certified by the American Society for Training and Development (ASTD)? What issues exist in the profession that you should have knowledge about? This part answers those questions.

Chapter 15

The Consummate Professional

*W*hat does it take to be a model of success and professionalism as a trainer? Probably the same thing it takes to be a model of success in any vocation, whether it's ballet, soccer, chemistry, plumbing, teaching, or writing. I once read that most people achieve only a third of their potential. Successful professionals in any field achieve more than a third of their potential because they work at it.

How can trainers maintain a professional edge? Professional trainers can become lifelong learners; they go the extra mile to be better than average; and they give back to the profession. Each of these topics is addressed in this chapter. In addition, you will not want to miss Bob Pike's thoughts about what it takes to be a master trainer.

Become a Lifelong Learner

You have an obligation to your participants and employer to continually improve your knowledge and skills. The rapid changes in the world today can turn today's expert into tomorrow's dolt if the person fails to keep up.

Trainers create their own development plan to ensure that they are lifelong learners. Several strategies can be included in a development plan.

Attend formal learning events

Probably the first thing you think about when becoming a lifelong learner is "What class or conference can I attend?"

Go back to school

You may not need an MBA, but courses at the graduate level are critical. Take courses in finance or marketing or organizational development so that you can continue to be a strong contributor to your organization. Take a class to bring yourself up to speed in the technology area. Take an adult-learning class as a refresher or to get another perspective.

Check your local community colleges and universities. Many have continuing educational programs that may offer topics to help you grow. I've benefited from programs such as "Dealing with Difficult People," "Project Management," and "Learning to Be More Creative."

Consider certification

Certification confers valuable credibility to anyone in the profession. The American Society for Training and Development has responded to the growing demand for credentialing. It initiated a certification program in 2005 based on the 2004 Competency Study. Certification benefits trainers by offering a means to prove their value and identify a path of continued professional development.

Seminars and workshops are available to help individuals prepare for certification. The next chapter discusses certification for trainers and others in the broader field of Workplace Learning and Performance.

Attend conferences

At the very least consider attending your professional organization's annual conference. It may be expensive, but you owe it to yourself to invest in your development. Sometimes local chapters also present conferences or daylong seminars. All of these add to your knowledge and skill base.

To get the most out of these events, network with others. Trade business cards. Offer to exchange information or resources. At least as much learning occurs during the breaks and informal networking opportunities as occurs during the formal sessions.

If you network with many folks, jot a note on the back of each business card to remind yourself about the topic, what you were to send, or why you want to stay in touch with the person.

Enroll in a train-the-trainer, preferably one in which you are videotaped and obtain feedback on your training style.

Ask others

Many other learning experiences exist, if you just ask.

Join an association or a group

Toastmasters, National Speaker Association (NSA), The American Society for Training and Development (ASTD), International Society for Performance Improvement (ISPI), and others are great groups for you to join. They provide opportunities for you to learn new skills, to stay on top of the latest happenings in the profession, and to network with others in the training profession.

Go to the *Training For Dummies* resource list at www.ebbweb.com to learn more about these and other groups. Find a chapter in your area. All will invite you to attend a trial meeting to determine if the group is right for you.

Create mentoring opportunities

Identify another trainer whom you respect and would like as a mentor. Ask the person if that would be possible. My mentor and I meet for breakfast four to six times each year. I pay for our meals. This has become the best $10 investment I make. I'm investing in myself.

Determine where the experts hang out. Then go there. Sometimes this is a related association or an informal group. More-seasoned people and those with different experiences can offer you priceless advice and knowledge.

Train with a partner

Training with a partner is a unique way to learn from someone else. It allows you to observe another trainer, elicit feedback about your efforts, and learn new techniques and skills. Even if you do not co-facilitate, invite other colleagues to observe you during a training session. Ask them to notice specific aspects of your training and solicit their input after the session.

Do it yourself

You don't have to wait for a class or a conference or a meeting to learn. You can establish your own pace by reading books and journals.

Read

I recently designed a training certificate program for ASTD. As a part of my data gathering, I asked top training professionals what they did to maintain their expertise. Everyone stated that they read. And they didn't just read a book or two. They read lots! They devoured the printed word. Some subscribed to (and read) dozens of journals and magazines. Others read upwards of 20 books every month. This behavior represents the experts in our profession; they must be on to something!

Subscribe to and read professional journals such as *Training Magazine* and *T&D Journal*. Read general business magazines such as *Fortune, Business*

Week, and the *Harvard Business Review.* Read the journals published by your company's or your client's industry. And read cutting-edge journals such as *Fast Company.*

Identify resources

Many other resources exist. Sign up for an online service. The World Wide Web is a dynamic source for professional development resources. Sites provide information as well as link you to other related sites.

You can listen to books on tape while driving longer distances. Organizations sell tapes of conference presentations.

You can be a resource to yourself. In fact, you will be your own best critic. Videotape an actual training session and play it back to identify what you like and what you do not like about your training style. If you think taping the session will be disruptive, you may wish to tape yourself during a practice session or just audiotape your session. Of course you will not have the visual portion, but you can hear how you sound and will be able to critique the audio portion of your training session.

Learning and growing are ongoing processes, even if you are at the top of your profession. Often it is what you learn after you "know it all" that counts. Aspire to the best of your profession.

Go the Extra Mile: Stay on Top of Your Game!

Go the extra mile? Gosh! Isn't becoming a lifelong learner enough? Well, learning new skills is just the beginning. Going the extra mile means that you are looking for ways to constantly improve. How can you be more than a good trainer, a great trainer? In addition, how can you keep your energy up ALL the time? Even if this is the 49th time you have conducted the same session? Is it really possible to be enthusiastic and energetic? Yes it is!

Good to great

A widely read book, *Good to Great,* by Jim Collins provides a format to think about how trainers can upgrade their skills (see Table 15-1). The left-hand column in the table lists attributes of good trainers. But good can be great. Several ideas that go beyond good to great are listed in the middle column. Space is available in the right column for you to add your thoughts about what you could do to move from the already good trainer you are to a great trainer.

Table 15-1	Good to Great Trainers	
Good Trainers	*Great Trainers Also . . .*	*To Be Great I Will . . .*
Design and deliver training that addresses all learning styles	Spend quality time with individuals to ensure that each participant's learning needs are met	
Know their content well	Constantly update and improve content based on organizational and industry needs	
Have excellent presentation skills	Seek opportunities for feedback; practice to fine-tune	
Are flexible when difficult situations arise	Have backup plans and options ready	
Are enthusiastic about the training topic	Inspire participants	
Are informed about the most recent developments in their fields	Become experts and contribute to the field by writing articles and books	
Effectively manage the learning setting	Provide feedback and implement improvements	
Ensure that participants learn	Ensure knowledge applies to the job; follow up after training	
Are good communicators	Are flexible communicators, moving into others' communication comfort zones	
Are a model of what they train	Ensure participants are models as well	

Great trainers do everything that good trainers do, but so much more and so much better. Invest in yourself. Go from good to great. Believe in yourself. If you don't, who will?

Where's your energy? Stay pumped!

Imagine this. You are about to go into a training program that you have taught countless times. You are starting to lose interest in the topic, and you are wondering how you will get through this without being monotonous and boring. Here are some thoughts about how you can make every training session seem as exciting as your first.

- ✔ Recharge your batteries every day. You owe it to your participants to give every session everything you have. Self-talk works well for me: "This will be the best darn training these participants have ever experienced!"

- ✔ Even though the topic is not new to you, it is to the participants. Remembering that they may be hearing the information for the first time is exciting. Determine how to have more participant involvement to experience the topic from another perspective.

- ✔ Do something that is just a little crazy; for example, if you are showing a video, serve popcorn; ask participants to use crayons for a particular activity; on a nice day, hold a discussion outside.

- ✔ Use previous evaluations for the program to determine an area for improvement. Then integrate improvements into the next program. By striving for continuous improvement, you will never have to train the same program twice.

- ✔ A day before the session, examine the part of the program you dislike the most. Chances are it never was right for you. In my case, it is usually more presenting and less interaction. Rework that part of the program so that you eliminate the reason you don't like it. In my case, it would be identifying a way to increase participation.

- ✔ Observe someone else conducting the session (or other sessions) to identify new presentation or facilitation techniques.

- ✔ Page through a *Pfeiffer Annual,* one of the *Games Trainers Play* books, or another activity book (see the *Training For Dummies* resource list on my Web site at www.ebbweb.com) to add a new or revise a timeworn activity.

- ✔ Experiment with activities you have not used before: funneling, an in-basket, or a relay.

- ✔ Try a new presentation technique or media; for example, use overhead transparencies or conduct a debate.

- ✔ Conduct research about the topic (the Web, journals, books) so that you have new information to share or so that you feel better prepared.

- ✔ Invite a guest speaker to conduct the part of the workshop that is most energy draining for you.

- ✔ Co-facilitate a portion of the session, perhaps role-playing with the other trainer or introducing a "point-counterpoint" type discussion.

- ✔ Get to know the participants personally. This helps you appreciate how much they need the information you have to give.

- ✔ Identify new energizers to use with the group each day. Energy is contagious. You will catch it from the participants.

✔ Find cartoons or quotes that relate to the session and introduce them after breaks or as energizers.

✔ The night before the session, pull out your Smile File that's filled with thank-you cards, fabulous evaluations, special notes, cartoons that make you laugh, clippings, or articles about you. Spend 20 minutes looking through it. What? You don't have a Smile File? Better start one today.

✔ Approach every training program as though you want it to be your best ever. Remember how good you feel after you have completed a training program and the participants loved it.

✔ Try reverse psychology: Think about the worst job you ever had (mine was making plastic wastepaper baskets on the midnight shift) and compare conducting the training to it.

✔ Determine a reward for yourself following the training session.

✔ Now identify two more things that keep you going and list them here.

- I could . . .

- I could . . .

Design

If you design often, take care that you do not fall into a rut of doing the same things over and over. Try something new. It keeps your designs fresh and keeps you inspired and interested.

Plan to include a new type of activity in each program that you design. If you have never used a game show to review material, build one in. If you rarely use guest speakers or role plays, consider them. There is such a wide variety of activities, you may never run out of ideas.

What does professional mean to you?

Every trainer needs to define what it means to be "professional." Take time to determine what it means to you to be a true professional. Write your thoughts out on paper. Share them with others. Consider it for a panel discussion topic at your local ASTD chapter meeting.

Develop your personal training code of ethics; that is, what do you intend to live by and honor as a trainer? It could include delivering only the highest quality training, always giving credit to others to whose work you refer, holding confidential information close, and respecting all learners. A code of ethics gives you a guide, something to live by and on which to base decisions.

To get you started thinking about what it means to be a professional, interview another trainer whose work you respect and who has been around the profession for a while.

Ten core skills of a master trainer

by Bob Pike CSP, CPAE-Speakers Hall of Fame

I believe that we make ourselves more valuable when we develop what I call CORE Skills. In management training we often refer to these as *soft skills*, but I think this is a misnomer. Why? Because people are most often hired for the technical skills (their ability to do the job — whatever the job maybe), and they are fired for their lack of personal skills — that ability to work with and through others. These personal skills are the ten CORE Skills I challenge you to master:

1. **Make and keep commitments.** This means that a "yes" is a "yes" and a "no" is a "no." Many people make promises and don't follow through. Or they overpromise and underdeliver. What if you and all the employees in your organization were known as people who made commitments and kept them. Do you think this would help you gain a competitive advantage?

2. **Face each day with a positive attitude.** It's been said that we burn three times as much energy when thinking negatively as when thinking positively. What if you and each person in your organization looked for ways things could be done, instead of reasons why they couldn't? What if we looked at the potentials and possibilities, instead of the problems?

3. **Persist until you succeed.** Most people quit one step short of success. Thomas Edison, who failed ten thousand times before successfully creating a practical, sustainable light bulb, said most people would not have failed if they had simply tried one more time. He also said that he didn't fail 10,000 times — he simply found 9,999 ways it wouldn't work!

4. **Have a clear positive self-image.** For years, I sold and conducted a program that thousands of others could sell and conduct as well. My price was even a bit higher. There were always those that were willing to cut the price a bit — even a lot — just to make a sale. I didn't. When asked what justified the difference I said, "All other things being equal, you get me with this." I didn't say it to brag or be boastful. My attitude was the same at 25 that it is at 55. What I mean is that I'm committed to getting you results, not just selling you a product. That attitude, that self-concept, that commitment, is worth the difference. I completed a "Faith at Work" program with Ken Blanchard of *One Minute Manager* fame. He talked about **EGO** meaning **E**dging **G**od **O**ut. He pointed out that this could happen with pride, thinking more of ourselves than we ought to — and also with self-doubt — thinking less of ourselves than we ought to.

5. **Multiply your value 100-fold.** Many people focus on the MDR — the Minimum Daily Requirement: what is the least I can do to get by? My focus is on the most we can give to add value to whatever we do. What if we had an organization made up of people who were constantly looking for ways to add value? What power! I consulted for an organization that had been forced to reduce salaries, cut jobs, and faced two years before things improved. We pulled a group of 150 managers together and in small groups led them through a process where they had to find ways to recognize and reward employees without using pay, promises, or promotions. In less than two hours we had a list of over 150 ways that managers could use cafeteria style — picking and choosing those that would work best with their individual employees. Using some of these would help all managers to increase their value by creating a more motivational environment.

6. **Treat this day as if it were your last.** What if everyone in your organization always focused on the highest priorities — both personally and professionally? What if we lived this day in a compartment, not letting yesterday's challenges creep in, not letting tomorrow's problems drain energy — just focusing on doing the absolute best we can right now? What do you need to do today that would cause you at the end of the day to have no regrets?

7. **Master your emotions.** Sister Kenny was founder of the Sister Kenny Institute and originator of innovative cancer therapies even though she was not a medical doctor. She faced harsh criticism for years until her methods finally proved themselves. How did she manage her emotions in the midst of unjust accusations? Perhaps it started at age 6 when she lost her temper over a difference with a playmate. Her mother took her aside and said, "Any one who angers you, conquers you!" Those words must have played back through her adult years until her methods were proven. Look at the work that would have been lost, the tens of thousands that would not have received treatment if she had not known how to rein her emotions in. Her refusal to explode kept her critics from having ammunition with which to destroy her work.

8. **Laugh at the world and yourself.** We take ourselves too seriously. We all make mistakes. Are we going to get down on ourselves or learn from them and laugh at them? Nurse educators have explained to me that often there is laughter in very serious training classes containing life-or-death content. Why? "Because," they say, "What we do is too serious to take seriously all the time." Can you laugh and learn even when things do not go your way?

9. **See a need, take action.** All too often people see a need and say, "That's not my job." Elbert Hubbard wrote a delightful small book over 100 years ago called "A Message to Garcia." It was about an army officer who took a message from Roosevelt to a Cuban revolutionary and emerged from the jungle after three weeks having delivered the message, no questions asked. What if everyone in your organization took action when the need arose, rather than passing the buck? Let's have a renaissance of initiative!

10. **Seek guidance.** Are we willing to ask for help — especially from a Higher Power? Are we willing to ask that we be guided to opportunities to use the talents that we've been given? Are we willing to ask for the wisdom to discern those opportunities that are great rather than those that are merely good? I keep a prayer journal. I spend time praying for world leaders, our nation's leaders, our teachers, our children, my extended family, and so on. As people share needs, I add them to my prayer journal. I pray for the companies that I'm involved in and their employees. And I seek guidance to use the talents and abilities that I've been blessed with.

So now you've had a look at all ten CORE Skills. If you want to put into practice some of these concepts let me offer the following: Read Og Mandino's book, *The Greatest Salesman in the World*. This book is less about selling and more about developing the personal skills needed to succeed in any job. In fact, they are really the principles of living life at the highest level. The book still sells over a million copies years after its first publication in 1968.

 Bob Pike has been a part of the training profession since 1969. He is the president of Creative Training Techniques International and has inspired hundreds of thousands of trainers through his Creative Training Techniques workshops and his *Creative Training Techniques newsletter*. Bob is also the author or editor of over 20 books including the best-selling *The Creative Training*

Techniques Handbook. The focus of his work is using involvement and participation at all levels to drive greater results. Bob is my model of a consummate professional trainer. He presents ten core skills all professional trainers should live by in the "Ten core skills of a master trainer" sidebar.

Give Back to the Profession

All trainers receive advice and ideas from others throughout their careers. Therefore, all trainers owe something to the profession. How can you do that?

✔ **Publish what you have learned or your ideas for others to consider.** *Training Magazine* and *T&D Journal* are two publications that print articles by practitioners. The *Pfeiffer Annual* publishes activities, articles, and instruments.

✔ **Write a book.** ASTD Press, Jossey-Bass/Pfeiffer, and HRD Press are all trainer-friendly.

If you are interested in publishing, write for a publication calendar from the periodicals or speak to an editor about the topics they want to publish.

✔ Accept invitations to be a part of a panel discussion, or present at your local professional chapter meeting.

✔ Submit a proposal to speak at a national conference.

✔ Be a contributor to your local chapter of NSA or ASTD: Present at meetings, volunteer to chair committees, or support the fund-raisers.

✔ Mentor someone entering the training field.

✔ Present at your local grade school or high school for career day.

✔ Provide pro bono work for a local nonprofit organization.

✔ Start a scholarship fund.

Training is a profession that gives a great deal to its members. Think about how you can give back to the profession, your community, and individuals. Yes, it takes a great deal to be a professional trainer. You can do it. Be all the things that you are capable of being. Astound yourself. Thomas Edison believed that "If we did all the things we are capable of, we would literally astound ourselves."

Chapter 16

Training Certification

● ●

In This Chapter

▶ Getting information about ASTD

▶ Finding out more about the ASTD Competency Model

▶ Understanding certification: What it means for you

● ●

*Y*ou may be feeling a bit overwhelmed about the number of skills and the amount of knowledge trainers require to do their jobs. It can be overwhelming. But support is available. The American Society for Training & Development (ASTD) is the world's largest association dedicated to workplace learning and performance professionals, and to providing content and resources to individuals, like you, who enter and work in the field.

Two ASTD initiatives are particularly exciting:

✔ The ASTD Competency Model
✔ ASTD's certification offering, based on that model

Both of these initiatives will continue to have a profound effect on the workplace learning and performance profession and on each member of the profession.

This chapter provides you with an introduction to ASTD and what the association offers. It also provides an overview of the ASTD Competency Study, *Mapping the Future,* and its value to the profession. Most exciting, however, is the introduction to the ASTD Certification Program and what it means to you. The Certification Program was a direct result of the study.

Due to its far-reaching effect, I am most excited about the topics in this chapter. Jennifer Naughton, ASTD Manager of both the ASTD Competency Study and the Certification Program, has graciously given her time to assist with writing this chapter.

All About ASTD

ASTD is the world's largest association dedicated to workplace learning and performance professionals whose job it is to connect learning and performance to measurable results for organizations. ASTD's 70,000 members and associates come from over 100 countries and thousands of organizations of all sizes and all industries: private- and public-sector organizations, government and academia, consulting firms, and product and service suppliers.

Why is ASTD's mission important?

ASTD's mission is: "Through exceptional learning and performance, we create a world that works better." ASTD's research has shown that people are the key to driving an organization's competitive edge. People are the chief asset in a fast-paced world where knowledge and service are the currency of success. The best strategic solution to meet these challenges is workplace learning that unleashes talent and leads people to peak performance.

What does ASTD do?

ASTD is a membership association for training professionals and others in the workplace learning and performance profession. ASTD provides content, resources, and professional development opportunities and serves as a forum to bring people together to learn, network, and grow. And ASTD sets the standard for best practices.

ASTD provides resources

ASTD provides resources for professionals in the form of research, analysis, benchmarking, online information, books, and other publications, including the following:

- *State of the Industry Report,* which annually analyzes U.S. organizations' training investments and practices

- *Training + Development magazine,* which keeps readers up-to-date on the latest ideas, trends, and best practices

- *Infoline* series, which gives short practical "how-to" guidelines on a range of training topics

- *Learning Circuits,* which offers online news and features about e-learning

- Buyer's Guide, which provides a searchable database of products and services

ASTD's history

ASTD celebrated its 60th anniversary in 2004. The seeds of the organization were sown in New Orleans, Louisiana, during a training committee meeting of the American Petroleum Institute in 1942. The United States was at war, and training was critical to meeting the needs of increased production and replacing workers gone to war. The following year, a group of 15 men met for the first board meeting of the American Society of Training Directors in Baton Rouge, Louisiana.

These training pioneers became the nucleus of a national group, which convened the ASTD membership for the first time in Chicago in 1945.

Other local, regional, and industry-specific training groups gradually aligned with ASTD.

ASTD adopted a constitution at its 1946 convention that established two goals: to raise the standards and prestige of the industrial training profession and to further the professional's education and development. These two goals have remained part of ASTD's mission even as the profession evolved and needs changed.

In 1964, the association changed its name to the American Society for Training & Development. In recent years, ASTD has widened its focus to connect learning and performance to measurable results.

Find out what ASTD offers firsthand. Check out the society's Web site at `www.astd.org`.

ASTD provides professional development opportunities

As a training professional, you should go to ASTD for your own professional training and development. Here are a few of the opportunities.

- ✔ Certification, as of 2005 (read more in the "Certification: What It Means for You" section later in this chapter)

- ✔ Training Certificate Programs that help practitioners discover what's required of trainers today

- ✔ Human Performance Improvement (HPI) Certificate that includes a five-course in-depth program

- ✔ Certified Performance Technologist (CPT) credential that recognizes practitioners who have demonstrated proficiency in ten standards (in affiliation with the International Society for Performance Improvement)

ASTD serves as a forum to bring people together

ASTD brings people together in conferences, workshops, and online.

- ✔ The ASTD International Conference & Exposition (ICE) occurs annually in the May/June time frame, drawing 9,000 attendees from all over the world

- ✔ ASTD TechKnowledge is a conference and exposition that focuses on e-learning and the use of technology in learning

> ✔ ROI Network conferences and workshops focus on developing the profession's ability to measure and evaluate return on investment
>
> ✔ ASTD supports 137 local chapters in the United States and 12 global networks around the world

To be a part of this rewarding profession, become a member of ASTD. You will be amazed at what a difference it makes to have the opportunity to grow and network with other professionals like yourself.

. . . and a whole lot more

ASTD recognizes a number of best practices in the profession through several awards programs: ASTD BEST Awards, Excellence in Practice Awards, Advancing ASTD's Vision Awards, Advancing Workplace Learning and Performance Awards, Research-to-Practice Awards, and ROI Network Awards. And, ASTD advocates on behalf of the profession to promote U.S. public policies that support a highly skilled workforce and provides the media with expertise on trends in workplace learning and performance.

ASTD has an online career center and job bank and offers a wide range of tools and information on workforce development, learning, and performance on its Web site at www.astd.org.

Introducing the ASTD Competency Model

The ASTD Competency Model — developed in partnership among ASTD, Development Dimensions International (DDI), and Rothwell & Associates (R&A) — provides a strategic model for the profession. With an eye toward the future, the model enables individuals and institutions to be prepared to align their work with organizational priorities. The model's comprehensive view of the field unifies the profession and defines various areas of expertise.

Overview of the model

Having a defined set of competencies is a hallmark of any profession. The ASTD Competency Model defines standards of excellence for trainers and others in the workplace learning and performance profession. The model, shaped like a pyramid (see Figure 16-1), displays three layers of knowledge and skill: foundational competencies, areas of expertise, and roles. What is contained in each of these layers? The following sections provide the details.

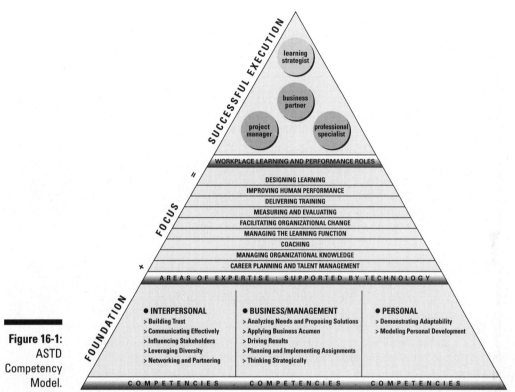

Figure 16-1:
ASTD
Competency
Model.

Competencies

Competencies encompass the clusters of skills, knowledge, abilities, and behaviors required for success in all jobs in the profession. In simple terms, this is what those in the profession collectively need to know and do to be successful.

Foundational competencies

Foundational competencies underlie the successful completion of many tasks, and are, therefore, found at the base of the model. The model defines each of the 12 foundational competencies and provides examples of actions that can be included in each. The 12 foundational competencies have been placed into three clusters: interpersonal, business/management, and personal.

✔ **Interpersonal:** Every job requires a certain level of interpersonal acumen. The ASTD Competency Model identifies a set of interpersonal competencies that are important to trainers and others in the workplace learning and performance profession. The interpersonal competencies include the ability to build trust, communicate effectively, influence stakeholders, leverage diversity, and take part in networking and partnering.

✔ **Business/management:** The training profession continues to strengthen its role in the boardroom. With that role comes an expectation of business and management competencies. The model includes five business and management competencies: analyzing needs and proposing solutions; applying business acumen; driving results; planning and implementing assignments; and thinking strategically.

Although you will certainly find these competencies in many professions, their existence in this model highlights the important role workplace learning and performance professionals play to help drive organizational success.

✔ **Personal:** The Competency Model identifies two personal competencies: demonstrating adaptability and modeling personal development. These two should not come as a surprise to you, given the emphasis of both throughout this book. Trainers are often expected to model appropriate behavior when change occurs whether it is global, cultural, economic, social, or political.

Trainers must be role models of the profession. Chapter 15 clearly states that it is the responsibility of members of the workplace learning and performance profession to create learning opportunities to upgrade our own knowledge and skills. As training professionals, we must ensure that we are in a continuous learning mode for two reasons: first, to serve as role models; second, because trainers must stay ahead of and on top of new developments in our profession and in the industries that we serve.

Areas of expertise

Areas of expertise are the specific technical and professional skills and knowledge required for success in the workplace and learning specialty areas. Although some professionals are highly specialized, many people demonstrate expertise in more than one area.

Areas of expertise are positioned above the foundational competencies on the model because they supplement them through specialized skills and knowledge. Nine areas of expertise are identified. Just below the nine, a narrow band depicting technology supports the areas of expertise. This represents the fact that all the areas rely on technology such as Web-based training to leverage and support their skills and knowledge.

The nine areas of expertise are listed here. This book covers several on the list.

✔ Career planning and talent management

✔ Coaching

✔ Delivering training

✔ Designing learning

✔ Facilitating organizational change

✔ Improving human performance

✔ Managing organizational knowledge

✔ Managing the learning function

✔ Measuring and evaluating

Roles

Roles are broad areas of responsibility within the profession that require a certain combination of competencies and areas of expertise to be effectively realized. The roles are at the top of the model because they require a vast body of skills and knowledge. The four roles and a brief definition of each are as follows:

✔ **Learning strategist:** Determines how training and other workplace learning and performance improvement strategies can best be leveraged to achieve business success and add value.

✔ **Business partner:** Applies business and industry knowledge to partner with clients to identify opportunities by evaluating and recommending solutions.

✔ **Project manager:** Plans, resources, and monitors the effective delivery of training and other learning and performance solutions to support the organization.

✔ **Professional specialist:** Designs, develops, delivers, or evaluates learning and performance solutions and maintains and applies an in-depth working knowledge in any one of more of the areas of expertise.

The value of a competency model

The competencies, areas of expertise, and roles identified provide a model for understanding the requirements of the profession. Although this is important, the real value of the model is its application to enhance and elevate the profession. Among other things, the competency model can be used to

✔ Attract people into the profession

✔ Evaluate individuals for selection or promotion

✔ Guide career-planning decisions

✔ Assess job performance

✔ Establish a foundation for credentialing programs

It is this last purpose, professional certification, that has created considerable excitement among trainers and others in the workplace learning and performance profession.

If you are serious about being a professional in the workplace learning and performance arena, you want to obtain your certification. To get started, obtain your personal copy of *The ASTD Competency Study, Mapping the Future* by Bernthal, et al.

Certification: What It Means for You

In the preceding section of this chapter, you find out about the ASTD Competency Study and how it provides a road map for guiding professional development and the future of the profession. Now, I switch gears and focus on certification and its implications. Before describing the value and components of ASTD's Certification Program, the following section starts with some context.

Certification versus certificate

Certification is a voluntary process whereby a professional body such as ASTD recognizes or grants a designation to professionals who have met certain qualifications or standards. Certified individuals are usually issued a designation recognizing that they have met those standards.

Certification and certificate are often used interchangeably, but they do not mean the same thing. Certification and certificate programs differ in their criteria and goals. In *certification*, the focus is on assessing knowledge and skills. In a *certificate* program, the focus is on the training provided to develop a certain knowledge and skill base (*e-Answers e-zine* "Credentialing, Licensure, Certification, Accreditation, Certificates: What's the Difference?" May 2002, Volume 1, Issue 3, ©Mickie S. Rops & Associates). Furthermore, certificate programs typically award a document signifying completion, with or without an assessment. Unfortunately, the lack of standardization in terms and inconsistent application creates mayhem in the marketplace and really muddies the water.

To determine which is which, ask yourself, Is the focus on the completion of a learning experience (certificate) or the measurement of attained knowledge and skills (certification)?

Certification: Why now?

Ninety percent of the nearly 2,000 academics, practitioners, and leaders in the workplace learning and performance profession surveyed indicated that they believed an ASTD professional credential would be beneficial to the field. ASTD then made the decision to move forward with the development of the professional Certification Program as a direct result of the demand. The consensus was that this certification would serve as a powerful tool to encourage professional development and a means to prove one's value.

Certification: Show me the value

So, what is the value of certification? In this section, I attempt to answer that question. There are many levels of value: to the individual, the employer, and the profession. I discuss some of the benefits to each group briefly.

Value to the individual

Typically, individuals seek to become certified because it adds to their credibility. It may also provide them with greater opportunities for employment, promotion, and increased earning potential. It can also help to provide a structured pathway for their professional development and encourages them to stay current in the field. Sometimes, certification is even preferred for a given job.

Value to the employer

Certification also provides value to organizations. It can help employers by providing a reference point when evaluating jobs and promotion candidates. In the January 2005 edition of *Training + Development magazine,* Jamie Mulkey, Ed.D., a test development and security expert from Caveon (a firm specializing in test security), explains that organizations request certification from employees for a number of reasons. "Primarily, organizations want to validate that their workforce is qualified. And a rigorous testing process, such as professional certification, helps them do this." She added that "certification has become the mantra for many organizations who want to ensure individuals in their organization are competent to perform in a given job role."

Value to the profession

According to the U.S. Department of Labor (DOL), there are a number of criteria that characterize a profession. One criterion includes having a set of defined standards for the field. Certification can help to codify a profession and establish these standards. In the case of training, the competency model and related body of knowledge directly relate to the fulfillment of the DOL definition. At the end of the day, certification can serve to raise the bar of professional practice and to help protect against incompetent performance.

In another sense, certification in the training field has intrinsic value. Because competency assessment and people development are at the heart of what people know and do in this field, certification is an important means to an end. In fact, it is often the training and education departments that are the first to outline the requirements for competent practice. Thus, this certification is merely echoing at a macro level what is already being done by those under its umbrella at the micro level.

ASTD Certification: A Quick Look

The Certification Program is new to the profession. The following sections give you a quick look at what it will look like.

Competencies and certification

The ASTD Competency Model provides a clear identification of skills, knowledge, and specific behaviors needed for success. In broader terms, it identifies what people across the field should know and be able to do collectively for success. So, how is this model linked to certification? And how does it provide a foundation for the Certification Program?

Actually, the answer is pretty simple. The model essentially defines what the relevant knowledge and behaviors are and answers the "what to certify" question. Standards are built later to answer the question "How well does one have to perform?" In combination, certification is based on the competencies and performance standards that are based on the model, and the certification designation indicates those standards have been met.

Certification design

At the time of writing, ASTD had defined the preliminary high-level certification design (subject to refinement). The highlights of this design include the following:

- ✔ Applicant eligibility: 2–3 years' experience/equivalent in the profession
- ✔ Exam covers all nine Areas of Expertise plus "specialty" component(s)
  - • Specialty measured by performance-based assessment (for example, portfolio, case example)
  - • Learning design and training delivery are among the more heavily weighted Areas of Expertise

✔ Signed code of ethics

✔ Precertification readiness and optional assessment

✔ Continuing education credits required as part of renewal

Applicant process and flow

The applicant process, depicted in Figure 16-2, is described in ten steps.

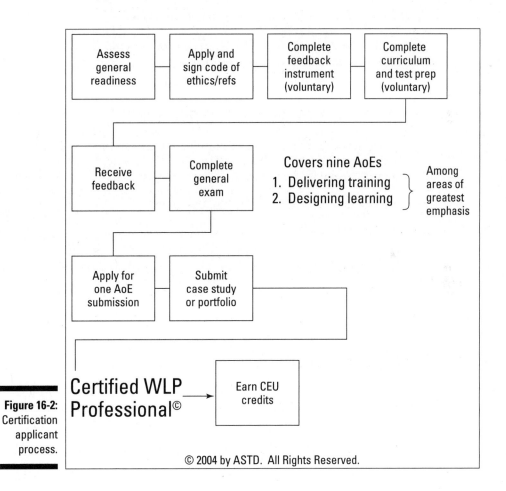

Figure 16-2:
Certification
applicant
process.

Step 1: Assess general readiness

Applicants are encouraged to assess whether they are prepared for certification and if certification (versus some other route, such as a college or university degree or a course or learning event) meets their needs.

Step 2: Apply and sign code of ethics/references

If certification is suitable, applicants complete an application, which includes submitting references and signing a code of ethics.

Step 3: Complete assessment instrument (optional)

If desired, applicants can opt to take a practice exam or a self-assessment instrument to pinpoint areas where additional work may be necessary. This step helps determine where gaps may exist between what the applicant currently knows and does compared to what is expected.

Step 4: Complete curriculum and test prep (optional)

Applicants can choose from a variety of means to prepare for the assessment. ASTD is developing supporting materials to help learners prepare for the exam.

Step 5: Receive feedback (optional)

Applicants can seek out or be provided with additional feedback. If a second practice test is available, it can be used to pinpoint any areas that remain and that need special attention.

Step 6: Complete general exam

After being assigned to a testing location, applicants take the general, knowledge-based portion of the exam.

Step 7: Apply for one Area of Expertise submission

Upon passing the knowledge-based portion of the exam, applicants are eligible to apply for the performance-based component.

Step 8: Complete case study or portfolio

The Area of Expertise performance submission provides an opportunity for applicants to demonstrate their expertise in one of the nine Areas of Expertise. Depending on the nature of the Area of Expertise selected, the assessment ranges from a computer-based assessment to a videotaped submission or role play.

Step 9: Designation awarded

Provided that applicants have passed both parts of the assessment and have met all of the requirements, they are eligible for becoming certified. Notification of certification designation will come from ASTD following the completion of all paperwork and requirements.

Step 10: Apply for continuing educational units

In order to keep current and to contribute to moving the profession forward, evidence of continuing education units are required for recertification. This can come from a variety of sources at the time of writing:

- ✔ Supplier certificates

- ✔ ASTD certificate programs (for example, Human Performance Improvement Certificate)

- ✔ Attending ASTD's annual conference (ASTD's International Conference and Exposition)

- ✔ Certification in related programs (for example, Certified Performance Technologist (CPT))

- ✔ ASTD chapter programs

- ✔ University programs or courses

- ✔ Volunteer services (boards or officer positions)

- ✔ Publications

Consult ASTD for specific point values and requirements pertaining to earning continuing education units.

The Certification Life Cycle

ASTD's Certification Life Cycle is displayed in Figure 16-3. You begin by assessing and building competencies to become certified. To ensure that you stay current, you develop a lifelong learning strategy.

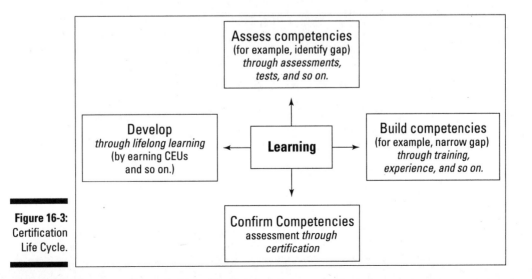

Figure 16-3: Certification Life Cycle.

Learning to be recognized

ASTD's leadership in the training field goes hand in hand with its leadership in developing certification for the broader profession and the continuous learning that's needed to keep skills relevant. In fact, learning is at the core of ASTD's mission and vision. Part of that responsibility includes providing ongoing education and assessment to help keep the profession current.

Failing to keep current can rob an individual of early warning signs that problems may lie ahead. If the demand for some of your skills is starting to increase, you may miss a valuable opportunity to make a course correction.

Staying current

What are your responsibilities as a member of the profession for keeping current? Keeping your certification status current through renewal indicates that you are up-to-date on industry standards. Lifelong learning and its importance is a popular concept these days. But the real challenge is not just talking about it but doing it and also serving as a model for others.

You can be a model of professionalism. Start your journey toward certification today. For more information about either the Competency Model or the Certification Program, visit www.astd.org/competency or send an e-mail to competencystudy@astd.org.

Your career depends on your continued ability to reinvent yourself and add value. Use both the ASTD Competency Model and professional Certification Program as a means to establish the value connection from where you are to where you want to go.

Certification is one of those small steps in your career that may make a huge difference. Achieving certification in your field can be an adventure, one of those life experiences you should not pass up. I live my life by a Helen Keller quote: "Life is either a daring adventure . . . or nothing."

Chapter 17

Training Trends

The 2004 American Society for Training and Development Competency Study identifies eight economic, social, and technology trends shaping the profession. Chapter 16 discusses the competencies that are required as a result of these trends.

✔ Uncertain economic conditions are driving organizations to be more efficient and productive.

✔ Organizations are becoming more flexible, networked, and virtual, requiring employees to be on call 24/7.

✔ A global economy is changing the marketplace, resulting in outsourcing and global collaboration and competition.

✔ Increased diversity, increased use of temporary workers, a greater demand for highly skilled workers, and an increasing number of retirees all contribute to major changes in the complexion of the workforce.

✔ The pace of change is faster than ever, requiring organizations and employees to be more flexible.

✔ Concerns about security are increasing anxiety.

✔ Technology is shaping how and where we work, live, and learn.

✔ Corporate ethics and are more important than ever.

Read more about the Competency Study trends (from the American Society for Training and Development, ASTD) in *Mapping the Future*.

You may see these trends as indicating a need to provide training better, faster, and cheaper. And you are right! Each of these trends lends itself to a trainer's need to produce better training, in a shorter time frame, and at a more reasonable cost than in the past.

This chapter addresses some of the ramifications of these trends. In an effort to provide better, faster, and cheaper training, one of the biggest changes is a move from training toward performance improvement, recognizing that training is not the solution to all problems.

This chapter also focuses on delivery formats available to trainers who will live with these trends, including team training, technology, and part-time trainers. And finally, the chapter addresses how to be successful with today's diverse learners.

The Changing Training Environment

The trends require all training departments to be more efficient and productive and to affect the bottom line in a positive way. This change has been coming for a long time and brings with it a need for trainers to partner with management, for training to be linked to a business need, and for trainers to rely on multiple solutions (as opposed to training only).

What you need to know about performance

by Dana Robinson

Learning and performance: How are they different? Learning and performance are *not* the same. Learning experiences develop skills and knowledge so people *can* perform. Performance occurs when people apply this skill and knowledge in the workplace, accomplishing results for the business. People can know *how to do* many things yet not apply those skills in the workplace. So, while knowing is important, by itself it is not enough to enhance performance of people on the job. Most studies of training programs indicate that people apply less than half of what they have learned on the job. Therefore, a significant investment in learning may not result in a benefit to the employee or to the organization.

Why do people learn a skill and not use it on the job? People do not use skills on the job when they return to a work environment which is nonsupportive. The work environment is the infrastructure which surrounds employees; while we cannot always *see* it, we can always *feel* it. Examples include the incentives and rewards within the organization, the amount of coaching and reinforcement which is available, and clarity of roles and expectations. People perform on the job when they have the required skills and knowledge *plus* the rewards and reinforcements for using those skills and knowledge. Keep in mind this formula:

(Skill and Knowledge) × (A Supportive Work Environment) = Successful On-the-Job Performance

If the skill and knowledge factor is "100" but the work environment is "zero," there will be *no* performance change following training.

What is the role of management regarding learning and performance? While trainers can control a great deal of the learning design and delivery, ensuring that people do acquire skill and knowledge, they cannot control the work environment to which employees return following a training program. This is where management must be active. There are really two levels of management to consider. The first level of management is the direct manager of the employee. This person will, more than any other individual, influence whether employees do — or do not — use their newly learned skills. This person can encourage employees to use the skills, coaching and guiding employees when they are having difficulty doing so; these actions will result in a higher use of skills. Unfortunately, this type of reinforcement is not always present. There is also higher-level management to involve. More senior managers can make changes at a broad level...such as ensuring people have the tools and equipment they need to use their skills and perform as required.

What motivates management to be involved? For management to ensure the work environment is supportive of training programs, the linkage between the skills being developed and the goals and requirements of the business must be evident. How will the skills people acquire in a specific training program benefit the organization? The greater the alignment between training and the business goals, the more likely management will actively support the skill building that is done.

So what's a trainer to do? Realize that training, by itself, will not change performance. Then include in the learning design and the implementation strategy for the program some or all of the following techniques.

✔ Ensure that the learning experience is directly linked to the business goals of your organization and is developing skills which are job-relevant for the participants. You accomplish both these goals by completing a quality needs assessment.

✔ Keep appropriate managers in your organization informed and engaged during the design and implementation process for your training program.

✔ Include in the learning design skill building experiences which are job-relevant to those attending. This will assist participants in identifying the linkage between the skills being developed and what participants need to do on the job with these skills. Ensure participants know the WIIFM factor . . . What's In It For Me when I learn and apply these skills?

✔ When applicable, provide job aids that assist the participants in applying the skills on the job. If you are developing people to conduct interviews, provide an interview guide to use. If people are to use a software program, provide a printed summary of the steps used to access and use the program.

✔ In the learning experience, encourage participants to identify one or two barriers they will encounter as they use their new skills. Then facilitate a discussion about actions the participants can take to overcome these barriers.

✔ Encourage participants to meet with their managers, when they return to their jobs, to discuss the skills they have learned and how they are to utilize them.

The change brings a broader definition of what trainers do, even changing the title from trainer to performance consultant. Don't despair. Many excellent trainers have always conducted business as performance consultants, working hand-in-hand with management to add value to the organization. Change may be huge for some trainers; it is less so for others.

 One of the early leaders in the area of performance consulting is Dana Robinson. Together with her husband and business partner, James Robinson, she has authored numerous books to help HRD functions to transition to a performance focus. Dana describes the change to performance in the sidebar.

Alternative Training Options

Alternatives for training are numerous and include everything from facilitated classroom to computer based with no facilitator, from one-on-one coaching to multiple participants, and from one site to a global Webinar. This section introduces some of the options available to you. The following section examines e-learning formats.

What's to know about e-learning?

In the late '90s many organizations jumped on the e-learning bandwagon thinking that instructor-led training was going the way of the horse and buggy. But it was a bit too early for instant success.

How much e-learning is actually taking place?

Training Magazine's annual industry report (October 2004) is a barometer of employer-sponsored training in the United States. It reports that classroom training continues to hover around 70 percent. The delivery of training utilizing a computer and no instructor averaged 17 percent. The remaining 13 percent delivery was instructor led from remote location and other miscellaneous delivery formats.

It is likely that the many formats of e-learning will continue to play a role in training delivery but probably not "take over" instructor-led training, as was once thought.

What is e-learning?

E-learning (electronic learning) is a term that defines a broad set of applications and processes with assistance from technology. It has many names besides e-learning, including computer-based training, Web-based training, distributed learning, virtual classrooms, and distance learning. E-learning is a partial answer to some of the trend issues above.

✔ Achieving higher productivity with fewer human resources, e-learning is a solution that reduces the number of hours spent in the classroom and time away from work.

✔ A global environment allows participants to be located anywhere in the world and receive some of the same training opportunities.

✔ Cost-cutting measures mean there is less money to be spent on training, and e-learning can be a solution.

✔ The accelerated pace of change may require more employees to gain skills faster than ever before, and an e-learning solution can accomplish that.

What is all this jargon?

The following list provides definitions to expose you to several e-learning solutions. Entire books have been written about most, so don't think you will have the knowledge to implement any as a result of this chapter.

✔ **Computer-based training (CBT):** A basic term for the use of computers in managing and presenting content to participants. The learning is self-paced and can be individualized. Frequently participants have choices in the mode, for example, video, audio, graphic, verbal, or a combination. Most computer-based training is interactive, including simulation, problem solving, games, and so on.

✔ **CD-ROM courses:** The original form of CBT, in the form of a read-only memory compact disc. This has given way to Web-based training.

✔ **Web-based training (WBT):** Web-based training is still CBT because it takes place on computers. Access to the Internet or corporate Intranet and a Web browser is required. WBT allows learners to be in control of the pace of their learning. It solves material distribution concerns, and updates to materials can be made instantly. Corporate firewalls can sometimes pose a problem but can usually be resolved by the corporate IT department.

To achieve success in Web-based training, ensure that the learners take responsibility for their own learning. This means that a trainer's job is to make certain that learners are adequately prepared.

✔ **Performance Support System (PSS):** A combination of expert coaches and mentor, documents, tools, and decision support tools that help employees make the right decision on the job. It assists performance at the job site.

✔ **Electronic Performance Support System (EPSS):** When the PSS uses computers to store, capture, reconfigure, and distribute information to assist the employee, it is called EPSS — on-the-job support and training at its finest. Major benefits of EPSS are to improve job performance, decrease training time and costs, and increase retention.

✔ **Distance learning:** Instructional delivery that does not require the participant to be physically present in the same location as the facilitator. In the past it may have meant a correspondence course. Today video, audio, and computer technologies are common delivery formats.

✔ **Distributed learning:** Similar to distance learning, but the resources are distributed, allowing learners to have more control over their learning by being able to access content, peers, experts, and services on their own timeline.

✔ **Webinars:** Live training or seminars delivered to a dispersed audience that uses real-time audio and video or scheduled online demonstrations. May use a combination of a telephone and computer.

Be sure to design any e-learning to engage the learners and promote meaningful interaction. Pique learners' curiosity through humor, games, puzzles, problem-solving exercises, self-assessments, checklists, and other novel design elements. Plan for frequent feedback in the design to reinforce learning.

How can you learn more?

If you are not familiar with e-learning, begin as a learner. I suggest you start by joining a virtual classroom experience. Vendors will often host free sessions to introduce you to their products. Note how the facilitator encouraged interaction and how the material was presented.

To keep yourself motivated, team up with another trainer who is in the same situation. Discuss what you learn, compare designs and delivery, and track product information or other things that are important to your organization.

It won't take long; soon you will be riding the technology wave rather than drowning in a sea of e-jargon.

Blended learning

Blended learning is a recent buzzword that mixes e-learning with other training formats. Imagine that you are at a salad bar, selecting all the best ingredients. Blended learning allows you to pick and choose what will work best to meet the organization's and participants' needs.

Blended learning is a natural evolution of e-learning that includes Web-based training, CD-ROM courses, videos, Webinars, EPSS, and simulations. It also includes the less glamorous media including classroom training, job aids, books, coaching, and conference calls. When designing a blended-learning solution, consider some of these points.

✔ Blended learning optimizes resources, providing the greatest impact for the least investment. Remember to consider the organizational culture and how receptive it will be to changes in delivery formats.

✔ The blended-learning solution should be solution focused — what is the business problem you are solving and what is the best way to solve the problem?

✔ Technology capabilities will drive at least some portion of the blended-learning solution, but remember to include the characteristics of the audience (time available, how motivated, their learning style) and the characteristics of the content (the subject-matter experts, type of content: skill-based or knowledge-based, how soon it will be out of date).

✔ Almost all blended-learning solutions will require a communication/marketing plan prior to deployment.

Considerations for one-on-one training

One-on-one training may have a number of names, but it can be chunked into two areas. On-the-job training and coaching or mentoring. On-the job training may include coaching or instruction. The distinguishing factor is that it takes place in the learner's workplace. Coaching is developing the skills and experiences of learners by providing them with progressively more difficult tasks that stretch them to perform. It is paired with continuous discussion, feedback, and counseling.

You would use one-on-one training when you need to personally involve the learner or when highly specialized training is required. Although some people believe that it is a good format because it is simple and fast and anyone can conduct one-on-one training, they are wrong. It is true that it is a good format, but more understanding is required.

It can be simple and fast during the time the trainer is with the learner, but this is due to a good deal of up-front preparation. In addition, "anyone" cannot conduct good one-on-one training. It requires someone who has good communication skills, is patient, has a high amount of content-related and contextual knowledge, and is easily approachable.

Remember to use media and visuals for one-on-one training, too. You probably would not set up a computer for a PowerPoint presentation, but you certainly could print off a hard copy of the presentation. If a video was useful to a group of participants, it will be useful to individual participants as well.

Often the responsibility for one-on-one training lies with the learner's supervisor. The person may be new to the organization or be presented with new work. If you are the supervisor/trainer in this case, think of this role as an extension of your leadership skills. Like a leader, you will steer learners in the right direction, guiding them to the correct decisions and helping them uncover new knowledge.

One-on-one trainers use some of the same learning strategies as classroom trainers; however, they have the advantage of focusing on only one learner. Build some of these learning strategies into your one-on-one training.

- ✔ Begin by describing the whole picture. What should it look like when completed correctly? Where does the learner fit in the process? Provide the big picture.

- ✔ Clarify the expectations and requirements. Be sure that the learner knows what is expected. Discuss the gap between where the learner is now and what is expected.

- ✔ Provide new information that the learner needs to know. Recommend people or other resources that can help with the new information. Provide documents or other data that would be helpful. Do not go beyond what the learner needs to know at this time.

- ✔ Demonstrate the process wherever possible.

- ✔ Present problems as a learning method. Provide feedback and suggestions for improvement.

- ✔ Plan time to follow up with the learner.

- ✔ Leave the learner with job aids that can be used for review or guidance after the session has ended.

You see that the process is not that different from a classroom situation in that you use similar techniques.

Team Training

Few things in the training field can be as frustrating and at the same time as enriching as team training. Having the opportunity to train with a colleague is a unique opportunity to grow. Trainers frequently are a one-person show and rarely have the opportunity to work with a colleague and to obtain feedback from someone in the same profession. It is also an opportunity to watch another person model new techniques and approaches, tell new jokes, and present content from a new perspective.

At the same time the experience can be very frustrating. The other trainer may take longer on a section, causing you to cut material. The other trainer's style may be opposite yours; for example, you keep the front table neat and orderly, while the other person prefers to spend time with participants and doesn't bother organizing until the end of the day. The other trainer presents content in a different way, and you wonder if one of you is incorrect.

The bottom line is that the participants must see you working as a team. They should see nothing but two professionals making sure that they are conducting the best darn training they've ever attended.

Meet prior to the session

Meet at least once prior to the session to review the schedule and content. At that time, assign responsibilities and negotiate ground rules. Spend time ensuring clear understanding of your expectations of each other and the outcome of the session. The following suggestions should be considered a minimum.

- ✔ Discuss your training style preference.
- ✔ Discuss the logistics: room setup and number and type of participants.
- ✔ Identify any modifications to be made to the design.
- ✔ Walk through the session, making notes about who will do what.
- ✔ Identify where the supporting trainer will be located physically in the training room.
- ✔ Request specific feedback from each other.
- ✔ Exchange contact information if necessary, especially cellphone numbers.
- ✔ Identify how and when to intervene during the session.

Make each other look good during the session

During the session, both trainers need to work as a team. Even if you are training only half the material, it is still a full-time job. Reading the paper in the back of the room while your partner is training in the front is not acceptable behavior. So what do you do?

- ✔ Remain in the room with your co-facilitator.
- ✔ Stay mentally engaged to ensure that you can assist when necessary.
- ✔ Take notes to provide useful feedback during the post-session debrief.
- ✔ Stick to the ground rules you established, for example:
  - Stand if you want to add something, but wait for the okay from the lead (person who is "on" at the time) trainer.
  - The lead trainer always makes the final call (if an error was made and the lead did not acknowledge the supporting trainer, it can be discussed at the next break and a decision made about how to handle it).
  - Do not correct the other trainer in front of the group.

If you must deliver a message to your co-trainer that is not content-related (such as "The lunch hasn't arrived yet; continue until 12:15"), write your note on a piece of paper, fold it in half, and unobtrusively place it on the table next to your partner. Few participants will notice. It won't interrupt the flow. Your partner will know that it is important but not to break into the content.

✔ Assist each other during fishbowls, in small-group activities, or by charting while the other is leading a discussion.

✔ Each of you should be responsible for an equal amount of the boring or difficult sections.

✔ If individuals are struggling with course content, one of the trainers can provide additional support off-line.

✔ If you are supporting, stay one step ahead of the other person. What's the next activity? Are all materials available? Can you hang a chart page on the wall?

Learn from your co-facilitator. Take advantage of training with another trainer to build your repertoire of skills. Observe new techniques, ask for feedback on specific delivery skills you wish to improve, and pick up stories, examples, and personal touches that seem to work with the participants. This is a golden opportunity. Grab it.

✔ Two trainers, working well together, establish a model of cooperation and teamwork for the participants.

✔ Use the advantage of two for modeling, role-playing, acting, or debating two points of view.

✔ Carry your fair share, whether you are the lead trainer in the front of the room or the supporting trainer in the back.

The supporting trainer has a perfect opportunity to watch participants' body language. This will provide insight about how well the content is being received and if adaptations are required.

✔ Show mutual respect, demonstrate listening, and display nonverbal agreement.

✔ Ensure that both of you have personal time during the break.

Provide feedback following the session

Meet immediately after the session to discuss how things went. If you have kept notes during the session, you will be better prepared and organized for the meeting.

If this is a multiple-day session, meet at the end of each day so that you don't lose valuable feedback. The next day will be filled with new experiences and will overtake the previous day.

- ✔ Provide a professional critique that includes both positive feedback as well as areas for improvement.

- ✔ Some organizations develop a checklist of skills and attributes they deem necessary.

- ✔ Give feedback on the items the other person has requested. Be honest, candid, sincere, and sensitive.

- ✔ Use specific examples to make your point.

- ✔ Identify areas in the training materials, content, or delivery that should be changed or improved; document these to forward to your supervisor.

- ✔ Use excellent communication, listening, and feedback skills. You will grow professionally and benefit from the opportunity (or even the challenge) to interact with another trainer having a different style, personality, pace, and viewpoint.

- ✔ Celebrate successes.

Training with a partner can be one of the best experiences you've ever had as a trainer. Use these guidelines to ensure it.

Help for the Part-Time Trainer

The trends in training lead to a need for more trainers. If you're good at what you do, you may be *rewarded* with the opportunity to show others how to do what you do so well. What do you do? Select the sections in this book that you think will be most beneficial to you. Then go out there and try it!

The art of managing both training and your real job

As a part-time trainer, one of the biggest problems you may have is managing both your training responsibilities and your real job. These tips will help you.

- ✔ Accept training projects that are consistent with the objectives of your position.

- ✔ When you know you will be training, keep a resource file on that topic handy. Clip articles and save other relevant information in these resource files. When you are ready to prepare, all your resources will be in one spot.

✔ Keep a list of points you want to make/things you want to do. Keep the list handy so that when you think of things, you can write them down. When you are ready to prepare, all your thoughts will be collected on your list.

Use index cards to collect your ideas. You can easily track each as you present it.

✔ Keep a training bag ready. Have markers, pens, masking tape (whatever you consistently use in training) stored in an old brief case. When it's time to train, just grab your bag. There's no need to scurry around for the things you need.

✔ Keep all your training manuals, handouts, and audiovisuals in one spot. This prevents you from having to assemble everything at the last minute.

Discipline yourself to replenish supplies in your kit immediately on returning from the current training session; it will always be ready to go.

✔ If you have just completed a program and you know you'll be doing it again, write a summary of what went well/what you'd do differently immediately following the program. Make any changes at that time too. If you do this while the material is fresh in your mind, it will save you time.

✔ Remember that investment pays off. If you spend adequate time preparing for your training the first time you do it, you will benefit every time you train.

Training on the run

What about those times that you are expected to design an interactive training session, based on data, on short notice? Or the times that management asks you to condense your session down from a day to two hours? Impossible you say? You may feel that way, but as the trends clearly show, efficiency and productivity take precedence now. Because this is more the norm than the exception, these suggestions will help you next time it occurs.

✔ Conduct a needs assessment that ensures you are training the most important knowledge and skills, and only the most important knowledge and skills.

✔ Make use of job aids that can be used during the training session and easily referenced after the session.

✔ Use a practical, yet simple-to-remember process to teach whatever you need to. Three steps should be the maximum.

✔ A shortened time frame does not mean that you turn everything into a lecture. If anything, it is even more critical that participants are involved and experience the skills they must learn.

✔ Identify how you will follow up with participants. Send an e-mail the next day with reminders of key concepts. Another e-mail or reminder letter a week later jogs memories.

✔ You may not have much time left for an evaluation, so ask one or two questions, key questions, such as, "What is the most useful concept you learned in this session?" or "What is one thing you wished you had learned but didn't?"

Next time you are asked to do the impossible, just smile and start running!

Planning for Today's Diverse Learners

As noted in the ASTD Competency Study, the future holds a more diverse workforce. Several factors contribute to this. The combination of an aging workforce whose hopes for early retirement have been dashed by an economic downturn find themselves working beside "Gen-Next-ers." Implications for training are obvious. The MTV generation may challenge more and have a shorter attention span. The near-retirement crowd may need to unlearn current practices first, thus taking longer, and may experience a decline in their vision or hearing.

Trainers may need to balance different pace preferences, different comfort levels with technology, and different levels of self-confidence.

Diversity will be displayed in other cultural differences including race, gender, ethnicity, and affiliations. Trainers will need to select materials and media, such as case studies and videos, that reflect a diverse audience and eliminate gender-specific language.

As a trainer, make an effort to learn about those from other cultures. Learn to pronounce names correctly. Respect personal preferences. If participants have written Ms. or Dr. on their table tents, there is a strong preference to be addressed in the more formal context. Recognize that a highly participative learning approach may be uncomfortable for some cultures. Some cultures do not view direct eye contact as positively as those who live in the United States.

Diverse cultures require additional effort. A diverse audience requires that trainers speak clearly, are careful about giving feedback, frequently check for understanding, give instructions in the same sequence they are to be followed, avoid single country references, take care with jokes or other offensive remarks, and repeat information when necessary.

Unique differences occur in any language. For example, using the colloquialism of "Are you pulling a fast one?" does not make much sense to someone just learning the language. Say instead, "Are you trying to trick me?" Similarly, sarcasm may be misunderstood as well. "Sure it is!" stated sarcastically will be better understood if you say, "I don't think that is correct."

Read a book that identifies common gestures and their meanings in other cultures. For example, a thumbs-up signal that to you indicates everything is okay is a rude gesture in Nigeria and Australia.

Participants who have disabilities will also add diversity to your training session. Be sure that you use the word disabled or the specific disability (as opposed to handicapped). Some disabilities may not be visible but may still create learning challenges, for example, dyslexia or diabetes.

Trainers cannot learn everything there is to know about disabilities. However, you should try to accommodate special needs. Attend to environmental aspects such as lighting, noise levels, refreshments served, and seating arrangements. Never assume anything, and get information about special needs prior to the training session. Identify what you can do to maximize the learning experience for everyone.

Having a diverse training group is a certainty. Equally as certain is that diversity will change the way your organization provides training.

Professional trainers deal with many different situations. Dealing with diversity in the classroom provides an opportunity to model appropriate behavior for participants. Participants who see trainers working effectively with a diverse group may see the benefits and learn skills through observation.

As with any profession, nothing is static. It makes me think of the words to Bob Dylan's song, "The times they are a changing."

Part VI
The Part of Tens

The 5th Wave   By Rich Tennant

"I was giving them a rousing motivational speech from my college football days, at the end of which everyone jumped up and butted heads."

In this part . . .

You find practical pointers for enhancing your training session. Wondering how to start your training session? Need ideas to increase participation, save time, or find new ways to form small groups? Want some tips for adding humor to your sessions? Looking for a new ice-breaker or two? Look no further. You've found six chapters guaranteed to increase energy, add fun, and make you look like a pro!

Chapter 18

Ten Tips to Start Off on the Right Foot

In This Chapter

▶ Learning how trainers catch and hold participants' attention

▶ Reviewing ten items a trainer accomplishes in the opening of a training session

*F*irst contacts create a lasting impression. Most people have discovered that the first ten minutes of any initial meeting between two people lays the groundwork for almost all assumptions and decisions about the ensuing relationship.

If first impressions are critical, how does a good trainer catch and hold participants' attention from the start? How do trainers start off on the right foot? This chapter identifies ten aspects of getting your training session off to a good start.

The American Society for Training and Development (ASTD) offers a Training Certificate Program. One of the objectives of the program is to teach trainers how to open their training sessions with PUNCH. ASTD believes that the opening is one of the most important sections of any training design. Training should open with a purpose, not just open. A training session can open with PUNCH if the trainer accomplishes these five things.

✔ **Promotes** interest and enthusiasm for the training-session content. Participants desire more after the opening. Perhaps there was an element of surprise built into the opening using props or introducing a creative activity.

✔ **Understands** participants' needs — both content as well as personal-esteem needs — by learning something about participants' experience and expertise.

✔ **Notes** the ground rules and administrative needs so that guidelines are established to ensure the training session runs more smoothly: what time lunch will be held, when breaks will occur, and where restrooms are located.

✔ Clarifies expectations by discussing the agenda and the objectives for the session. The opening also identifies other expectations participants have that may or may not be addressed.

✔ Helps everyone get to know each other through the use of icebreakers, discussions, or other activities. Getting participation early sets the stage for full participation throughout the session.

How do you add PUNCH to your training? These ten aspects of starting off on the right foot guide you in the right direction.

Establish a Climate Conducive to Learning

Creating rapport and establishing a climate conducive to learning cannot be overemphasized. When done right from the start, it means that participants will be open to and enthusiastic about the learning events that follow. They will know what to expect. You can set the tone for the rest of the training session by what you accomplish at the beginning.

The opening should indicate whether the rest of the session will have participants up and moving about or sitting or a combination of the two. It should set the tempo and tone of the session. Fast paced? Slow? Jovial? Serious? Interactive? Passive? Creative? Cerebral? Exciting? Calm? All of these describe a potential training climate. Decide what yours will be, and then begin to establish the climate during your opening.

If you desire a participative climate, the opening should put people at ease — including the trainer. Participants may be reluctant to get involved unless the trainer provides structure that includes a purpose. They may be shy or may not want to appear vulnerable in front of their peers or strangers.

Think through the climate that will be the most conducive to learning. Then begin to establish it from the first moment the session begins.

Clarify Participants' Expectations

Participants expect you to ask about their expectations for the session, and numerous ways exist for you to accomplish this. Of course, the most straight-forward way is to simply ask, "What are your expectations for the session?" List them on a flipchart page and post them on the wall. There are other ways to get the same information. You can twist the question a bit to assist learners to get at their questions or concerns from a different perspective. Try some of these.

✔ Ask for hopes and fears. Post on two different flipcharts.

✔ Ask for dreams and desires.

✔ Ask "Why are you here?"

✔ Ask "What questions did you bring with you today?"

✔ Ask "What do you need to happen today for this training to be worth your investment of time?"

✔ Ask "How well do your needs match the learning objectives?" and "What else do you need?"

What if the participants' expectations go beyond the scope of the training design? Better to let them know now how you intend to handle it. You may respond in three ways. First, you can add time to the agenda to address the additional expectations. This most likely means eliminating or shortening something else. Second, if the additional expectation is something that concerns only one or two individuals, you may choose to meet with them after the session or during a break to discuss their needs. Third, you may need to tell them that you're not prepared or time doesn't allow for the added content, or whatever is the truth, but that you will follow up with them following the session. This may mean that you e-mail them additional resources, put them in touch with someone who has the expertise, or whatever will address their concern.

Possibly the most important thing you can do for participants is to help them understand "What's In It For Me" (WIIFM). Some trainers describe this as helping participants tune into station WII-FM. Participants who understand why they are involved in a training session, how it will help them do their jobs better and faster, and how the content relates to them will get more out of the training session.

Introduce the Content

Related to clarifying the participants' expectations is introducing the content. You provide an overview for participants by reviewing the agenda and the objectives for the training session. Telling them what's to come provides a foundation for the content and establishes a common starting point for everyone in the room.

Ensure that participants know other aspects of the content as well. They may want to know whether they will be required to take a test, whether they will receive a grade for the course, or whether the grade will affect their jobs. They may want to know what kind of participation will be expected and whether there will be assignments. Explain each of these as you walk them through the agenda.

I generally present the content and then ask participants whether they were anticipating different or additional content. You can do either first. I find my process saves time because I do not have to repeat the content later as I present the agenda. On the other hand, sometimes it is more important for the participants to establish their own agenda than to save time. During instances such as a team-building effort, I facilitate a discussion of their expectations and needs first. It takes a bit longer, but there is more buy-in that leads to better end results.

Surprise!

Add an element of surprise right from the start. Add something unconventional to send a message to participants that this session may not be the same thing they have experienced in the past. You may introduce props in your opening or state something unusual or shocking about the topic (that you can prove later, of course). You can also start with an activity first, rather than addressing the logistics of the session.

- ✔ During introductions, most trainers start at the front and go clockwise around the room. Plan to start someplace else, such as the middle back and go counterclockwise. Even better, ask for a volunteer to start, ask for a second volunteer, and select or call on folks all over. This takes a bit of practice on your part to remember who was introduced. When all else fails, you can always end by saying, "Who has not been introduced yet?" to pick up anyone who was missed in this scatter approach.

- ✔ Save housekeeping issues until just before break. No one needs to know most of the information until then anyway. Because most sessions start off with a discussion about lunch, parking, and sign-up sheets, you will surprise your participants when you do not begin the same way.

- ✔ Ask participants to use crayons instead of pens or pencils to generate lists, draw something, write their names on their table tents, or anything else they would typically complete with a pen.

Doing something just a bit differently or in a different sequence introduces an element of surprise that energizes participants, adds interest and excitement to the session, and communicates that this session will not be boring.

Introduce Participants

An opening is not complete unless participants learn who else is attending the session. Whether you use an icebreaker or a quick round of introductions will depend on the amount of time you have available and how participants will need to interact during the rest of the training session.

Allow participants to become acquainted with one another. Establish a way that they can begin to understand who else is in the training session and what their attitudes, values, experience, and concerns may be. Use this time wisely. Before selecting how participants will meet each other, determine what you want participants to be able to do as a result. You may just want them to be able to match names and faces, but you may want to consider other results that will help to further the training session. What else do you want participants to know about each other? Make a list of what you want to accomplish. These may help get you started.

- ✔ Have a continuous contact for other content.
- ✔ Practice solving problems.
- ✔ Understand attitudes, beliefs, likes, and dislikes.
- ✔ Practice a creative experience.
- ✔ Begin to build a team.

Many legitimate aspects exist for what you hope participants will learn about each other and how they will interact later based on this introduction experience. At the least, I suggest that everyone in the group accomplish two things.

- ✔ All participants hear all other participants' names.
- ✔ All participants speak up at least once.

This is a good time to mention the use of table tents — the cards folded like a tent that have people's names written on them. Use them; they will help you remember participants' names and help participants remember and use each others' names. Have participants place their names on both sides during the introductions. This allows you and other participants to see their names from any angle.

Learn About the Group

Be sure to build time into the opening so that you can observe the group and learn something about the group's dynamics and the individual personalities. Conducting an icebreaker provides you with this opportunity.

It may be tempting to have your head in your notes during the icebreaker to prepare for the next section. If you do, you will be doing participants and yourself a disservice.

Take time to determine how you perceive the group as a whole. Circulate among the participants, observing how they work together. Listen to conversations. Who seems to be taking the lead? Who is still reluctant to join in? What strong personalities exist in the group? Who seems to be dominating the discussion?

This time gives you a chance to think ahead to the rest of the design and to be aware of potential difficulties where you may consider changing the process. For example, if you have planned a risky activity and the group appears to be risk-adverse, you may make a mental note about it. It is certainly too early to make the change now, but you may give yourself a personal heads-up that a change may be required.

Make it a practice to use this time to discover as much about the group and individuals as you can.

Establish Ground Rules

Establishing ground rules as a part of your opening shapes the parameters of behavior the participants expect of each other and from the trainer for the session. I generally present the group with a few to get started, or the givens, such as start and end time. (See Chapter 9 for suggested ground-rule categories.) I sometimes make a commitment such as "If we start on time each day (or after each break), I guarantee we will end on time."

Capture the same words that participants have used. You need buy-in to the ground rules from everyone, so you may need to modify the list in order to get agreement.

As you facilitate development of the ground rules, be sure to refer to responsibility for them. For example, while establishing ground rules, I may make the point that the participants must share in the responsibility of learning, emphasizing that my role is to present content and that their responsibility is to ask questions if I have not been clear or did not provide enough information.

Post the ground rules in a location where everyone can see them, usually near the front of the training room. This facilitates your ability to reference them if you need to use them to manage disruptions or as a reference point to facilitate group dynamics.

Confront Any Issues

If you know issues exist around the training session, confront them during the opening and plan time to address them. In fact, your icebreaker may incorporate the concerns.

If something is happening in the organization that led to this training session, address it head on. If it is troublesome to participants, allow enough time to discuss. You will find that if you do not address it immediately, participants will not be able to focus on the content you're presenting. And besides, you will most likely address it later anyway.

Establish Your Credibility and Style

Just as you want to know about participants, the participants will be trying to learn something about you, your expectations, your style, and your credibility. You have a number of things to cover in the introduction. How you cover them and in what order will tell the participants as much about your expectations as anything. You will be modeling your style. My preference is to weave them in throughout different parts of the opening.

If participants have not met you before, they will want to know something about you. Begin to share something about yourself during the opening. If you ask participants to divulge something about themselves during an ice-breaker, you should divulge the same information. If you ask them to draw a picture that depicts something about them, you should draw a picture, too. This ensures that you share the same information that they do. It also keeps you at a similar level with your participants. Follow Rudyard Kipling's advice: "Don't lose the common touch." Let people know you care about their success and that you're there to guide them; as someone once told me, be a "guide on the side, not a sage on stage." You will be a more successful trainer if you're genuine.

Your expectations for the time together may be covered at the same time that the group establishes its ground rules. Be sure that you build your expectations in as well. For example, if you expect the participants to assist with balancing participation, say so. If you do not, many participants will assume that it is your job to manage all disruptive behaviors. Be sure participants understand your expectations up front.

Your style will come across in the opening — whether you want it to or not. Participants observe how you approach the opening and will make assumptions about your style. Did you take time to listen to participants and clarify what they meant? Did you check your watch?

Some trainers use a bio sketch or have someone else introduce them to establish their credibility. Credibility is a combination of what you know (your expertise), what you have done (your experience), and how you present yourself. Those who present themselves best come across as humbly self-confident. I try to avoid having someone introduce me. If I cannot avoid it, I make sure that it is short and appropriately related to the training I am about to present. I like to add a personal element or a lighthearted statement that relates to the participants. For example, I may say that I have been conducting training for more years than I want to admit. To establish credibility, I will mention my experience and expertise as introductions to stories. I may say, for example, "One of the things I have learned working in the manufacturing arena for the past 20 years is. . . ." This statement has the same effect as reading it from a resume but is more subtle and is positioned where it makes more sense to the participants.

Take a Break!

Yes, take a break. If the opening was an hour in length, take a break. It maintains the energy level, gives participants an opportunity to follow up with other participants, and gives people a chance to take care of personal needs before you begin the content.

Remember, your opening is one of the most important segments of your training session. Be sure it adds PUNCH to the entire design.

Chapter 19

Ten Ways to Increase Participation

In This Chapter

▶ Identifying practical ways to increase participant involvement

▶ Ensuring that increased participation also increases the learning that occurs

"*L*earning is not a spectator sport!" Quoting John Newstrom, coauthor of the *Games Trainers Play* series, he is quite serious about the purpose of increasing involvement through games or any other means. Retention is enhanced with an increase in participants' involvement.

Increasing participation is something that the trainer controls. And it all comes down to being prepared. The topic of increasing participation has been woven throughout this book. From a big-picture perspective, it includes such things as creating and maintaining a safe learning environment, being flexible enough to accommodate the range of needs and preferences in the room, and appealing to all learning modes.

The ideas presented in this chapter include how to lay the foundation of a participative environment, how to build on that foundation with participative activities, how to frame your comments to encourage participation, and how to continue constructing a participative session.

Begin to Encourage Participation Right from the Start

Creating and maintaining a safe environment starts the moment the first participant enters the room — no matter what time it is. Greet the first person, introduce yourself, and learn something about him or his drive to the session or other local information. As participants continue to arrive, introduce yourself to as many as you can. Invite them to have a cup of coffee if available. This small gesture sets the stage for creating an environment that encourages learning and participation. It demonstrates that you are open, accessible, human!

Once the session starts, get people up, moving about, and participating in the first few minutes. The icebreaker should at the least provide an opportunity for everyone to get to know each other by name. Don't immediately worry about the logistical information (location of the bathrooms and the time for lunch); however, be sure that you take care of it before the first break.

Also, as a part of your introduction, express your interest in and the value of participation and the benefits of learning from one another. Ensure that participants have an opportunity to express their needs and/or expectations of the session. If you do these things, you will lay the foundation that encourages participation right from the start.

Cards for the Shy and Faint of Heart

Index cards can be a lifesaver for increasing participation. The participants in your sessions have different communication styles and preferences. Some participants are forming their thoughts as they quickly respond. Some need time to think about their responses before they say anything. And some participants just do not like to speak up at all. Most will respond if they have had time to think about what they will say. Unfortunately, if you ask a question, at least one-third of your participants will have an answer ready before the question mark punctuates it.

If you want everyone to have time to think about their responses to a question without being influenced by others in the session, have everyone jot down their answers on index cards. Then call on those first who usually do not speak up first. This is safe for the quieter participants because they have had time to think about their responses.

You may use index cards to increase participation in many ways. These are a few of my favorites.

- Take a poll.
- Ask for an opinion.
- Ask for their concerns, questions, or issues.
- Administer a mini-quiz (keep it fun).
- Conduct a midcourse evaluation.

What to do with the cards? Try these.

- Collect and compile them and report the responses.
- Collect, shuffle, and redistribute them, having participants read the card each received to the rest of the group.

✔ Pass them around the room and ask participants to add more information or answer the questions; then read them or return them to the original authors.

✔ Collect, sort, and prioritize the cards to create a customized learning module.

Give Your Role Away

Find ways in which participants can take on the role of the trainer. A good trainer acknowledges that the collective group of participants in the room knows more than any single trainer. Creating ways that allow participants to take on the training role is a great way to gain participation and distribute the wealth of knowledge.

✔ Ask someone to facilitate a discussion. You can give the discussion a format; for example, ask how participants will apply this to their jobs.

✔ Encourage participants to speak with each other, rather than directing all comments to you. For example, if Maggie asks a question, ask Mario to respond by saying, "Mario, how would you answer Maggie?" After a few times, participants view this as "permission" to converse as a group. If the discussion is going well, you may even want to sit down or move to a side wall, providing further evidence that you approve.

✔ Have participants form teams of three or four participants and write review questions in an attempt to stump the other teams. Keep score numerically or use a graphic such as the old "hangman" game to track errors or a baseball diamond to track "hits."

✔ Assign various sections of the content to small groups who create and present the information. This not only allows for more participation, but it also demonstrates that the participants know the material. You can always add a fine point if something is missed at the end of the presentations.

Participation; Repeat, Participation

As you gain verbal participation, you want it to continue. How do you ensure that those who got involved and spoke up once or twice will continue? And how do you get those who have not been involved to jump on the participation wagon, too?

How you respond to participants who contribute to the session can encourage them to repeat their involvement and will serve as a model for those who have not yet participated. Try these three things.

✔ Thank the participant for the contribution. Use the person's name and make eye contact.

✔ Restate the comment and expand upon it. You can also use it later in the session: "As Suki mentioned earlier. . . ."

✔ Acknowledge the contribution and then encourage others to add to a response or to share a different perspective. If it is a different perspective, always return to original participants to affirm their initial contribution.

On Your Feet!

Move participants around to encourage discussions with other participants. Physical movement keeps the blood flowing to the brain and prevents the afternoon blahs. In addition, you will find participation will increase.

✔ **Form small groups.** You do participants no favors by keeping them in the same area of the room. Most new groups you form should have a different number of people, include different participants, and be located in a different place in the room. If the room is large enough, have tables set around the room with chairs so that you can occasionally direct groups to the tables.

✔ **Include activities that have people standing.** Relay races, moving groups from place to place, recording information on a flipchart, or portions of a game show, for example *Jeopardy!,* in which reviews could be completed while standing.

✔ **Post flipcharts with issues and have participants move around in pairs to address and add their comments.** Sharon Bowman is a firm believer in moving participants around. She conducts an activity she calls a gallery walk. Participants complete an activity on a flipchart page and hang it in a hallway. Groups visit the charts and may add written comments to them. This allows people a different location and different vantage point. It may even encourage seeing the information from a different perspective.

✔ **Have participants stand for part of your presentation, but be sure you have a reason.** You could conduct a verbal pop quiz in which participants could find someone in the room who knows the answer. You could have them discuss something in pairs and constantly change the pairs.

Say a Lot without a Word

Certainly what you say verbally, your compliments, thanks, paraphrases, elaborations, and even your disagreements, will encourage participation. However, your body language may speak louder than words. Use the power of nonverbal communication to encourage participation.

Use physical body language: Make eye contact with all participants. Fleeting eye contact will not obtain the involvement you desire. Allow your eyes to linger. Nodding your head shows that you understand and encourages participants to continue. Avoid defensive postures such as folding your arms. Stop talking and do not interrupt. Avoid distracting movements. Get out from behind a table (never use a podium) and move toward people to draw them into the discussion. Don't just listen. You need to *look* like you're listening. Avoid checking your watch — even if you're innocently trying to determine the time.

Learn to determine the time without obviously looking for it. For example, you could practice reaching for something (a glass of water, your notes) while stealing a glance at your watch. Or you can have your watch or other clock sitting unobtrusively on the table. I like to use the plastic stick-on clocks that are slightly larger than a quarter and stick them to the projector.

Don't just say you are interested. Look like you're interested. Later prove that you heard what was said by reiterating the comment or building on the idea with comments such as "Marlo's question earlier. . ." or "To build on what Andre suggested. . . ."

Remove the Tables

I use this technique when I really want to heat up the environment and send a message that the participation stakes have been raised considerably. Remove the tables from the participants. You may take them out of the room or push them against a wall in the room. I usually do this while participants are out of the room: during a lunch break or at the end of a day if participants are returning the next day. You could have participants assist if you want. I place the chairs in a circle, leaving only one chair width open for participants to move in or out of the circle.

This arrangement creates an informal atmosphere and encourages a high level of participation. The drawback is that participants no longer have a place to write. Plan this technique carefully in your design. Tearing down and resetting tables can use up quite a bit of time. So it may be possible that you have little writing and more group activity during a specific portion of your training session, that is, a full afternoon or even between the final break for the day and the end of the session. This allows you to reset the tables before the next day's session.

Attention-Getting Answers

When asking questions, don't stop at the first answer — even if it is correct. This is a great way to start an interesting dialogue and get participants' minds engaged. The other more obvious reason is that those who have the fast, right answer will do most of the talking. Pausing after answers — even right ones — is a unique way to encourage more participation.

Sometimes when participants answer a question, you may feel a need to simplify their roundabout answer. If it is necessary, you could on occasion say, "Gee, I must be a bit slow today. Could you explain that again?" Two things will happen. First, you encourage the participant to reexamine the response and simplify it for the group. Second, you will gain the group's attention as members are drawn into the challenge you have just presented.

Use round robins regularly to encourage a word or two from everyone. Ensure that the responses asked for are short. For example, "Tell me one thing required for excellent customer service."

The Quietest

After the environment in a training session seems to be safe for even the shyest person, I request that the group decide at the beginning of the assigned activity who in the group has spoken the least up to that point in the session. The chosen individual will be the person who leads and/or reports out for the small group. Don't wait too long to use this technique. I am always surprised about the increased participation from that previously "quiet" person.

Participation Right to the End

There is no need for you to take over at the end. End your session with as much participation as you started. Ask participants to share something.

- One action each will implement immediately
- The most interesting fact they learned
- New questions they have as a result of the training session

Allow time for participants to say goodbye to others in the session. This could be an informal walkabout, or participants could have an assignment such as writing and distributing messages to others. If consistent teams were utilized throughout the session, have the teams create a goodbye skit, song, or cheer to present to the larger group. Encourage continued participation by distributing contact information for all participants.

Chapter 20

Ten Ways to Save Time in the Training Room

● ●

In This Chapter

▶ Identifying ways to save time while encouraging participation

▶ Identifying ways to catch up if you have fallen behind schedule

▶ Determining how to save time without diminishing learning

● ●

*A*s a trainer, you will want to keep everything moving along in your session. You recognize the importance of maximizing participation yet are concerned about how much time you have available. At times you may need to address issues that your learners are focused on before you move forward with the designed learning experience.

✔ How do you save time while increasing participation?

✔ How do you save time without diminishing any learning experiences?

✔ How do you catch up if you have fallen behind schedule?

Consider the Relationship of Time to Small Groups

If you need to save time during the small-group exercise, form more groups with fewer people. A smaller group will accomplish the task faster than a large group. If you need to save time during the report-out stage, form fewer groups with more people. You will have fewer reports to hear.

You could also have groups report just one item at a time in a round-robin fashion. You save time because duplicate ideas are not reported.

Groups may be able to summarize their ideas on flipchart pages posted around the room. All ideas can be viewed and discussed by the large group. Depending on the activity, each group could select the one or two best ideas to report on. All ideas on flipcharts are viewed as participants leave for or return from break.

One Activity, Two (or More) Objectives

Time. There is never enough of it. Therefore, way back in the beginning of your training cycle begin to think about how you can save time in the design. One of the obvious ones is to use one activity to achieve two or more objectives. For example, participants may be practicing the skills used to conduct performance evaluations. Observers could be taking notes about how well the process was demonstrated. They could also be observing how nonverbal communication affected the skill practice. The next module may be about communication. Later in the day when you want to discuss feedback, you could ask the folks who received feedback from their observers, "What worked; what didn't?" One activity, three different skills.

You may also save time by using "work" that participants need to complete back on the job. When I work with teams, I use real-life projects that they need to accomplish as the basis for creating experiences in which they can evaluate their effectiveness as a team. In your design consider whether participants could bring projects with them to complete as a part of an activity.

Gentle Prods

When you establish small groups to complete a task or activity, always assign a specific amount of time to complete the task. But people lose track of time. The task needs to be completed in order for the learning to occur. First, be sure that you have designed the appropriate amount of time to complete the task. If you're sure of that, you may do two things to help groups stay on time.

First, you could ask them to select a timekeeper within their groups to manage time.

Second, you may wish to give them time cues throughout the task. Examples may include these:

- ✔ "You should have started the second step."
- ✔ "You should be halfway through the task."
- ✔ "How much time do you need to finish?"

✔ "The second person in your group should be providing feedback."

✔ "You have about five minutes to go."

✔ "You should be wrapping up."

✔ "Sixty seconds left."

These gentle prods keep the groups moving and on time.

Different Pace for Different Folks

Always plan a reasonable amount of time in a training design so that it can be completed. However, in real life, some participants simply take more time to complete individual projects than others. If you have a design element where you expect that to occur — for example, completing a self-assessment or quiz — schedule it just prior to a break.

Those who finish early can leave and those who take longer have control over whether they would like to continue at the same pace or try to wrap up more quickly. Those who use most of the break time to complete the task may return late to the session. Again, that is a decision they make, and you should not delay the start if they are still out of the room.

Don't forget to also use the gentle prods throughout the activity to keep them informed of how much time is available.

Divvy Up the Work

All work doesn't need to be completed by all people. If a small-group activity is not dependent upon a specific sequence, assign different groups to complete different parts of the activity. For example, if I have given a group a worksheet that has a list of concepts or components, I will ask some of the small groups to start at the top and work down and some of the groups to start at the bottom and work up. Sometimes, just for fun, I ask one of the groups to start in the middle and go either way.

All of the concepts or components are addressed by one group or another. Learning is not lost because everyone becomes familiar with all of the components of the activity during the debriefing. During the debriefing I encourage all groups to take notes about what the other groups have produced.

The Time Is Now

Time cannot be bottled to save for the future, so use it well. You cannot save time. Don't waste it. Use your time resource wisely.

- ✔ Start the session on time.
- ✔ Start on time after every break.
- ✔ Distribute materials and handouts efficiently. If participants are sitting in a U shape, start stacks at both ends and in the back middle. If participants are at separate tables, place the right number of materials for each table in stacks prior to the start of the session or at breaks.
- ✔ Watch carefully the time you spend in large-group discussion. Time can run away from you here. Establish time limits for discussions that are either scheduled or unscheduled.
- ✔ You do not need to hear from every person every time. If you skip a group or individual, catch them on the next question.

Be Prepared

Examine your behaviors to ensure that you're as well prepared as possible and that you're not the cause for falling behind.

- ✔ Provide clear, concise, complete directions. You may be held up by a group that hasn't finished because they did not understand the instructions. If the instructions are complex, put them in writing.
- ✔ Prepare your flipcharts and other visuals before the session begins.
- ✔ Be sure you know the objective of the discussion. When the point is made, move on. Don't let discussions drag on.
- ✔ Test new activities with colleagues to estimate the timing.
- ✔ If you don't want participants to worry when you're behind, put only general times on their agendas; for example, break the agenda up based on morning and afternoon.
- ✔ Provide examples that will give small-group discussions a jump-start.

Cut Out the Fat

Examine the training. Understand the objectives and your audience well enough so that you know what information is "must know" and what information is "nice to know." Then be prepared to cut out anything that is "nice to know" when you're short of time. I usually identify the least important activity in each module so that I can set priorities as I go along.

Do job aids exist for some of the content? If yes, you probably can cut some time out in that area by providing the information once and then referring to the job aid for future use.

Often, training materials have lists of things to do or remember. When I get to a page of lists, I ask participants to grab a marker or pen and highlight or circle the ones that I think are essential for them to remember. This provides a quick way to address the list in a time-efficient way.

When prioritizing what to keep, remember to keep anything that will help them learn more after the session or help them find information later. No one remembers everything they learn in a training session. However, if they know how to find the information later, you will have done your job.

Use Timekeepers

You may wish to act as a timekeeper yourself. Or assign timekeepers to small groups to ensure that the groups finish their tasks on time.

You can use timekeepers during breaks. Ask for a volunteer who will round up people who have not returned from break. Sometimes, just closing the door to the training room signals those who have lost track of time that the session is ready to start again.

Pre-Training Strategies

Face-to-face time in the training room is getting shorter and shorter. Therefore, you may wish to consider how you can use time before the training begins. You could, for example, assign pre-reading, electronic tutorials, or exercises to the participants.

Pay close attention to the training assessment to identify skill level, experience, and special needs. Doing so ensures that you're prepared for the variation within the group.

Add techniques to support the training. You may need to develop checklists, job aids, e-mail tips, Web-based learning, brownbag sessions, mentors or user support groups or plan to introduce a buddy system during the training.

Chapter 21

Ten Quick Ways to Form Small Groups

In This Chapter

▶ Clarifying the importance of using small groups

▶ Identifying creative ways to form small groups

Small groups are critical to a well-designed training program. They are one of the best ways of promoting involvement and participation. The value of small-group activities include these.

✔ Small groups provide an opportunity for more people to have more "air time" to express opinions, add ideas, and ask questions.

✔ Small groups allow individuals to receive feedback more quickly.

✔ Small groups allow participants to learn from each other.

✔ Small groups create opportunities for more people to practice skills or apply knowledge at the same time.

✔ Learning becomes more dynamic and active in small groups.

✔ Small groups encourage participants to know each other better, breaking down barriers and creating a more positive learning atmosphere.

Small groups are a great way to encourage participation, but using the grade-school method of counting off by fours or fives is not a very creative process. You will actually find more than ten ways to form small groups because there are several variations to each theme.

Whatever technique you use to form small groups, there is only one decision you need to make. Which is more important, how many groups you have, how many people are in each group, or neither one? Let me give you a couple of examples.

✔ The activity may require a trio, such as a role-play between two people plus an observer. You need three people in each group, but it doesn't matter how many groups.

✔ The activity may have five areas, each to be covered by a small group. You need five groups, but it doesn't matter how many people are in each.

✔ Sometimes, you can provide flexibility such that participants can select their own groups, but you still have enough control so that everything is covered. For example, you may have five issues posted on flipcharts that need to be addressed. You could say, "To form small groups, stand next to the issue you want to address. When five people are standing next to one issue, stand next to your second choice." In this case, if you had 22 people in your session, all five issues would be covered, and potentially the smallest group would have two members. Most often, the distribution is quite even.

What if you don't have the exact number of people? Additional participants can always be observers. If there are too few, you may fill in occasionally, although this is not a preference of mine because it takes you away from other groups who may need your assistance.

A little planning before you form small groups ensures that the participants will be successful and all content is addressed.

Arrange participants in small groups prior to giving activity instructions. If you begin with activity instructions and follow with instructions about how you want small groups to form, many participants will have forgotten the initial instructions by the time they have settled into their small groups.

Count Off

Of course you can count off. But do it backward instead. To break into five groups, count off backward from five, "five, four, three, two, one, five." Be sure to stay with the group. Adults can get really confused on this one!

You may also teach participants to count to five in a foreign language — Spanish, German, French, Chinese — and ask them to count off in their new language. This adds a nice touch if the language is one of your participant's first language. It also creates interesting discussion in a diversity training session.

If one of your goals is to provide participants with the opportunity to meet and work with a variety of people, change small-group formations from activity to activity.

Noise Level

Identify sounds that participants could make to form small groups. For example, have participants think of the first vowel sound in their names. Have them make that sound and find others making that same vowel sound. When they find their group, they find a place to sit prior to receiving instructions.

You could have participants think of their favorite color. Have everyone stand and say their color out loud, finding others who are saying the same color.

Have participants think of the last digit of their phone number. Have them say the number until they find others with the same number. Realize that you may have ten small groups anytime you request something as open-ended as this one. You may also have participants whose digit doesn't match anyone's. Quickly pair up strays or assign them to one of the smaller groups that has already formed.

Go to Your Corners

Identify reasons for people to go to separate places in the training room. For example, you could have them go to one of four corners depending on whether they are a first born, last born, middle, or only child in their family. They could go to the corner of the room that is closest to the direction they would head to go home (as a crow flies).

You can connect the corners to content. For example, if you're training a business-communication class, you could have them select the method of communication they prefer, for example, e-mail, face-to-face, telephone, or notes.

Personal Data

Form small groups based on some tiny piece of data about them. You could use birthdays for four groups by using first, second, third, and fourth quarters of the year. Several others are last digit in their Social Security numbers, color of shoes they are wearing, favorite season, first letter of their middle name, or height. For the last two, have participants stand in order (alphabetically or by height) and then split at the quarter or one-fifth point depending on how many groups you desire. If you need two groups, form groups of those wearing glasses or not.

Note that you may need to modify some of these to achieve the number of groups you need for your activity. Even better, come up with your own ideas.

Secret Codes

Code the participants' materials in various ways. Purchase stickers and place them on the training materials, under the participants' chairs, on the outside or inside of the table tents, or on name tags. If you distribute a limited number of different-color markers for participants to use to write their names on their table tents, you can refer to the color marker they choose. Handouts for an activity can be copied on different colors of paper. Put participants into groups based on the color of paper they choose. You may also write numbers or letters on the back of participant notebooks. Use several colors of pens or folders.

Puzzling Participants

Purchase or make four- to six-piece puzzles. Participants select a puzzle piece and find the rest of the pieces to their puzzle to form a small group. More puzzle pieces than participants? Paper-clip two pieces together from the same puzzle.

Small blank puzzles are available from a party goods or office supply store. Add a personal message that is revealed after the small group puts all its pieces together.

Puzzles do not always have to "fit" together physically. You could write the names of people (or fictional characters) who "fit" together on index cards. You could use, for example, Alice, Cheshire Cat, Mad Hatter, and the Queen of Hearts; or you could use Snoopy, Charlie Brown, Lucy, and Pig Pen. You could select television characters, political figures, movie characters, or even "characters" from your organization.

Dog Days

Put people into small groups using sounds. Use as many index cards as you have people. Determine how many people you want in each group. Then write the same sound on each card. For example, you have 20 people in your session and you want groups of four. If you select dog sounds, write "woof woof" on four cards, write "yap yap" on four cards, write "arf, arf" on four cards, and write "ruff ruff" and "bark bark" on the rest. Have participants stand and tell them that when you say go, they should walk around the room and find the other dogs that are speaking the same language. If you use this in a communication session, you can create all sorts of language analogies.

You can vary this by using familiar songs: "Happy Birthday," "Jingle Bells," "Row, Row, Row Your Boat," and so on. You could use sounds you make without opening your mouth: humming, clapping, snapping your fingers, stomping, and so on. You could also use advertising slogans, different animal sounds, words from business: "You've got mail," "One moment please," "If this is correct, please press one," and so on. Sounds made by vehicles, instruments. Well, you get the idea. I suggest that unless you have a strong risk-taking group, you may not want to use it until after the first day.

Small Groups Where None Dares to Go

All the techniques are great you say, but what about the times that you're (unfortunately) providing training in a classroom setting. You know the one with long tables, everyone facing the front of the room, furniture so close participants can barely move between rows? Do what you can with what you have. The best idea is to have the odd-numbered rows turn to the back of the room, facing participants in the even-numbered rows. Decide whether you want small groups of two, four, or six and have participants split the groups accordingly.

If you want participants to work with different people the next time, have the even-numbered rows turn to the back of the room. And if you really want to mix things up, you can have everyone get up and rearrange the room to be more suitable for learning. Just remember to be careful of what you ask for. You'll get a room that looks nothing like it did when you made the offer.

Pick a Prop

It takes a bit of preplanning, but there are hundreds of props you could bring for forming groups. Trinket catalogs like Oriental Trading sells miniatures of almost everything — toys, various-shaped erasers, cards, party favors, and so on. You could bring miniature lifesaver candy or miniature candy bars in different flavors. Have participants select one and then find the other individuals who have selected the same (color, flavor, toy) whatever.

I once took bubble-gum cards from four different sports: baseball, football, basketball, and soccer. Participants were supposed to form the team of the same sport. You could use a regular deck of playing cards. Sort the cards into sets of matching numbers and have participants find their set.

Using props works well around holidays, when it is easy to find little, inexpensive, yet cute items. You may use something as simple as colored index cards or shapes cut from construction paper.

Make Mine Different

You don't always need to form a group based on what is similar. You could form by what is different. This is particularly good for times when you want to form pairs and you have already had them work with the individuals to their left and their right.

Have participants find someone to work with who is different in some way. Find a partner who has different-colored hair or eyes from yours. Wearing shoes with laces? Find someone who is not. Find someone whose birthday is in a different month from yours.

Chapter 22

Ten Tips for Adding Humor to Training

In This Chapter

▶ Identifying ways to interject humor into a training session

▶ Avoiding bombs when telling a joke

▶ Making humor a natural part of your presentation

Thomas Edison once said that he had never worked a day in his life. It was all fun! Wouldn't it be great if you could always say that? Adding humor to your training is one way in which you can add fun to your participants' days.

I have always believed that people should not have to get up and go to work in the morning. We should all love our jobs so much that we get up and go to play each day. Learning should be like that. People seem to learn more when they are having a good time. This chapter provides you with ideas for how to add humor and fun to your training session, how to feel like everyone has come to play for the day.

Laugh and Learn

When humor and playfulness are suppressed in traditional education and training, other traits are lost as well. Creativity, imagination, and inventiveness have a hard time surviving in a mirthless environment. Incorporate humor into a training session in several ways.

Use humor that matches your style. What works for your favorite stand-up comedian or even another trainer may not work for you. Relate humor to something that participants know. It is difficult to find humor in something that must be explained.

Focus on funny stories as opposed to jokes. Stories usually fit into the flow of events and have a purpose in training because they are generally used to make a point. So even if your participants do not find the story funny, you have made a point and not wasted participants' time. Unless the trainer is very skilled, jokes, on the other hand, tend to break the flow of the training. On top of that, if the joke bombs, you may have wasted participants' valuable time.

Relate humor to the training. Forget adding extraneous humor, such as an irrelevant joke at the beginning. The best humor happens as a result of what occurs naturally in the classroom. Trainers can have ready-to-go funny comments that work when a certain situation pops up in a classroom. Trainers can also relate humor to content in the session or to the processes used to deliver the training. Trainers should also be ready to laugh at themselves. Several ideas follow later in this chapter about how to build humor naturally into the session.

Follow the lead of good comedians and paint a picture for participants. Using concrete, real-world descriptions that relate to them helps them see and hear the humor.

Keep it simple. Shakespeare said, "Brevity is the soul of wit."

Whatever humor you use, be sure to practice. Be sure to practice your punch line. Be sure to practice your punch line with a pause just before it.

Start Off on a Funny Foot

Establish the atmosphere right from the start. Every session should start off on a high note to set the stage for the rest of the session. Be positive. You want to send the message that this will be fun. Your opening comments can have some planted humor such as when I let participants know how long I have been in the business.

Icebreakers are discussed elsewhere in this book. Icebreakers must induce a sense of fun in the session. Icebreakers should never be drudgery for participants. I like to use props in the opening at some point. Icebreakers seem to lend themselves to the use of props: blocks, t-shirts, bags, flashlights, tools, or dozens of other things.

Unless you are a professional comedian, forget the jokes. Tell a funny story but no contrived jokes. If you bomb, it may seem like a long time until lunch.

When listing the ground rules in my training sessions, if someone says, "We should have fun," I grab a red marker and write over the top of all the rest of the ground rules the word FUN, stating, "Above all, have fun." This drives home the message that I encourage humor and believe learning should be fun.

Why add humor to the opening of a training session?

✔ Relieves nervousness participants may feel

✔ Establishes the environment for the rest of the session

✔ Gets participants' attention

✔ Models that although the session is serious, the trainer does not necessarily believe in being glum

I'm Lost!

Use humor to defuse unexpected situations. Here are some examples you may want to try.

✔ If you lose your place or pause too long, you can say, "I just wanted to wait a moment in case any of you have lost your place." Steve Martin's favorite for this situation, "Where was I? Oh yes! I was here!" (Take a step to the side.) Or, "I'm just going through a mental pause!"

✔ When you garble a sentence, you can say, "Later on I'll pass out a printed translation of that sentence."

✔ If you tell a joke and it bombs, you could say, "Okay, I'll just go back to my desk (Wisconsin, home office, or wherever you call "home") now!"

✔ If you are using a microphone and it goes dead, you can say, "Evidently someone has heard this presentation before."

✔ If people are talking during your presentation, you can say, "Feel free to talk among yourselves." Or, "I see you're starting to break up into small discussion groups ahead of me."

✔ If someone points out you misspelled a word, you could say, "Mark Twain once said he never respected anyone who couldn't spell a word more than one way!" Another response when informed you have misspelled a word is to look around the flipchart as if you are missing something and then say, "Does anyone know where the spell check is on one of these?"

Or my favorite. When I misspell a word or need to write a word that I can't spell on a flipchart, I quickly write 10 to12 arbitrary letters in an empty corner of the flipchart, for example, Q, B, R, J, Z, D, N, A, and say, "I'm not the best speller in the world, so if you notice that I have missed a letter someplace, just take it from this group of letters and place it wherever it belongs in the word!"

✔ If you give incorrect instructions, say, "Does everyone understand? Good. Now forget it. That was just a test to see if you can follow instructions. Now I will give you the actual instructions."

- If a participant answers a question incorrectly, you could say, "right answer, wrong question!" (Be careful with this one.)

- If the lights go out, you can say, "Why do I have the feeling that when the lights come back on, I'll be alone?" or "You thought you were in the dark before this session!"

Humor can turn an awkward situation into an enjoyable experience. The participants laugh. The laughter makes them feel good and eases the tension of a difficult situation for the trainer.

Get Participants in the Act

Don't feel as if you need to be the one responsible for all the laughs. Get participants in the act so all enjoy themselves. How can you do that?

Many games and energizers exist where everyone is laughing at the end. Relay races can have that effect on participants. "All Tied Up" is an energizer in which participants stand in close proximity to one another. Everyone grasps everyone else's hand in no particular order. Next, participants begin to untangle themselves.

One game that results in everyone laughing is called "Did You Shower Today?" Place one chair for each participant in a circle. Have all participants sit in the chairs. Begin giving directions for participants to change chairs. I have started you off with a few, but you can add or change them to personalize for your group. This activity helps participants get to know each other better and leaves them laughing because at times four of five people may be trying to sit on the same chair.

- If you showered today, move 3 chairs to the left.

- If you read a newspaper regularly, move 2 chairs to the right.

- If you traveled abroad within the past year, move 1 chair to the right.

- If you like chocolate, move 2 chairs to the left.

- If you have a pet, move 3 chairs to the right.

- If you like snow and winter weather, move 1 chair to the right.

- If you are a gourmet cook, move 2 chairs to the left.

- If you like to paint, move 3 chairs to the left.

- If you play a sport, move 1 chair to the right.

> ✔ If you are involved in a sport that does not require a ball, move 1 chair to the left.
>
> ✔ If you like Mexican food, move 5 chairs to the left.
>
> ✔ . . . add your own ideas.

When participants say something funny, be sure that the entire group has heard it so everyone feels a part of the humor.

Practical Humor

Sometimes trainers facilitate energizers that are unrelated to the content or the process. You can do this, but with time often short, think of ways to energize the participants yet make it useful. Humor can be practical, such as when you are forming small groups or designating a leader for a small group. Here are two suggestions for designating a leader. Both get laughs. The first is to ask for someone to volunteer from each group. Tell them that you cannot say what they are volunteering for until after they volunteer. This always gets a laugh. After you get a volunteer from each group, tell them that they can select the leader for the group. That usually brings on lots of groans.

I learned the second method for selecting a leader from Bob Pike. Have each small group stand in a circle. Ask all participants to point their index fingers to the ceiling and to think of whom they can select as their group's leader. Then tell them that on the count of three they should all point to the person for whom they are voting. Each group counts the number of "votes" each person received. The person with the most votes is the leader.

Add humor when you are forming small groups. One way I have done this is to place table tents around the room that have funny activities printed on them. Participants are asked to stand next to the card that describes something that they do. Items can include these or others you identify.

> ✔ Has eaten an entire batch of cookies
>
> ✔ Has gone skinny-dipping
>
> ✔ Squeezes toothpaste from the middle

Don't Be Original!

All of your humor does not need to be original. In fact, it may be better if someone else has tested it for you.

The HUMOR Project, Inc. in Saratoga Springs, New York, is a great place to start. It is the first organization in the world to focus full-time on the positive power of humor. Its mission is to "make a difference by being a unique, pioneering, and cutting-edge organization that touches the lives of individuals, organizations, and nations." The organization wants people to get more "smileage" out of their lives by applying the practical, positive power of humor and creativity. Check its Web site at www.HUMORproject.com for publications including books, *Laughing Matters Magazine,* and an e-newsletter. The organization holds an annual conference in Saratoga Springs, where they are located. You will also find props that can add humor to your training. The least you should do is to get on their mailing list, and they will send you a fabulous catalog.

Many books are available for finding anecdotes or stories to make your point. One of my favorites is *Braude's Treasury of Wit and Humor for All Occasions,* published by Prentice Hall. And, of course, you should ever be on the lookout for cartoons (remember to obtain permission if you intend to print them in your materials) and jokes that will fit in your content.

The Sunday comic strips are often closer to real life than you may imagine. If it is a simple concept, you may be able to describe the cartoon without the image. Tear jokes, cartoons, and advertising out of magazines and start a file of content. Join a daily joke list on the Internet.

Get ideas by reading or listening to current and classic comedians. Several of the classic comedians whom I enjoy are Mae West, Groucho Marx, Henny Youngman, Jack Benny, and W.C. Fields, who said, "Comedy is a serious business. A serious business with only one purpose — to make people laugh."

Referencing something that most participants will remember can add humor. For example, sometimes television ads will make a point that you can use. You may not need to say anything much more than referring to the ad, such as, "Remember the X company ad where they were herding cats?" You can also reference lines in movies that make a point and add humor. You can state the movie, the actor's name, and the punch line to get a laugh.

Remember who is in your audience. Don't do as I did once, referencing a movie that was over 30 years old. Because most of the participants in my training session were in their late 20s and early 30s, none had seen the movie!

Phunny Props and Puns

Add fun with props. Sometimes a prop can represent a concept within your training session. For example, I use a flashlight when I teach creativity skills in a variety of ways to add fun to the session. I refer to the fact that their "creativity may be in the dark" but there are ways to "ignite their spark." I challenge them to "harness their creative energy" and state that there is a "ray of hope." I tell them that the session will "illuminate" their natural creativity.

Notice the use of puns in the creativity example. You can't just add props without making a point. For example, I once saw someone use a rubber chicken to point to content on the flipchart. There was no purpose, except to make people laugh. He was successful. People laughed. Maybe I'm too uptight, but I just did not think it was funny. There are many other ways you can make people laugh that relates to the training content.

Props may be used to review content material and increase energy. Many trainers have participants get in a circle and toss a tennis ball or a koosh ball as they review material. In addition to relating to content, props can be used as prizes during the session after games or activities or as rewards when someone volunteers to be a leader or observer or to play another role that goes above and beyond expectations.

Other props that will make people smile may be related to an upcoming holiday. Sparklers for the Fourth of July or candy hearts for Valentine's Day will make people smile without your saying anything. You can go beyond the traditional holidays by using props related to Mardi Gras, the Super Bowl, Groundhog Day, May Day, the first day of spring, and so on.

Another logical prop is anything that has a yellow smiley face on it. Smiley faces have become quite common place, so items displaying them are easy to locate. They do make people smile. Whatever you use, try to tie it to the topic, the area, or your audience. Use puns to stretch the meaning a bit.

Ten Tips to Make a Joke Bomb

How many trainers does it take to make a joke bomb? Just one. But once is enough! Telling a joke is easy. Making people laugh is hard work. Professional comedians make it look oh so easy. But the truth is that few have ever ad-libbed a line in their life. They practice and prepare — just like great trainers do. If you are going to tell a joke, heed the following ten things that can go wrong. If you want your participants to laugh, *don't* do them!

✔ Announce that you are going to tell a joke.

✔ Don't practice; rely on your natural skills and your ability to ad-lib.

✔ Ensure that the joke has nothing to do with the content.

- ✔ Insult someone or, better yet, everyone.
- ✔ Use a sexist, ethnic, political, racist, or religious joke.
- ✔ Extend the joke, making it drag out.
- ✔ Garble the punch line.
- ✔ Don't research your audience; everyone loves a joke.
- ✔ Laugh your way through the joke.
- ✔ If your joke bombs, be sure to try to explain the punch line.

Here's to having only good belly laughs following all your jokes.

But I'm Not Funny!

When I first started in the training field, a friend of mine gave me advice about using humor. He said, "Don't try to be funny; just have fun." I know I don't need to be a comedian to be seen as having a great sense of humor. Don't take yourself too seriously. You need to be able to laugh at yourself to be seen as someone who has a sense of humor. Mess up in front of the class? Make a joke and write it off as an opportunity to add humor to the session.

Focus on the participants. When you care more about the participants and the experience you are creating for them than you care about yourself, it frees you of a huge responsibility. You do not need to be perfect. Things will go wrong in your training session. Participants will not behave the way you want them to; the room will not be set up as you wanted it to be. There's not much you can do about anything that goes wrong, but you can have fun with it while you are fixing the problem. Find humor in the unpredictable.

Identify the humor that is natural to you. I can't spell worth a darn; I make a joke about it. I am 4'11" short; I make a joke about it. I've been in the training field for a quarter of a century; I make a joke about it. I am not a computer whiz; I make a joke about it. What's funny about you?

Learners are desperate for humor, but it is virtually absent in the learning environment. I have found that learners will appreciate any attempt at humor.

Participants often walk into a training session expecting a boring experience. I know because they have told me so. If you can surprise them by removing most of the boredom, you will be a star. Remember, you do not have to be funny, just have fun.

Austere Attitudes

Everyone who walks into your training session will not be interested in being humored. Some will bring attitudes that are barriers to having a good time.

- ✔ Training is serious business — just like work.
- ✔ Humor is a waste of time.
- ✔ Employees who have fun at work are not productive.
- ✔ We can't possibly accomplish our goals with all this raucous laughter.

What can you do to try to turn these attitudes around? Well, nothing new: Build trust, encourage participation, respect others' opinions, and ensure that participants take responsibility for their own learning. When using humor, it should flow naturally from the content. Humor should support, not replace, the learning objectives. Always have alternatives to humorous activities available if the humor isn't right for a particular group of participants.

Chapter 23

Ten Icebreakers That Work

*T*he room is set. Participant materials are in place. The projector with your PowerPoint presentation is focused, and the participants have arrived. It's time to begin your training session, and first impressions will set the stage for the rest of the time together.

Chapter 18 introduces you to a number of elements that should be included in your opening. One of those is to help everyone get to know each other better. That is the key purpose of icebreakers.

I am convinced that training sessions are better when they start out with an icebreaker. Whether you use icebreakers created by someone else or you design your own, I suggest that you pay attention to some advice based on lessons I learned the hard way.

✔ **Never ask anyone to do anything you would not want to do.** This is cardinal rule number one. Isn't it amazing that participants will almost always follow a trainer's direction and do what they are asked to do? They believe that trainers always know what they're doing and that the things a trainer asks them to do will further their learning. If you hesitate for even a moment about conducting a particular icebreaker, don't use it. Your hesitation is a sign that it may not feel good to other participants as well. Participants trust trainers and trust that what we ask them to do is in their best interest. Don't break that trust.

I was once a participant in a training session in which the trainer asked us to get down on our hands and knees, make animal sounds, and find others who were imitating the same animals. As I was on the floor growling like a lion, I spotted the trainer laughing away. I felt duped and had much less respect for that trainer from that point on. Lesson learned? Be careful what you ask participants to do; it should maintain their self-esteem, build trust, and enhance what they are learning.

✔ **Select icebreakers based on the type of group you're training.** The participants who attend your training should help guide your decision. Executives will respond differently than factory employees, and employees in sales will react differently than those in engineering. Ask yourself a few questions about the participants to assist with your choice.

At what level are they in the organization? What jobs do they have? What is their cultural background? What is the age range? What gender? What educational level are they? What expectations will the participants have? What past training experiences have they had? Early in my career I did not take the time to ask these questions. I was asked to provide communications training to a group of engineers. Although I customized the training for the engineers, I used the same icebreaker that I had developed for a communication module for a sales staff. It fell flat. The analytical engineers were the exact opposites from the gregarious sales folks. Lesson learned? Know your audience.

✔ **Relate the icebreaker to the content.** I have always believed that icebreakers should relate to content so that they serve as the introduction to the topic. Today there is a more practical reason for relating the icebreaker to the content: time. In almost all organizations there seems to be more to do with less time to do it. Participants are busy, and it is a good possibility that the organization has asked trainers to squeeze more content into shorter sessions.

This means that it is wise to make every minute of your training session count. For example, if you're conducting a diversity session, select an icebreaker that spotlights differences. If you're conducting a team-building session, select an icebreaker that addresses individual team skills or characteristics. When I relate the icebreaker to the content, the flow of the session is natural. However, when I don't, I create a problem for myself because I must force a connection. Lesson learned? Make every minute in your training sessions count, starting immediately with a related icebreaker.

✔ **Use icebreakers to set the tone and to demonstrate the level of participation you expect.** The icebreaker can set the stage for how much involvement you expect of the participants. If you want them to interact with each other, you can select an icebreaker that gets them out of their seats and moving around meeting as many people as they can. In fact, the number of people participants meet during the icebreaker can be a part of the challenge. If you want participants to work in teams, you may design an icebreaker that encourages teamwork.

I remember using an icebreaker that was so funny it was difficult for any of us to stop laughing. Unfortunately, the topic was a serious one, and it was a challenge to make the switch for both me and the participants. Lesson learned? Select an icebreaker that sets the tone for the environment you're trying to create.

✔ **Observe the group during the icebreaker to learn something about the group and the individuals.** Icebreakers provide trainers with a perfect opportunity to learn about the group as well as individuals. In some cases the group will be outgoing and fun loving. In other cases the group may be defensive and negative. Trainers can observe individuals in the group to determine who seem to be the natural leaders, who has a tendency to dominate, or who is competitive.

At times I have gotten so involved in the icebreaker that I did not take advantage of this opportunity to learn more about the participants in the session. Later when I have had a problem behavior in the training session, I question whether I would have been able to head off the problem earlier if I had given more attention to the right things during the icebreaker. Lesson learned? Attend to the personalities during the icebreaker — the individual participant personalities, as well as the group's personality.

✔ **Watch the time during an icebreaker.** You will have determined how much time you will spend conducting an icebreaker. However, if you have selected an energizing icebreaker, it is easy for time to get away from you in a couple different ways.

First, if you have individual report outs (as some of the icebreakers in this chapter call for), set a limit on the amount of time allowed for each. If a participant takes too much time, intervene tactfully to get the group back on track. If you have 20 participants and each report-out takes just 2 minutes more than you planned, you will be 40 minutes behind schedule before you have even completed the introduction! Individual report-outs in groups over 25 become tedious and boring. Try another format, for example, individual introductions, but reports by small group. Or you could have the individual report-outs occur in subgroups.

Just recently I had a time problem in a group of 18 in a training certificate program. The final step of the icebreaker involved participants introducing themselves: name, city they lived in, how long in the job, and the slogan that defined them. The first person stood and provided at least 25 percent of his life story. I did not (though I knew I should have) cut him off. His one-minute introduction lasted at least five minutes. Unfortunately, everyone else in the group expanded their introduction to be in line with the first person. At the end of the icebreaker, we were almost an hour behind schedule. Lesson learned? Time can evaporate during an icebreaker. Watch your time carefully.

Remember, an icebreaker's success depends on the trainer in two ways: ensuring that you have established a comfortable climate and that you have selected the right icebreaker. You must be able to quickly establish a climate that gives participants permission to step outside their comfort zone. When you announce that time has been set aside for participants to meet each other, you may look about and see some rolled eyes or hear some groans.

That means that a couple of participants would rather sit in their chairs than go out to meet others. Use a tone right from the start to establish a climate that ensures people feel comfortable: a pleasant voice, a friendly smile, welcoming gestures, appropriate eye contact, and short, clear instructions all tell your participants that it is okay to play.

Finally, heed my advice throughout this chapter. It is based on the lessons I've learned over the years. Ask yourself these questions about the icebreaker you intend to use. Did you select one that is appropriate for the participants? Does the icebreaker allow you to establish a climate that gives participants permission to follow your lead? Have you simplified the directions so that everyone will experience success? If you can answer yes to all of these questions, your icebreaker will achieve the objectives you desire.

Good luck with your icebreakers. May they warm your training sessions immeasurably.

 Avoid using the word "icebreaker" when introducing the exercise. Even though that's what it is, remember that the word itself is trainer jargon that may not be understood by everyone. Even more important, however, is that you will appear more professional if you smoothly introduce what you want participants to do and why you want them to do it without labeling it as an icebreaker, an exercise, an activity, or any other "thing" you want them to do. You can say something like, "During the training session, we will be working together and tapping into the expertise in this room. Therefore, it is important that we find out who else is here and what experiences they bring with them."

Bingo

Bingo is probably the most used icebreaker of all the icebreakers. And the reason is, that it works. It has been around forever, and I do not know where it originated. Reproduce a Bingo card on a sheet of paper. Instead of having B-3 or N-13, each square has information. The information can be so specific that it matches individuals in the group, such as "drives a red Corvette" and "played a saxophone with Kenny G." The information can also be general so that it could match any number of people, such as "likes to drive fast" and "plays a musical instrument." Figure 23-1 provides an example of a Bingo card.

Participants move around the room and find a match to each of the criteria. In the first example, they would be looking for a specific person. In the second, several people may match the criteria. Individuals sign the appropriate square that matches their descriptions. It is a great way to meet and greet and learn something about others in the session to encourage additional discussion at the next break.

Drives a sports car	Exercises regularly	Voted in the last election	Has attended a training for trainers	Has season tickets
Plays a musical instrument	Plays poker	Has run a marathon	Likes to ride horses	Enjoys working with wood
Teaches computer classes	Is a gourmet cook	Likes to eat spinach	Has owned a surfboard	Plays golf
Likes to fly	Plays tennis	Collects something	Plays bridge	Painted a house
Has written a book	Is a closet poet	Has a pet	Is counting carbs	Has a garden

Figure 23-1:
Bingo
icebreaker.

You can easily tie these questions to the content, if you want. For example, if you're conducting a stress-management class, you could include squares that say "attends yoga classes," "goes for a walk at lunch," or "has used visualization successfully."

Expectations

If Bingo is the most used icebreaker, Expectations may very well run a close second. I learned this one from Ed Scannell and John Newstrom, authors of the wildly successful, very useful, and creative *Games Trainers Play* series. Buy any of them; you won't be disappointed.

In Expectations, participants identify what they really want to learn in the training session to make the day (workshop, training, week) valuable and useful to them. After you tell them what the objectives are for the session, have them form groups of two to four. Give the groups five minutes to list two or three expectations on a sheet of paper. As a trainer, you're trying to tap into their initial thoughts. If you allow more than five minutes, they will begin to go beyond the scope of the training. Also as a trainer you need to be prepared to adjust your training session to accommodate those that you can. You may be surprised that most of the participants' expectations will be covered.

Hopes and Fears

The Expectations icebreaker taps into the cerebral desires that the participants bring with them to the training session. Hopes and Fears taps into the participants' feelings about the training.

Provide a handout to participants that provides space for them to list their hopes and fears as they relate to the training session. Tell them that whenever people find themselves in a new situation, it is natural to begin thinking about the things they hope will happen and the things they hope will not happen. This exercise is an opportunity to find out how similar everyone is. Allow about three to four minutes for them to complete the handout.

Have participants pair up with someone they do not know or do not know well to discuss their lists. Conduct a round robin, obtaining one item from each column from the pairs. You may want to post them on a flipchart. Discuss the items, informing them of the hopes that will occur or what you may be able to do about those hopes that are not planned into the session. Also, reassure them of the fears that are unfounded or quell fears that are not really going to be as bad as they anticipate. For example, if participants in a speaking class will be videotaped and that is a fear that arises, you can discuss the benefits of the videotaping and let them know that no one will watch it except them (if that is true).

Post the flipchart pages on the walls during the first break.

Introduce Me, I Introduce You

It is sometimes easier to introduce others than it is to introduce yourself. In this icebreaker, pair participants up and have each interview the other to learn enough about the person to introduce him or her to the larger group. You may want to suggest the information you would like them to obtain, for example, their names, how long they have worked for the organization, where they attended school, something interesting about them that may be just a little different than anyone else in the room, or what they are hoping to improve as a result of this training session.

Provide paper for participants to conduct their interviews. After five to ten minutes for the interviews, have participants begin to introduce each other. In an exercise like this, I generally ask for a volunteer to go first as opposed to assigning someone to start. Some people prefer to have a model.

Go to Your Corners

This is another icebreaker that has been around a long time. It is used for discovering participants' common interests. Place four flipcharts in the four corners of the room. On the first page of each, write one of four words or phrases. They should be topics that would generate curiosity and/or tap into the interests of the group. You may use travel, reading, running, and gourmet cooking. Ask participants to choose one. After they select a corner, have them discuss why they chose that corner.

Have someone turn the first page on each chart to reveal the second round. These four pages could include something around the current events of the day. Again, have participants read the charts and select a new corner. Repeat the process.

I generally have the third and fourth pages relate to the content of the session. The third round may focus on needs the participants have and can be stated as "I hope we learn to . . ." followed by four things participants may want to learn. Conduct a short debriefing, asking someone in the group to summarize why they made that choice.

The fourth round can again relate to the content. You may use "I feel good about . . ." or I think I am pretty good at. . . ." These show the rest of the participants where the experts are in the group.

This icebreaker can also be used as an energizer if the pace bogs down, such as after lunch in a warm training room. When used as an energizer, identify content items that they can review in the four small groups.

Little White Lie

Allow participants a couple of minutes to think about this before putting them into groups of three. In the small groups, each person makes three statements about themselves: Two are truthful, and one is a lie. For example, my statement may be: I love to drive on icy roads; my hobby is gardening; and I think sleep is a waste of time and do not sleep at least one night each week.

The other two individuals guess which one is the lie. After a few minutes, the trios introduce themselves, playing off what happened in the activity.

I use this icebreaker to introduce a communication-styles workshop. The relationship is that if you know something about people's styles, you will be able to tell something about their preferences.

Personal Coat of Arms

Creating a coat of arms is an icebreaker that is a true classic. Although it has been around for many years, it is just as effective as the first time it was used. Creating a Personal Coat of Arms is more serious than most other icebreakers. In it, the trainer asks participants to draw a coat of arms that represents who they are. Participants may want to use words or draw symbols or pictures.

You may want to distribute a shield-like sketch that is divided into four quadrants. Have participants address a different item in each of the four quadrants. For example, participants may identify themselves on their coat of arms by answering who they are at work, at home, at play, and in the future. The coat of arms could also display something about what they like to do at work, at home, at play, in the community. You may request four specific aspects, or you may ask for something more generic: "Draw a coat of arms that tells us who you are."

In this icebreaker, it is a good idea to draw your own coat of arms and display and explain it to the group. I may share a coat of arms that looks something like the one in Figure 23-2. I would tell participants that I am a positive person who loves to write. I live on the water and am learning to play tennis.

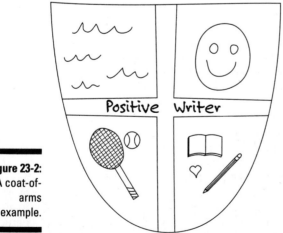

Figure 23-2:
A coat-of-arms example.

You can do many things with this icebreaker, including relating it to the content or focusing all of the quadrants in the future instead of the present and/or the past.

Autographs

Autographs is one of the most practical icebreakers. It is straightforward and serves as a perfect bridge from introductions to content. You can easily design your own Autographs to match the content in the training program you're designing. I first heard of this icebreaker from Michele Wyman, a colleague and trainer. The goal of this icebreaker is for each participant to meet many participants by obtaining as many autographs as possible.

To customize Autographs for your use, create a handout that lists 15 to 25 questions or statements that can be "autographed" by participants who match the description. Provide a combination of personal statements and content-related statements. Personal statements may include "Has been to Europe," or "Has performed on stage." Content-related statements will match the training topic. A communications training session may include statements such as "Have been told I am a good listener" or "Spends at least 50 percent of on-the-job time communicating."

After brief hello-my-name-is introductions, distribute the handout that you created. Tell participants that they will walk around and meet others in the session. When they meet a participant who matches one of the descriptions, he or she will sign the sheet. To encourage participants to meet as many people as possible, they must have a different autograph after each statement.

Name Association

Name Association has the unique quality of using a method to help participants remember each others' names. This may be one of the oldest icebreakers ever developed. I remember playing a game similar to Name Association — and that was before icebreakers were even invented! Two alternatives are presented here.

The first is to have participants introduce themselves using a characteristic that helps to identify them. The characteristic could rhyme with the participant's name, such as Duane the Brain or Tall Paul. The characteristic could start with the same letter as the person's name, such as Happy Harry or Timely Terry.

The second association can be related to an imaginary event. Participants introduce themselves and identify something they will contribute to the event that rhymes with their names. For example, if the event is a party, participants may introduce themselves like this:

- ✔ "My name is Ned, and I'll bring the bread."
- ✔ "My name is Mark, and I'll ensure a spark."
- ✔ "My name is Linda, and I'll bring the Splenda."
- ✔ "My name is Maggie, and I'll bring the baggies."

Note that the names do not need to rhyme perfectly and the items don't even need to make much sense. The real reason for using a name association icebreaker is to help participants remember the names of the others in the session.

Ask a Question

There may be times when you're looking for something quick and easy. Perhaps you do not have much time up front, but you still want everyone to know something about each other. If the session is only a couple of hours long, you have only a few minutes for an icebreaker. And if you plan for interaction among participants, you may actually save time by conducting a quick icebreaker up front that allows participants to meet each other.

There may be other times when your participants all work together and know each other, and you may want to get them to a similar level of knowledge or take them to a personal level of knowing each other. In these situations you may decide to ask a question of participants. Again, remember you can use this technique and relate it to the content as described in the introduction to this chapter. However, if you're simply looking for a question to ensure that everyone knows something new about the rest of the participants, these questions have worked well for me over the years.

- ✔ What do you like to do for fun?
- ✔ If you could be any animal, what would it be and why?
- ✔ Can you describe your dream vacation?
- ✔ What do you like best about where you live?
- ✔ What would you do if you suddenly became a multimillionaire by winning the lottery?
- ✔ What was the last book you read, and would you recommend it to the rest of us?

- If you could have a party and invite any three people of your choosing, alive or deceased, who would you invite?

- What historical person could teach you something, and what would they teach you?

- How do you like to spend your Saturdays?

- If you could change the world, what would you do?

- What do you believe was the turning point in your life?

- What opportunity did you miss, and how would it have changed your life today?

- What fictional character do you relate to most? Why?

- Whom do you most admire, and why?

- What's the most unusual thing that has ever happened to you?

- How do you like to celebrate success?

- What do you have in your billfold, pocket, or purse that none of us would expect to find there and why?

- If you were wearing a T-shirt that displayed your life slogan, what would the words on the T-shirt say?

- What is one interesting fact about you that most of the group would not know?

- What is your all-time favorite movie and why?

This is just a small sample of the questions you could use. Perhaps this list will start you thinking of others. (I try to tie even these questions to the content, if at all possible.) These questions can be used at other times during a training session. For example, if you need a quick energizer right after lunch, try one of these.

Which icebreaker to use? The decision is up to you. Consider the time you have available, who's in your audience, the content of the training, what you want to accomplish, the location where the training will occur, and what you feel comfortable doing.

What should you accomplish with an icebreaker? There are many things to consider, but I try to accomplish the following as a minimum.

- Grab participants' attention

- Establish a participative climate in which everyone is involved

- Set the pace for the rest of the training session

- Put people at ease, and this includes me, the trainer

✔ Initiate personal interaction between the participants

✔ Complete introductions of all participants that go beyond just their names and where they work

✔ Ensure that everyone speaks at least once in the large group

✔ Observe the group to define its personality

✔ Identify the individual personalities in the group

✔ Share enough information so that everyone learns something about the other participants

✔ Establish a starting point for or a transition to the content

Create your own list of what you want to accomplish with the icebreakers you conduct.

Index

BUSINESS, CAREERS & PERSONAL FINANCE

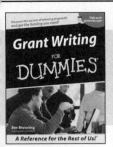

0-7645-5307-0

0-7645-5331-3 *†

Also available:

- Accounting For Dummies †
  0-7645-5314-3
- Business Plans Kit For Dummies †
  0-7645-5365-8
- Cover Letters For Dummies
  0-7645-5224-4
- Frugal Living For Dummies
  0-7645-5403-4
- Leadership For Dummies
  0-7645-5176-0
- Managing For Dummies
  0-7645-1771-6

- Marketing For Dummies
  0-7645-5600-2
- Personal Finance For Dummies *
  0-7645-2590-5
- Project Management For Dummies
  0-7645-5283-X
- Resumes For Dummies †
  0-7645-5471-9
- Selling For Dummies
  0-7645-5363-1
- Small Business Kit For Dummies *†
  0-7645-5093-4

HOME & BUSINESS COMPUTER BASICS

0-7645-4074-2

0-7645-3758-X

Also available:

- ACT! 6 For Dummies
  0-7645-2645-6
- iLife '04 All-in-One Desk Reference
  For Dummies
  0-7645-7347-0
- iPAQ For Dummies
  0-7645-6769-1
- Mac OS X Panther Timesaving
  Techniques For Dummies
  0-7645-5812-9
- Macs For Dummies
  0-7645-5656-8

- Microsoft Money 2004 For Dummies
  0-7645-4195-1
- Office 2003 All-in-One Desk Reference
  For Dummies
  0-7645-3883-7
- Outlook 2003 For Dummies
  0-7645-3759-8
- PCs For Dummies
  0-7645-4074-2
- TiVo For Dummies
  0-7645-6923-6
- Upgrading and Fixing PCs For Dummies
  0-7645-1665-5
- Windows XP Timesaving Techniques
  For Dummies
  0-7645-3748-2

FOOD, HOME, GARDEN, HOBBIES, MUSIC & PETS

0-7645-5295-3

0-7645-5232-5

Also available:

- Bass Guitar For Dummies
  0-7645-2487-9
- Diabetes Cookbook For Dummies
  0-7645-5230-9
- Gardening For Dummies *
  0-7645-5130-2
- Guitar For Dummies
  0-7645-5106-X
- Holiday Decorating For Dummies
  0-7645-2570-0
- Home Improvement All-in-One
  For Dummies
  0-7645-5680-0

- Knitting For Dummies
  0-7645-5395-X
- Piano For Dummies
  0-7645-5105-1
- Puppies For Dummies
  0-7645-5255-4
- Scrapbooking For Dummies
  0-7645-7208-3
- Senior Dogs For Dummies
  0-7645-5818-8
- Singing For Dummies
  0-7645-2475-5
- 30-Minute Meals For Dummies
  0-7645-2589-1

INTERNET & DIGITAL MEDIA

0-7645-1664-7

0-7645-6924-4

Also available:

- 2005 Online Shopping Directory
  For Dummies
  0-7645-7495-7
- CD & DVD Recording For Dummies
  0-7645-5956-7
- eBay For Dummies
  0-7645-5654-1
- Fighting Spam For Dummies
  0-7645-5965-6
- Genealogy Online For Dummies
  0-7645-5964-8
- Google For Dummies
  0-7645-4420-9

- Home Recording For Musicians
  For Dummies
  0-7645-1634-5
- The Internet For Dummies
  0-7645-4173-0
- iPod & iTunes For Dummies
  0-7645-7772-7
- Preventing Identity Theft For Dummies
  0-7645-7336-5
- Pro Tools All-in-One Desk Reference
  For Dummies
  0-7645-5714-9
- Roxio Easy Media Creator For Dummies
  0-7645-7131-1

* Separate Canadian edition also available
† Separate U.K. edition also available

Available wherever books are sold. For more information or to order direct: U.S. customers visit www.dummies.com or call 1-877-762-2974.
U.K. customers visit www.wileyeurope.com or call 0800 243407. Canadian customers visit www.wiley.ca or call 1-800-567-4797.

SPORTS, FITNESS, PARENTING, RELIGION & SPIRITUALITY

0-7645-5146-9   0-7645-5418-2

Also available:

- Adoption For Dummies
  0-7645-5488-3
- Basketball For Dummies
  0-7645-5248-1
- The Bible For Dummies
  0-7645-5296-1
- Buddhism For Dummies
  0-7645-5359-3
- Catholicism For Dummies
  0-7645-5391-7
- Hockey For Dummies
  0-7645-5228-7

- Judaism For Dummies
  0-7645-5299-6
- Martial Arts For Dummies
  0-7645-5358-5
- Pilates For Dummies
  0-7645-5397-6
- Religion For Dummies
  0-7645-5264-3
- Teaching Kids to Read For Dummies
  0-7645-4043-2
- Weight Training For Dummies
  0-7645-5168-X
- Yoga For Dummies
  0-7645-5117-5

TRAVEL

0-7645-5438-7   0-7645-5453-0

Also available:

- Alaska For Dummies
  0-7645-1761-9
- Arizona For Dummies
  0-7645-6938-4
- Cancún and the Yucatán For Dummies
  0-7645-2437-2
- Cruise Vacations For Dummies
  0-7645-6941-4
- Europe For Dummies
  0-7645-5456-5
- Ireland For Dummies
  0-7645-5455-7

- Las Vegas For Dummies
  0-7645-5448-4
- London For Dummies
  0-7645-4277-X
- New York City For Dummies
  0-7645-6945-7
- Paris For Dummies
  0-7645-5494-8
- RV Vacations For Dummies
  0-7645-5443-3
- Walt Disney World & Orlando For Dummies
  0-7645-6943-0

GRAPHICS, DESIGN & WEB DEVELOPMENT

0-7645-4345-8   0-7645-5589-8

Also available:

- Adobe Acrobat 6 PDF For Dummies
  0-7645-3760-1
- Building a Web Site For Dummies
  0-7645-7144-3
- Dreamweaver MX 2004 For Dummies
  0-7645-4342-3
- FrontPage 2003 For Dummies
  0-7645-3882-9
- HTML 4 For Dummies
  0-7645-1995-6
- Illustrator cs For Dummies
  0-7645-4084-X

- Macromedia Flash MX 2004 For Dummies
  0-7645-4358-X
- Photoshop 7 All-in-One Desk
  Reference For Dummies
  0-7645-1667-1
- Photoshop cs Timesaving Techniques
  For Dummies
  0-7645-6782-9
- PHP 5 For Dummies
  0-7645-4166-8
- PowerPoint 2003 For Dummies
  0-7645-3908-6
- QuarkXPress 6 For Dummies
  0-7645-2593-X

NETWORKING, SECURITY, PROGRAMMING & DATABASES

0-7645-6852-3   0-7645-5784-X

Also available:

- A+ Certification For Dummies
  0-7645-4187-0
- Access 2003 All-in-One Desk
  Reference For Dummies
  0-7645-3988-4
- Beginning Programming For Dummies
  0-7645-4997-9
- C For Dummies
  0-7645-7068-4
- Firewalls For Dummies
  0-7645-4048-3
- Home Networking For Dummies
  0-7645-42796

- Network Security For Dummies
  0-7645-1679-5
- Networking For Dummies
  0-7645-1677-9
- TCP/IP For Dummies
  0-7645-1760-0
- VBA For Dummies
  0-7645-3989-2
- Wireless All In-One Desk Reference
  For Dummies
  0-7645-7496-5
- Wireless Home Networking For Dummies
  0-7645-3910-8

ASTD MEMBERSHIP APPLICATION

5093026

Please indicate whether this is for ☐ A New ASTD Membership ☐ Membership Renewal or ☐ Membership Upgrade
(Please do not use this form for ASTD Chapter or Global Network dues.)

Chapter & Global
Network Code: ☐☐☐☐☐☐

1. Please print: (* indicates a required field)

Last Name*_____ First Name*_____ Initial _____

Title*_____

Company/Organization*_____

Billing Address*_____

City, State or Province*_____ ZIP/Postal Code*_____ Country*_____

Shipping Address (if different from Billing Address)_____

City, State or Province_____ ZIP/Postal Code_____ Country_____

Daytime Phone*_____ Fax _____ Email Address*_____
ASTD DOES NOT SELL EMAIL ADDRESSES

How many years of experience do you have in the industry? _____

		Shipping and Special Handling Charges		
		Canada/ Mexico	Other	Total

2. I want to enroll or renew as an ASTD member:

☐ **Classic Membership** .... $180/year — $25 — $70 — $_____

Enjoy a wide range of career-enhancing products and services: publications and research reports, extensive online resources, members-only discounts, and more. (ASTD Classic Members receive *T+D* magazine, our flagship publication, at an annual subscription rate of $60 as part of their membership dues.)

☐ **2-year Classic Membership (Save $40)** — $320 — $25 — $70 — $_____
☐ **Senior Membership (Age 62 or older)** — $90/year — $25 — $70 — $_____
☐ **Student Membership (Full-time student)** — $90/year — $25 — $140 — $_____

3. I want to add even more value to my Classic Membership with my choice of additional features – priced at significant savings.

☐ **The ASTD Books Plus** .... ~~$129~~ $79 — $25 — $70 — $_____
New ASTD published book four times a year. A $129 value for just $79.

☐ *Infoline* **Plus** .... ~~$129~~ $79 — $25 — $70 — $_____
1-year subscription (12 issues) to ASTD's premier "how-to" publication. A $129 value for just $79.

☐ **Training Professionals Plus** .... ~~$275~~ $130 — $25 — $70 — $_____
1-year subscription to *Infoline; The Annual Training and Performance Sourcebook*, and two ASTD published books for training professionals. A $275 value for just $130.

☐ **Organization Development/Leadership Professionals Plus** .... ~~$350~~ $200 — $25 — $70 — $_____
Annual *Team and Organization Development Sourcebook* and subscription to ASTD's OD/Leadership e-newsletter (10 issues). A $350 value for just $200.

☐ **E-Learning Professionals Plus** .... ~~$275~~ $175 — $25 — $30 — $_____
Unlimited access to *Training Media Review's* 24x7 online database; a bimonthly e-newsletter; and one leading edge e-learning publication. A $275 value for just $175.

☐ **Consulting Professionals Plus** .... ~~$125~~ $75 — $25 — $70 — $_____
Annual subscription to *C2M* (Consulting to Management), a quarterly journal for consultants, plus one cutting edge new title to enhance your career and business. A $125 value for just $75.

☐ **ROI Network**.. ~~$150~~ $75 — $25 — $30 — $_____
Quarterly newsletter, one specially published title on evaluation and ROI, access to the ROI online bibliography and network of practitioners. A $150 value for just $75.

Total: $_____

4. Payment method:

☐ My check, drawn on a U.S. bank and payable to ASTD, is enclosed.

☐ Please charge my: ☐ Visa ☐ MasterCard ☐ American Express ☐ Discover

Card # ☐☐☐☐☐☐☐☐☐☐☐☐☐☐☐☐ Exp. Date ☐☐☐☐
M M Y Y

Print name as it appears on credit card _____ Signature_____ Date _____

5. Return this application with payment to: ASTD, Box 1567, Merrifield, VA 22116-1567.

If you are using a credit card, you may fax this form to **+1.703.683.1523.**
For faster service, please call an ASTD Customer Care Associate at **1.800.628.2783 (U.S.)** or **+1.703.683.8100.**

Linking People,
Learning & Performance

080445-31610